THE BATTLE OF PLASSEY 1757

The Victory That Won an Empire

THE BATTLE OF PLASSEY 1757
The Victory That Won an Empire

Stuart Reid

Frontline Books

THE BATTLE OF PLASSEY 1757
The Victory That Won an Empire

First published in 2017
and reprinted in 2022 by Frontline Books,
an imprint of Pen & Sword Books Ltd,
47 Church Street, Barnsley, S. Yorkshire, S70 2AS

ISBN: 9-781-39902-087-9

CIP data records for this title are available from the British Library

For more information on our books, please visit
www.frontline-books.com
email info@frontline-books.com
or write to us at the above address.

Printed and bound by 4edge Limited, UK
Typeset in 10.5/12.5 Palatino

Contents

Introduction   vii

Chapter 1   Mercantile Soldiering   1
Chapter 2   Calcutta   17
Chapter 3   Into the Black Hole   34
Chapter 4   To Fulta and Back Again   51
Chapter 5   Drums along the Hoogli   66
Chapter 6   The Battle of Plassey   85

Epilogue: Patna   101

Appendices
Appendix 1.   East India Company Forces in Bengal 1756–1757   105
Appendix 2.   The Bengali Forces   129
Appendix 3.   Captain Alexander Grant's Accounts of the Fall of Calcutta   135
Appendix 4.   The Black Hole of Calcutta   156
Appendix 5.   Clive's Headquarters Journal of the Expedition to Bengal   167
Appendix 6.   Captain Eyre Coote's Journal   186
Appendix 7 .   Various Contemporary Accounts of the Battle of Plassey   202
Appendix 8.   Orme's Account of the Pursuit of the French up the Ganges   219
Appendix 9.   A General Return of all the Troops Under the Command of   226
               Lieutenant-Colonel Robert Clive
Appendix 10.   A General Return of the Sepoys Under the Command of   229
               Lieutenant-Colonel Robert Clive
Appendix 11.   A General Muster Of The Troops Under The Command Of   231
               Colonel Clive In Camp Near Chinsura
Appendix 12.   A General Muster of the Troops in the Train Under the
               Command of Colonel Clive in Camp Near Chinsura   234

Notes   237
Bibliography   267
Index   268

Introduction

Once upon a time, as the saying goes, every schoolboy (and schoolgirl too) knew the awful story of the Black Hole of Calcutta, where 146 British prisoners were cruelly packed into a tiny prison and how only twenty-three of them emerged alive next morning. And they knew too how Robert Clive avenged the dreadful deed at the Battle of Plassey, and so founded the British Empire. However, although empires and the stirring deeds that won them are not much in fashion these days, it has always been one of history's ironies that the British Empire should indeed have been founded in a muddy field in Bengal on a wet June day in 1757, but even then it was arguably more by accident than by design.

The British Army was represented that day by a mere detachment of 215 officers and men drawn from a single regiment of the line, and instead most of those who wore red coats at Plassey were actually the mercenary employees of the United Company of Merchants trading to the East Indies; the famous East India Company. And nor was the Company setting out to conquer India, or indeed any part of it. Its goal was a quiet and profitable trade, but it was to be secured by supporting a coup against the then Nawab or viceroy of Bengal and replacing him with a more compliant successor.

Perhaps inevitably, by so intervening in local politics to ensure that its preferred candidate won, the Company itself became a political power in its own right and as such it would eventually come to rule first Bengal and then, through it, India itself. There is no doubting the pivotal moment in Indian and Bangladeshi history represented by the Battle of Plassey, but yet at one and the same time it is arguably a little-studied one. Given the attention paid to the battle by historians on all sides, this might at first seem an odd statement, yet those historians have by and large quite understandably concentrated on the complicated tale of 'tricks, chicanery, intrigues, politics and the Lord knows what',[1] which brought the rival armies to Plassey, rather than the fighting along the way, and the battle itself which dictated the outcome. The drums and trumpets have been forgotten.

Yet the military history of the affair is a fascinating and curiously intimate story in its own right, and a proper accounting of it is long overdue. This present study then is a straightforward record of the thirteen months of campaigns and battles which set a rather bemused set of Company directors on the road to acquiring an empire. Notwithstanding that the Battle of Plassey itself is routinely dismissed as an insignificant affair hardly justifying the name, men fought there and men died there and in the battles which preceded it – on both sides. This therefore is *their* story rather that Robert Clive's.

It is customary to round off introductory remarks such as these by gratefully acknowledging all those individuals and institutions who assisted the author in the writing of the book. In this case, the very deepest gratitude is owed to a gentleman long dead named Samuel Charles Hill, late Officer in Charge of the Records of the Government of India, who in 1905 published his three-volume *Bengal in 1756-1757: A Selection of Public and Private Papers Dealing with the Affairs of the British in Bengal during the Reign of Siraj-Uddaula.* Whilst Hill prefaced the first volume with a substantial history of those affairs, it is the more than comprehensive selection of papers, ranging from narratives and letters written by those involved on all sides, through short notes, lists of individuals and military returns, all gathered together in one accessible collection, which is truly indispensable. Its value may be gauged by the frequency with which the papers transcribed therein are cited in the footnotes of the present work.

More conventionally, I have to acknowledge the assistance and encouragement of Martin Mace and John Grehan of Frontline in bringing this book to a successful conclusion; the staff of that extraordinary library maintained by the Literary and Philosophical Society of Newcastle upon Tyne, and others too numerous to mention, except perhaps for a forgotten soldier of fortune, Captain Alexander Grant, an ancestor whose story served as my inspiration.

Note on Spelling and Terminology

Anyone reading European letters and journals of the time will find the spelling by Europeans of Persian, Hindi, Bengali and other words used by the diverse peoples of India to be eccentric and far from consistent. In the present text, quoted passages are rendered as originally written, but otherwise, whilst acknowledging post-colonial sensitivities, a certain degree of consistency has been attempted. Madras, for example, was officially re-named Chennai in 1996, just as Bombay had become Mumbai a year earlier and Calcutta became Kolkata in 2001, but in all three cases the earlier names are retained in this study simply because that is how they were known by those involved. On the other hand, it should be noted that the Nawab's capital of Murshidabad was most commonly spelled Muxadavad (or something like) by Europeans at the time.

By the mid-eighteenth century there was already a substantial Eurasian population in India, referred to by a variety of terms: the term *topass* is generally believed to derive from the Hindi word *topi*, signifying a hat, the wearing of which appears to have been regarded as a status symbol, distinguishing Eurasians from the wider native population. They were also frequently referred to as *Portuguese*, in part because there was a large Eurasian population in and around the Portuguese colony of Goa, but largely, no doubt, because they could affect to pass as such in European society, although often distinguished from actual Europeans as 'Black Portuguese'. Except when quoting contemporary texts, all are referred to here as Eurasians.

One particular oddity requires explanation. The various campaigns and battles recounted here were fought up and down a single river; a distributory of the Ganges properly named the Bhagirathi, although the French rather confusingly preferred to simply call it the Ganges. At the port of Hugli, however, it changes and the river then takes the name of the port, just as mariners commonly referred to the Thames Estuary as the London River. Hugli was variously rendered at the time by most Europeans as Hughly, Hoogli or Hoogly, so in the present narrative it has been arbitrarily decided to avoid confusion by referring to the port as Hugli and to the river as the Hoogli.

Distances were commonly expressed at the time as miles, which will no doubt be familiar to readers; yards and feet. Broadly speaking, a yard is the equivalent of a metre and there were three feet in a yard.

The principal unit of currency throughout Moghul India was the silver rupee, which seems to have traded at the time at around 8 rupees to £1 sterling.[2] Large sums of money were expressed in *lakhs* of 100,000 rupees.

Dedicated to the memory of

Captain Alexander Grant, E.I.C. (1725–68)

Chapter 1

Mercantile Soldiering

Originally chartered by Queen Elizabeth on 31 December 1600, the East India Company or 'The United Company of Merchants of England Trading to the East Indies', as it became in 1708, was certainly the first and arguably by far the most successful multinational trading corporation the world has ever seen. Within less than fifty years of the strange affair at Plassey related in these pages, the Company would not only be astonishingly wealthy but, under the direction of a government-appointed Board of Control, it would be unashamedly governing vast tracts of the Indian subcontinent as a sovereign state in all but name.

Yet, the Company, or at least its directors and shareholders meeting at the India House, their sprawling, and surprisingly ramshackle headquarters in London's Leadenhall Street,[1] never set out to be empire-builders, and indeed almost frantically tried to avoid it. On the contrary, in a proper pursuit of profit, the directors of the Company were ever anxious for nothing more than a 'quiet trade', undisturbed by alarums and 'brabbles'. However, to their oft-expressed distress and occasional angry disapproval, the Company's servants half a world and many months away from London, constantly fell foul of commercial rivals such as the Portuguese, the Dutch and latterly the French, and discovered a destructive talent for getting embroiled in local politics and thereby upsetting the local rulers, on whose goodwill that quiet trade ultimately depended. Conversely of course, many of those on the ground were wont to complain with good reason that many of the troubles could have been avoided, were it not for the interference of a board of directors in London, as ignorant of local conditions as they were ungrateful for the efforts of its servants!

1

India

The Company's very earliest voyages at the beginning of the seventeenth century had been directed all the way to the South China Sea and to what is now the Indonesian Archipelago, primarily in search of nutmeg and other high-value spices. The trade was lucrative enough while it lasted but a murderous competition with the Dutch, who had got there first, eventually found the Company effectively forced out of the area. Instead the main focus of its activities soon shifted northwards to a far more broadly-based trade with the Indian subcontinent and a receptive Mughal Empire, which was at that time still strong enough to enforce some order amongst its often quarrelsome European guests, and keen to embrace a trade which brought the large quantities of silver needed to maintain its numerous armies.

There the East India Company dramatically expanded its commercial operations, quickly eclipsing the older Portuguese *Estado da Índia* by opening its own entrepots, first at Surat on the north-west coast, Masulipatnam on the east and the port of Hugli in Bengal. All three ports were already established and thriving as great trading centres long before the Europeans came, but for various reasons, by the beginning of the eighteenth century the Company had acquired three entirely new settlements of its own, dignified by the title of Presidencies and serving as regional headquarters for an increasing number of factories or trading stations planted all over the interior.[2]

The oldest of these Presidencies was Madrasapatam, commonly rendered simply as Madras. It was no more than an insignificant fishing village on the east coast when it was purchased by the Company on 8 August 1639. At first sight, Madras was an odd spot for an international trading centre, for it was very awkwardly sited; in effect sitting on an open beach with no proper supply of fresh water and a great bar lying just offshore.[3] This may have explained the cheerful readiness with which the local ruler had disposed of what was then a near-worthless asset, but it also meant that for the next two centuries and more rather than tie up at proper wharves to discharge or take on cargoes, or otherwise lie in a secure anchorage, shipping had to stand off the beach in good weather while everyone and everything was precariously ferried across the bar in small boats. In bad weather ships had to avoid it entirely. Yet astonishingly, Madras thrived. Soon the level of trade being carried on with the interior was such that despite this seemingly crippling disadvantage, Madras rose to pre-eminence amongst the Company's other stations and, for most of the eighteenth century, it was to all intents and purposes its head office in India.

Next in order of importance came Bombay. Very largely confined at this time to a pestilential island on the west coast, it was once a Portuguese colony before reluctantly coming to the British Crown as a part of Queen Catherine of Braganza's dowry. In contrast to Madras, it had a very good, well-sheltered harbour, but Catherine's husband King Charles II, who was no fool and quick to recognise a liability when he saw one, very promptly sold it on to a curiously ungrateful Company. Although relatively convenient to the imperial capital of Delhi, as a commercial establishment it never attained as much importance as Madras, especially when it came to trade with the Indian interior. On the other hand, it was very well placed to tap into the considerable local shipping trade with Arabia and the Persian Gulf and the 'country trade' all the way up and down the west coast of India. Consequently, although provided with a proper garrison it found itself largely dependent for its security on a small Company-run naval squadron, popularly known as the Bombay Marine, which began as an ad hoc anti-piracy patrol and would eventually evolve into the present Indian Navy. Moreover, having no significant landward territories attaching to it at this time also meant that Bombay was frequently in the happy position of being able to lend some of its troops to assist the other two Presidencies in time of need.

The third and most recently-founded of the Presidencies was Calcutta. Away from the west coast shipping lanes, most commerce within India quite naturally flowed up and down the great rivers. Of these the mighty Ganges was obviously the most important and so the Company hastened to establish a factory at Hugli, a port in its delta which in turn lent its name to the lower part of a distributory of the Ganges really called the Bahgramiti river. From here, goods and specie were at first transhipped to and from Madras, but by 1676 the Bengal trade was substantial enough to justify turning the factory into a presidency, capable of dealing directly with England. So far so good, but as we shall see in the next chapter a combination of overweening arrogance and an unhappy involvement in local politics, culminating in an ill-fated attempt to seize the port of Chittagong on the other side of the Bay of Bengal, saw the Company effectively expelled from Bengal in 1685. Such was the value of the European trade, however, that having made its peace with the perpetually cash-strapped Mughal Emperor, Aurangzeb, the Company was welcomed back with open arms just five years later. Nevertheless, in the circumstances, a re-establishment of the Hugli factory was considered imprudent, and so instead the site chosen by the Company for its new operational base was a fishing village named Kalkata situated on the left or east bank of the Hoogli River, some distance downstream from the port itself.

The Military

To protect all of these settlements great and small, and more importantly the Company's goods and treasure accumulated therein, some kind of security force was grudgingly acknowledged to be necessary. Yet anyone inclined to doubt the assertion that in the eighteenth century the East India Company still had no ambitions for territorial conquest in the Indian subcontinent, need look no further than the state of its 'military' companies immediately prior to the events about to unfold.

Whilst most of its soldiers were obviously employed as garrisons for the three principal settlements, the term companies was something of a misnomer for they were rarely if ever mustered as such, and instead small detachments, and even individual soldiers, were scattered up-country, providing security details for the factories and no doubt occasionally serving as armed bodyguards for the factors.

At Madras in 1721 there were just three such companies based in Fort St. George, and another at Fort St. David,[4] near Cuddalore, mustering a total of 545 men of all ranks, of whom only 245 were Europeans and the rest Eurasians. In addition there was an even more motley band officially known as 'the gunroom crew', but which, according to the garrison paymaster in 1724, was 'lookt on as a lodging workhouse to relieve poor sailors and at the same time be of use to the garrison'. What he neglected to add was, as it turned out in 1740, the fifty-six Europeans, fifty-two Eurasians and thirty lascars (native Indian labourers) then belonging to the gunroom crew were expected to look after some 200 guns of various calibres.

Bombay's original garrison, on the other hand, had actually been four companies of regular infantry sent out by King Charles II in 1662, but most of them, alas, quickly succumbed to fevers long before both colony and surviving soldiers were transferred from the Crown to the East India Company. Thereafter the comparatively strong military establishment maintained on the island varied between four and eight infantry companies, largely comprised of Topasses or Eurasians. In a return of 1742, the soldiers at Bombay were reported to number a total of 1,593 men of all ranks – but of those only 346 were Europeans.

Similarly, by the mid-1750s there were in theory six companies of infantry in Bengal and one of artillery, but one of the companies had been sent to Madras and was never seen again, while the rest were chronically understrength, not least because during the wars with the French the authorities in Madras were all too often guilty of intercepting and skimming off recruits bound for Calcutta. Consequently, as late as February 1756 there were only a total of 647 European officers and soldiers in Bengal, although once again a surprisingly large number of the latter were actually Eurasians.[5]

This was largely because during much of the eighteenth century the Company was not allowed to openly beat up for military recruits within the British Isles in competition with the Regular Army. Consequently, it had to find its soldiers in strange and unusual places and often by dubious means. As to those sent out from England, they all too often turned out to be of dubious quality physically as well as morally – often being men who were too short or too weakly to be of interest to the Regulars. As late as 1787, it was complained that one recent draft from England included 'broken gentlemen' and half-pay officers, both from the army and the navy, made redundant by the ending of the American War. There was even a former clergyman amongst them, although the circumstances of his misfortune are unrecorded! Otherwise, the rest were the depressingly familiar collection of undersized or disabled men, foreigners, deserters, criminals and even a few sailors who had jumped ship once too often. 'I did not think,' protested Lord Cornwallis on looking them over, 'that Britain could have furnished such a set of wretched objects.'[6] In the circumstances, there was probably some justification for the apocryphal story of the complaint made to the Directors that whilst it was no doubt inevitable that some of the Company's soldiers should be recruited in Newgate Gaol, trawling them from the Bedlam Mad House was going too far!

Consequently, many of the Company's European recruits were in fact found locally in India itself. In the early days, the term Europeans was exercised very broadly and a fair number of them were enlisted from the inevitable floating population of 'poor whites' of various nationalities. In Bengal, for some reason, most of the genuine Europeans at first appear to have been Dutchmen. Most of those would desert during or after the siege of Calcutta in 1756 and instead enlist with the French. Ironically, however, after the British capture of Chandernagore in the following year a sizeable number of the defeated French were enlisted in their place. So-called Portuguese were also enlisted – although in this case the term was in reality a very common euphemism for Eurasians, 'most of whom we are obliged to take tho' good for little'. But at least, as the Directors approvingly noted, they were 'cheaper by one half' than Europeans.[7] Later, in the nineteenth century, these cut-price Eurasian recruits would be rigidly segregated and often employed only as bandsmen, but in the early days this was rare, and while drummers appear to have normally been 'black Portuguese' or 'blacks', the rank and file were more generally found promiscuously mixed with Europeans.

Faced with the perennial difficulty of finding sufficient suitable recruits for its army, the Company even decided in 1751 to hire some Swiss mercenaries. In July of that year, a contract was signed with a military entrepreneur named Schaub for the provision of two companies, each comprising four officers, six sergeants, six corporals, a drum major and two drummers, and 120 soldiers. All of the officers and men were to be Protestants, and although the contract specified that they were to be raised in Zurich, Geneva and Basle, recruits from Alsace and Hanover were also to be accepted. Between 1751 and 1754, it seems that some 500 men were sent out, including artillerymen. Initially the Company agreed to maintain the traditional Swiss mercenary privileges in regard to discipline, drum calls and other practices. The contract or contracts appear to have lapsed in about 1754, although the Swiss companies maintained their identity for some time afterwards and one of them, commanded by a Captain Guapp, would fight at Plassey.

Nor, often enough, were their officers in much better shape and on the whole they were men who could not afford to purchase a commission in the Regular Army. In a letter written the night before his death at the storming of Conjeveram in 1759, Captain Robert Bannatyne wrote that, 'My Father had no great Estate and dying whilst his Children were young you May guess Whether five of us did not find use for small inheritance'.[8] As another bitterly put it, 'we are not, generally speaking, men of interest, else we should not have preferred a service in which seniority [in other words length of service] gives command'.[9] As with the rank and file, even some of the officers were men who had left their country for their country's good. One notable example we shall meet shortly was Captain Alexander Grant, a Highland Jacobite who had been 'out' in the '45 but afterwards arrived in India in 1747 as a lieutenant with one of Boscawen's Independent Companies, where he took the opportunity to transfer to the Company's service.

As we shall shortly see, this reliance on seniority meant that when hostilities commenced in the 1740s, some of the Company's officers were very old indeed in years, but not alas, in rank or ability. Indeed it could hardly be otherwise given the Directors' peevish opposition to granting anyone a higher commission than that of a lieutenant before the reforms of 1748. Even then, whilst the rank of captain afterwards became more common, the responsibilities piled upon officers were still rarely consistent with their small rewards. Just as lieutenants were commanding companies prior to 1748, afterwards it was not uncommon to find captains leading battalions, and majors, although existing, were decidedly rare. Pay was chronically low and, notoriously, officers were forced to rely on a wide and varied collection of allowances (and private trade) in order to make ends meet.

All in all, therefore, when our story opens, the Company's soldiers, both officers and men, were in reality no more than a dubious rabble of second-rate armed security guards, probably little removed in character and effectiveness from those euphemistically-titled 'security contractors' seemingly so ubiquitous in the present day. They were adequate enough to protect godowns or warehouses from pilfering and to present a suitable show when required, but not surprisingly all too many of them were at first found to be wanting when calamity fell and proper soldiering was the order of the day.

War in the Carnatic

At first, no matter the wars raging in Europe during the long years of Louis XIV – the Sun King – both British and French traders in India had recognised the dangers of engaging in national conflicts when there was no good reason to do so. This was partly a matter of a sensible recognition that it was bad for business and partly because in any case the Great Moghul forbade Europeans from disturbing the peace of his dominions in the name of whatever might be going on at the other side of the world. In 1744, therefore, when the governor of the French settlement of Pondicherry, Joseph-François Dupleix, learned that war had again broken out in Europe between Britain and France, he courteously wrote to Nicholas Morse, his British counterpart 100 miles away in Madras, suggesting that in accordance with past practice, neither party should engage in hostilities 'east of the Cape'.[10] With equal courtesy, Morse responded that he would be happy to concur, but as a mere servant of the East India Company he obviously had no authority over any of his sovereign's officers who might happen by. In this, Morse was equivocating for he knew perfectly well that the Royal Navy was already on its way to seize Pondicherry. Whether or not this was discreetly conveyed to Dupleix, or whether he was more than capable of reading between the lines, the Frenchman immediately appealed for the protection of the Nawab or imperial viceroy of the Carnatic, a gentleman named Anwar-ud-din. The Nawab, equally concerned to maintain a quiet and profitable trade, promptly responded by reminding both parties that it was strictly forbidden to undertake hostilities anywhere within the Emperor's dominions.

At this stage in the game, Mughal authority was still something to be respected. Commodore Curtis Barnet of the Royal Navy might indeed have been instructed to fight the French, but he was not authorised to start a war with the Mughal Empire. Pondicherry was therefore safe for the moment, but on the other hand French shipping on the high seas was still a different matter entirely. The patriotic zeal of eighteenth-century naval officers was deliberately encouraged and sustained by the prize money awarded for captured enemy ships, and Barnet found the Indian Ocean to be a very happy hunting ground indeed. A number of ships belonging to the French *Compagnie des Indes*, and of course their valuable cargoes, were very quickly snapped up, and this provocation goaded Dupleix into marching against the East India Company's Fort St. David, which lay a tempting 14 miles south of Pondicherry. He might easily have carried the place out of hand but fortunately the Royal Navy turned up in time to save the day. This time it was Morse who appealed to the Nawab and no doubt derived a smug satisfaction from Anwar-ud-din's repeated injunction in the name of the Emperor, forbidding the Europeans to disturb the peace. The French, for the moment at least, were egregiously in the wrong, but the complexion of the game changed dramatically when Commodore Barnet died suddenly in May 1746.

Of itself this was a setback, but one made all the worse by the fact the senior surviving naval officer, Captain Edward Peyton, was completely overwhelmed by the responsibility so suddenly thrust upon him. He was only too conscious that his ships were by now two years out from England and badly in need of refitting. Consequently, rather than risk a fight with an avenging squadron which arrived fresh from France a few weeks later, he hastily retired from the scene entirely to refit them at Trincomalee in Ceylon.[11] This was doubly unfortunate because the French commander, François Mahé de La Bourdonnais, the governor of Mauritius, also convoyed a substantial reinforcement of 2,000 French and 1,000 African soldiers destined for Pondicherry, and with Peyton now conspicuous by his absence Dupleix, felt confident enough to go to war with the British in spite of the Nawab and the Emperor.

Not that had he much to fear from the British. When La Bourdonnais appeared off Madras on 3 September 1746 and started landing his troops, there were only some 200 men in the military companies stationed in Fort St. George and about 100 more in the gunroom crew.[12] Even with the addition of a hastily mobilised European militia cobbled together from the Company's writers and other able-bodied civilian staff (including a surly Shropshire lad named Robert Clive) numbering about 150 men, and another 400–500 locally recruited peons,[13] this was hardly an adequate garrison to defend the place.

Nevertheless, the real weakness of the settlement was not the inadequate garrison or its equally inadequate fortifications,[14] but the simple fact that the fort itself lacked its own water supply and its inhabitants were dependent on freshwater springs now under French control. They, for their part, having established their camp at the south of the lagoon and safely out of range of the fort's guns, then proceeded to swing around to the north. There La Bourdonnais began raising two batteries to bombard the landward side of both the fort and the adjoining 'Blacktown'. At this point, some enterprising soul in the garrison saw an opportunity to attack the French camp, which was assumed to be poorly guarded. Unfortunately this happy inspiration was compromised by the decision to entrust the operation to the locally-recruited peons, who duly sallied out of the gate on the morning of 6 September, fired off their muskets with great enthusiasm, and promptly placed as much distance as possible between themselves and the beleaguered fortress.

Next day, La Bourdonnais retaliated by uncovering his batteries and commencing a bombardment, not directed against the walls, but instead using mortars to drop explosive shells inside. Some of the garrison's guns replied uncertainly, but the climate proved as deadly as the French and after just a few rounds were fired, their rotten carriages collapsed. In the circumstances, it is hardly surprising that the chief gunner thereupon relieved himself of his problems by succumbing to a heart attack. As one of the garrison unsympathetically observed: 'Mr Smith our Chief Gunner, having by this time discovered that he was ill-used by his wife, and likewise that much would be laid to his charge for having hardly anything that belonged to his province in that readiness that had all along been expected of him, died the day the enemy landed.'[15]

There is some slight uncertainty as to exactly when Smith shuffled off this mortal coil, but his demise was certainly symbolic: for with most of the garrison fled, and the rest drunk and mutinous, the guns useless, the gunner dead; and drinking water running out fast (which may have provided an excuse for the alcohol), a continued defence was clearly hopeless. On the evening of 8 September, after having lost just six men killed, Morse asked La Bourdonnais for terms and so Madras was surrendered at two o'clock on the afternoon of 10 September 1746.

Having briskly achieved what they set out to do, the French then proceeded to fall out amongst themselves in a truly spectacular fashion. True to his word to Morse, La Bourdonnais eventually offered a surprisingly moderate composition or ransom. A sum of £400,000 was agreed, which although substantial in itself was effectively no more than a fair compensation for the French shipping earlier seized by Commodore Barnet. Predictably, down at Pondicherry, Dupleix reacted to the news of the settlement with fury, for he wanted the British expelled from the Carnatic entirely. Denying that La Bourdonnais had any authority to make a treaty, and darkly insinuating that bribery had been involved, he sent some of his own officers to take charge of the town and re-visit the negotiations. As the royal governor of Mauritius, La Bourdonnais was having none of this high-handed treatment and flatly denied that Dupleix had any authority over him whatsoever. What was more he underlined the point by ordering the Pondicherry contingent aboard his own ships and arresting Dupleix's officers. Peremptorily deprived of his army, Dupleix had no alternative but to give way, but then providence intervened for him on 2 October in the form of a storm which dramatically demonstrated the dangers of Madras as an anchorage. Three of La Bourdonnais' ships were wrecked on the bar, including those carrying the mortars which he intended to use against Fort St. David, and four other ships were dismasted. Recognising that this was only a forerunner of worse weather to come, the French admiral hastily completed the capitulation, under the terms of which Madras was to be returned to the British by the end of January 1747, and took his leave, first for Mauritius and afterwards for France.

That left Dupleix in sole charge once again and, reinforced by the soldiers the admiral was forced to leave behind for lack of shipping, he was emboldened to once again defy Anwar-ud-din. Earlier he had grandly announced his intention of handing Madras over to the Nawab rather than to the British, but that bluster was seemingly just for La Bourdonnais' benefit and when the Nawab's son, Mafuz Khan, arrived there to take possession, the new French garrison very properly refused to hand it over to him without written orders from Pondicherry. They never came. Dupleix was resolved to hang on to the place and instead despatched a reinforcement for the garrison under a Swiss officer, Major Louis Paradis. By so doing he unknowingly changed the face of warfare in India.

At San Thomé, just outside Madras, on 4 November 1746, Paradis found himself facing a substantial Indian army under Mafuz Khan. Posted behind the Adyar River, the reputed 10,000-odd Carnatic troops were a typical Moghul force. Supposedly the best of them were the numerous and well-equipped cavalry, but the infantry were for the most part peons, such as those who had performed so dismally during the all-too-short defence of Madras. Against them Paradis could muster just 350 European soldiers, not unlike those serving the East India Company, and another 700 locally-recruited Indian troops. These 'cypayes', however, were very different from the peons standing behind the river. In 1740, Dupleix's predecessor, Pierre Benoît Dumas, faced with a growing threat from the warlike Maratha Confederation, had made the experiment of arming his hired peons not with the traditional matchlocks, but with firelock muskets and bayonets. Now his initiative was about to be justified.

Finding the Nawab's men showing no immediate inclination to advance, Major Paradis decided to attack at once. With those 350 blue-coated Frenchmen[16] formed in four ranks in the centre and the 700 *cypayes* deployed on either flank, he splashed straight across the river. Mafuz Khan's artillery greeted them with an ineffective salvo, and in response Paradis had his men fire a single volley and then immediately led them forward again with fixed bayonets. He was literally outnumbered by ten to one at this point but to the astonishment of all he won a swift and stunning victory as the Nawab's infantry, reeling from that thunderous volley and thoroughly intimidated by the bayonet charge that followed, scattered and fled, throwing their own cavalry into confusion. They too broke and ran as Paradis continued to storm forward, and to be fair to them were also hurried on their way by the French garrison of Madras, which sallied out and attacked their rear. Notwithstanding that well-timed assistance there is no doubting, however, that the gallant Paradis, as the historian Sir John Fortescue memorably wrote, had; 'showed us the secret of how to conquer India – with [firelock] musket and bayonet'.

Elated by the easy victory, Dupleix thereupon formally renounced La Bourdonnais' treaty and when the garrison commander in Madras had the termerity to declare such conduct dishonourable, he replaced him with the far more compliant Paradis. In doing so Dupleix was over-reaching himself for there was still a British garrison in Fort St. David, no great distance to the south of Pondicherry itself. La Bourdonnais had intended to deal with it after the capture of Madras but that plan was scuppered by the loss of the bomb vessels, wrecked on the bar. Therefore a straightforward escalade or storming of the walls was determined upon. Even allowing for the addition of Robert Clive and a number of others who escaped from Madras after the repudiation of the treaty, the fort had only some 200 defenders, and so the 1,700 men Dupleix sent against the place ought to have been sufficient to overwhelm them without any great difficulty. Fortunately, they never allowed the opportunity to try.

Having marched through the cool of the night and peremptorily scattered some peons manning an outpost in nearby Cuddalore, the French halted to cook a hearty breakfast before commencing their operations in earnest. No sooner had they relaxed, however, than Mafuz Khan and his brother, Muhammad Ali, turned up like the devil at prayers, eager to avenge their earlier defeat at San Thomé. Caught completely unawares, this time it was the French who broke and ran for Pondicherry, all of 16 miles away. Had Mafuz Khan pursued them vigorously none would have escaped, but the lure of the French baggage train proved irresistible. With the Nawab's cavalry busily engaged in plundering it, the French were granted a respite. A ragged battle line was somehow scraped together but then the appearance of some of the East India Company's troops hastening up from Fort St. David was sufficient to remind them of their mortality, and so off they went again. This humiliation was sufficient to persuade Dupleix that it was time to make his peace with the Nawab. A gift of 150,000 rupees secured the temporary withdrawal of Mafuz Khan and his men, but there was no question of an alliance and the best Dupleix could hope for was that the Nawab would stand aside long enough for him to settle matters with the British once and for all.

Alas for French hopes, it was already too late. At sea the ineffective Captain Peyton had been relieved by the much more aggressive Commodore Thomas Griffin. This was literally in the very nick of time, for no sooner did Paradis arrive at Cuddalore on 3 March 1747 for a renewed attempt on Fort St. David, than he saw to his chagrin the masts of Griffin's squadron rise over the horizon. Another hasty, albeit more dignified, retreat followed and the security of the fort was assured by the landing of 500 sailors and 150 marines. Dupleix, for his part, stubbornly refused to give up and when a small French squadron arrived, he used it to lure Griffin away from the coast while a third attempt was made to capture the British fort. Once again it came to grief; the French were ambushed in Cuddalore on the night of 27 June and this time fled all the way back to Pondicherry before they could be rallied.

Worse was to follow. Such was the influence wielded by the East India Company in London that Griffin was just the forerunner of an expedition led by Rear Admiral Edward Boscawen, who was acting on instructions not from the Admiralty but rather from the East India Company, and at their behest was tasked with the capture of Pondicherry. The unorthodox nature of his effective subordination to the Company was reflected in his surely unique title of Admiral, General, and commander-in-Chief of all forces in the East Indies.[17]

The core of his land forces comprised twelve newly-recruited Independent Companies of Foot, and a staggering absence of operational security is revealed by their being openly advertised as raising for a 'secret expedition' to the East Indies. At any rate the twelve companies were duly formed into two provisional battalions, one of 'Scotch' companies commanded by Major William Muir and an English one under Major Park Pepper, with both of them serving under the overall command of Major John Mompesson.[18] The temporary nature of these Independent Companies is emphasised by the fact that whilst they were built up around the usual cadre of recruits drafted from regular units, most of the personnel appear to have been Jacobite rebel prisoners pardoned on condition of enlistment, with an admixture of recaptured deserters hauled out of the Savoy prison. Some few of them may even have been genuine volunteers, but if so they were very much in a minority and it might not be going too far to refer to the companies as penal units. In addition, Boscawen had a regular company of the Royal Artillery and would also form a third provisional battalion comprised of marines from his ships, and a fourth battalion of seamen. For its part, the East India Company's contribution would comprise a newly-raised artillery company, an infantry battalion to be organised in-country under a Major Stringer Lawrence, and a contingent of locally-raised mercenaries, making a total of some 3,000 Europeans and 2,000 peons.[19]

After an unsuccessful attempt to take Mauritius on the way, Boscawen arrived off Fort St. David on 27 July 1748 and duly set about landing his troops and stores. Remarkably, the admiral had brought all his soldiers halfway around the world without losing any of them – in very marked contrast to some later voyages. Once on land, alas, he found himself in a different element and suffered a number of mishaps at the very outset of his siege of Pondicherry, not the least being the incompetence of his engineers who first opened their parallels too far from the walls and then found themselves sapping forward into marshy ground. Soon the monsoon was approaching, but just as importantly, news arrived that in Europe the preliminaries of peace had been signed at Aix-la-Chapelle on 19 April 1748 and that hostilities beyond the Cape were to cease within six months. The respective positions of the interested parties had already been adjusted by their far-off governments and it was agreed that Madras should indeed be returned to the East India Company per the treaty made by La Bourdonnais.

Stringer Lawrence

The loss of Madras, which was not actually handed back until 21 August 1749, had come as a profound shock to the commercial gentlemen in Leadenhall Street and for once they not only agreed that something must be done but actually proceeded to do it. First they persuaded the government to put together that secret expedition, but for their own part they rounded up about 150 new recruits and hired a Regular Army officer to command them. Whether they fully appreciated what they were doing is open to question, for on arriving in India in January 1748, armed with the appointment of Major and Garrison Commander of Madras, Stringer Lawrence embarked on a complete re-organisation and expansion of the Company's forces.

Lawrence was no ordinary line officer. His first commission was as an ensign in Clayton's 14th Foot, signed on 22 December 1727, and he was subsequently advanced to a lieutenancy on 11 March 1736 and became captain-lieutenant of the regiment on 22 June 1745.[20] He served in that rank at the Battle of Culloden in the following year, but by then it will have been clear that he was unlikely to go further in his chosen career. The fact of the matter was that he was all of 30 years old when he obtained that first commission back in 1727, which means that he had almost certainly started out in the ranks. With no financial backing with to purchase his subsequent promotions, he relied upon seniority alone; in effect stepping into dead men's shoes. In all fairness, promotion within the army at large was extremely slow in the 1730s and there was actually nothing in the least exceptional in his taking nearly twenty years to become captain-lieutenant, but by then, having started late, he was getting nigh on 50 years of age and certainly too old to wait his turn for the next death vacancy. The Company's service therefore looked more than attractive.

To the commercial gentlemen of Leadenhall Street he probably appeared no more than a safe pair of hands, who was not likely to commit any egregious blunders or otherwise embarrass his employers. Instead, they found they had hired a sergeant major who discovered his command to be an offence to his profession, and proceeded to do something about it.

Thus far the Company's forces had done little beyond guard the posts to which they were assigned, but the war with the French required something quite different. The few surviving Madras Europeans, formed the cadre of what was to going to be a proper infantry battalion and to bring it up to strength Lawrence pragmatically added some 300 Eurasians as well as those 150 recruits brought out from England. A contingent borrowed from Bombay eventually gave Lawrence a full 700 men, including, as was right and proper, an elite grenadier company formed from the best of them.[21] The Bombay troops had to be returned there in due course, but they were easily replaced when Boscawen sailed for home and several hundred men from his Independent Companies and Marines volunteered into the Company's service.[22] The necessary additional officers, including a Lieutenant Alexander Grant, were also found amongst departing Independent Companies and from the bolder young writers and other Company servants, whereby Robert

Clive gained his first military commission. The near-useless gunroom crew was also disbanded, and those gunners judged to be fit for proper service transferred into new artillery companies capable of operating efficiently either in garrison or in the field as required.

Hand-in-hand with these reforms, Lawrence also profited by the French example and undertook an equally radical re-organisation of the Company's local troops, replacing the unruly gangs of peons with properly-disciplined companies of sepoys, still serving under their own officers but now armed and disciplined in the European manner. They still had some way to go, but it was a start, and with Dupleix determined that no matter the peace in Europe the war in the Carnatic would go on, they would truly be forged in battle.

By now the focus of the conflict had completely shifted. The French needed local allies of their own and tried to go one better by establishing themselves not as clients but overlords. This was easily done for the superiority of European training and fighting methods was so obvious as to make the rival Companies indispensable. Dupleix soon found his opportunity in the wars which followed the death of Asaf Jah, the Nizam of Hyderabad, in 1748. On behalf of the Mughal emperor the Nizam had ruled the greater part of the Deccan, a vast plateau occupying most of southern India. The French promptly pledged their support for his grandson Muzaffar Jang and following the death of Anwar-ud-din at the Battle of Ambur in the following year, Dupleix also helped place a certain Chanda Sahib on the throne of the Carnatic.

Following the Battle of Ambur in 1749, Anwar-ud-din's son, Muhammad Ali, fled to Trichinopoly, while the French and their allies marched boldly into the Deccan. There they were equally successful at first. The British-backed candidate, Nazir Jang, was surprised and killed and Muzaffar Jang was duly installed as Nizam. Alas, Dupleix's triumph was short-lived, for an unexpected setback followed when Muzzafar Jang was in turn killed in a skirmish with the Afghans shortly afterwards, but the French were equal to the occasion and their military commander, the 30-year-old Charles Joseph Patissier, Marquis de Bussy-Castelnau,[23] promptly found a pliant replacement in Muzzafar's uncle, Salabat Jang. Once he was installed, to all intents and purposes thenceforth the French controlled the political fortunes of Hyderabad and in the process gained as a reward four rich districts on the Coromandel coast known as the Northern Circars.

For its part the East India Company was alive to the danger and resolved to stick by Muhammad Ali who was still besieged in Trichinapoly by Chanda Sahib and the French. At this crucial juncture, in mid-1751, Robert Clive suggested a diversionary attack upon Arcot, the capital of the Carnatic. His plan was all the more extraordinary in that at the time he was being employed not as a military officer but as a commissary running supplies up from the coast. Notwithstanding, the new governor of Madras approved and Clive made a bold dash for Arcot with a scratch force of regulars and sepoys. Famously marching through a prodigious thunderstorm, he seized the city in the name of Muhammad Ali by a bold coup de main on 1 September 1751. This had the desired effect. A thoroughly alarmed Chanda Sahib sent a large portion of his army from Trichinapoly to recapture Arcot, but Clive once again surprised everyone by maintaining a gallant defence of the place for some fifty days. Two further victories quickly followed, at Arni on 3 December 1751 and Conjeveram twelve days later, to secure both the Carnatic and Clive's growing reputation. More fighting inevitably followed but by now both the British and French governments were growing uneasy at the increasingly complicated twists and turns. Dupleix was recalled and a peace treaty signed at Pondicherry in January 1755. By this treaty Muhammad Ali was recognised as the Nawab of the Carnatic and Salabat Jang as the Nizam of Hyderabad, and thereafter the British and French also agreed 'not to interfere in the internal disputes' of the Indian princes.

While it would be wrong to cast the French as the begetters of all the troubles in India – the mismanaged business about to unfold in Bengal was to be proof enough of that – the fact remains that they had wholly upset the balance of power in southern India. In 1746, the respective Companies were no more than traders and tenants of the local rulers. Now, within less than ten years they were fast becoming territorial powers in all but name and in the process their security guards had become very effective private armies capable of taking on and beating any native army that came against them.

Princes all over India could not but take note of this growing power and were beginning to look upon the Europeans and their ambitions with some concern, and no more so than in Bengal, where the British were seemingly intent on challenging the authority of the new Nawab.

Chapter 2

Calcutta

As noted in the previous chapter, the East India Company's presence in Bengal stretched all the way back to 1633 and by 1685 the Company had a healthy network of factories scattered along the Hoogli river with the principal station established in the port of Hugli itself. An Imperial *firman* or charter exempted the Company from customs duties in return for a consolidated annual payment made to the Nawab of Bengal, but this payment had to be renegotiated annually and the accession of a new Nawab, Shaista Khan, in 1680 required some particularly hard bargaining by one of the Company's most experienced negotiators. The eventual settlement was tough, fair and immediately denounced by the Company's chief at Cossimbazar, a colourful character named Job Charnock. What followed can most charitably be described as sheer farce, which saw the directors in London decide to go to war with a Mughal Empire which was then still at the height of its power – and suffer a humiliating climbdown on every front. By some oversight the Company's declaration of war on the Empire in 1685 was not delivered to the Nawab of Bengal and although his troops surrounded Hugli, no attempt was made to seize the English factory, far less fight anyone. Consequently Job Charnock, who was by then in charge there, successfully withdrew both the Company's people and its goods without interference. Shaista Khan was in fact very sorry to see them go and when they defiantly fetched up a short distance away on a riverside mudbank which would later become the site of Calcutta, he was only too happy to enter into negotiations to formally allow Charnock and his people to settle there and begin trading again as soon as possible. Instead, alarmed by the advance of the Nawab's troops, Charnock piled everything and everyone back on to the ships and fled a further 70 miles downriver to the pestilential island of Hijili at the very mouth of the Hoogli. There, everyone started to die of fluxes and fevers as Shaista Khan's troops opened a desultory siege which only ended with the arrival of a small fleet of Indiamen, fresh out from England.

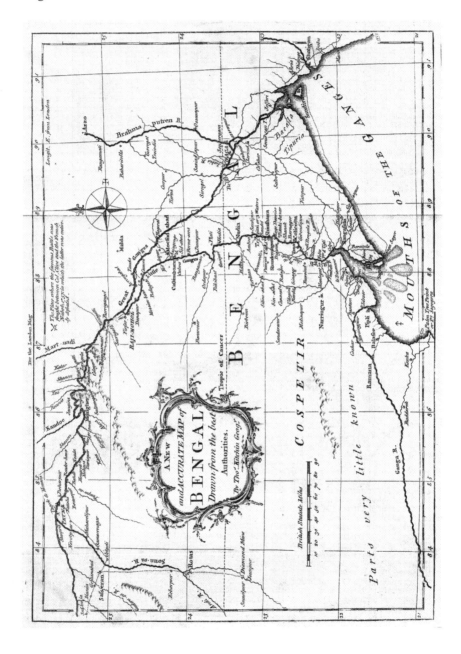

At this point, common sense intervened. Charnock still had possession of the cargo they expected to pick up. The Indiamen carried the specie to pay for the next year's cargo. Clearly it was in everyone's interest to resume business as usual. After some hesitation, Charnock moved back upriver to re-establish his nascent settlement of Calcutta, but no sooner was he ashore, clearing land and building huts and godowns than another fleet turned up from London with peremptory orders to evacuate the place and instead seize Chittagong, on the other side of the Bay of Bengal! This unexpected move was predicated on the mistaken belief that the port lay at the mouth of the Ganges and so controlled access to the interior. Perhaps, predictably, the expedition ended in a complete fiasco, with those concerned declining to attack the place on the not unreasonable grounds that it was indefensible and once captured could not be held.[1] Instead, they all retired unhappily to Madras, but in the end the pursuit of profit once again prevailed on both sides and by 1690 the Company was back trading at Calcutta and there at last it stayed, building Fort William to serve as its head office in Bengal.

To tell the story of this debacle properly would require a book in itself[2] but what the episode underlined to all concerned was that in Bengal at least, the relationship between the Company and the Empire was a symbiotic one, immensely profitable and indeed vital to both parties. So profitable was it that in 1717 the Emperor was persuaded to grant to the Company the privilege of issuing *dustucks* or passes to its carriers, exempting them from any tolls and duties which might otherwise be levied by enterprising local officials en route. In theory this ought to have been straightforward, but 'we under that pretence protected all the Nabob's subjects that claimed our protection, though they were neither our servants nor our merchants, and gave our dustucks or passes to numbers of natives to trade custom free, to the great prejudice of the Nabob's revenue; nay, more, we levied large duties upon goods brought into our districts from the very people that permitted us to trade custom free.'[3]

As the Company responded to all complaints by waving their Imperial *firman*, the only real redress for the Bengali authorities was to periodically blockade one or more of the Company's factories until they were quite literally paid to go away. Whilst of itself this long-standing and growing abuse of the Company's privileges did not provide a sufficient *casus belli* in itself, it was dangerous in that on the one hand it created a lingering resentment against the Company at the Nawab's court, while on the other hand the failure of the Nawab to act decisively, for fear of trespassing on Imperial authority and upsetting the considerable income streams generated by the Company, only reinforced the long-standing belief on both sides that the Company was a law unto itself and could therefore behave as it pleased with impunity.

The Company and the Nawab

It is possible that this behaviour might have gone on almost indefinitely but in early 1756 a succession crisis arose in Bengal. The then Nawab, Aliverdi Khan, lay dying. Of itself this was entirely unremarkable since he was all of 82-years-old, and notwithstanding Robert Orme's sour comment that 'twould be a good deed to swinge the old dog',[4] it was dropsy rather than an assassin which carried him off in the end.

The crisis arose because he had no sons to succeed him. Sensible of the difficulties likely to arise as a result, he had long since married off his three daughters with some care but alas all three husbands predeceased him. His acknowledged heir was now a 19-year-old grandson named Mirza Mohammed; rather better known to the world by his honorific title, Siraj-ud-Daula – the Light of the State. Unfortunately, while the young man had been allowed to increasingly assume the reins of power during his aged grandfather's last illness, he was reputedly arrogant, dissolute and consequently by no means popular.[5] With good reason, he recognised that any show of weakness at this point in time might literally prove fatal. A good deal of infighting aimed at eliminating or at least neutralising his most obvious rivals at court therefore took place during the months leading up to Aliverdi Khan's death.

The most immediate danger was reckoned to come from his aunt, the Ghaseta Begum, the eldest and most formidable of Aliverdi Khan's daughters. Moving quickly, Siraj-ud-Daula succeeded in arresting her, and perhaps just as gratifyingly seized upon a considerable part of her treasure. This was doubly fortunate, for an Imperial army, led by the Nawab of Oudh, was reported to be advancing towards Bengal intent on collecting a large sum of money promised by Aliverdi Khan to the Emperor six years earlier. No doubt there was some concern in Delhi that if the money was not squeezed from Aliverdi while he was still living there would be precious little chance of collecting it once he was dead. Having bought off this particular menace with the old lady's money, Siraj-ud-Daula then bethought himself to deal with the other threats to his imminent accession, but when Aliverdi finally shuffled off on 9 or 10 April 1756, his heir's immediate priority was to turn against a cousin named Shaukat Jang, the governor of the province of Purneah.

At the same time, the new Nawab also sent letters to both the French at Chandernagore and the British at Calcutta, warning them off from interfering in the crisis and inter alia demanding that they demolish their unauthorised fortifications built during Alivardi's illness. The French for their part were suitably conciliatory and diplomatically pretended that they were only repairing the damage to a bastion caused by an unlucky lightning strike! Their ready apologies and this unlikely explanation were duly accepted, as too for the moment were some urgent but equally insincere protestations of loyalty from Shaukat Jang, but at Calcutta the Governor, Roger Drake, was rather too blunt and dismissive in replying to the Nawab that the works to Fort William were being carried out because:

> in the late War between our Nation and the French, they had attacked and taken the Town of Madras contrary to the neutrality we expected would have been preserved in the Mogull's Dominions; and that there being at present great appearance of another War between the Two Crowns, We were under some apprehensions they would act in the same way in Bengal, to prevent which We were only repairing our Line of Guns to the Water-side.[6]

No matter that fears of General Bussy and his colourful army might frighten the Company officials to sleep of a night, this excuse was unjustified by the neutrality which had thus far been preserved in Bengal during the last European war. While no such works had actually been carried out as yet, this answer was exactly what Siraj-ud-Daula did not want to hear. Not only were the British intent on fortifying themselves in defiance of his authority, but they were also very publicly thereby proclaiming a lack of confidence in the Nawab's ability to preserve the peace in his own dominions. What was more, the British response to his accession had so far been confined to little more than a polite letter of acknowledgement. It is unlikely that Drake or his colleagues appreciated the very real pressures which the new Nawab was contending with – his succession still had to be formally ratified by the Imperial court in Delhi for a start – otherwise they might have proceeded with more circumspection. As it was, they had been ignoring local sensibilities for too long. While the old grievance over the matter of the *dustucks* was genuine, those lukewarm congratulations on Siraj-ud-Daula's accession, allied to the matter of the fortifications and to reports that the British were actively intriguing with his rivals, was altogether a much more serious matter. Whether or not any such interference was actually contemplated, far less underway, the Nawab was only too well aware of what had been going on in the Carnatic during the last ten years as a direct result of the British and French Companies ignoring injunctions to keep the peace in the Moghul's dominions. In particular, he and everyone else around him could hardly avoid noting how the rival European Companies had hadfirst interfered in local politics by supporting their own chosen candidates and then turning them into virtual puppets. Therefore the numerous reports from his spies, mistaken or exaggerated as they generally were, of the British strengthening their fortifications at Calcutta and conspiring with his rivals understandably led him to believe that unless he acted quickly and firmly, the British and the other Europeans would use the pretext of war between themselves to interfere with and ultimately dominate the governance of Bengal. The tragedy from a Bengali point of view is that not only was he right, but in acting to forestall such an outcome, Siraj-ud-Daula brought about the very domination which he foresaw and feared.

It certainly did not help matters that at this inauspicious moment the British gave refuge to a fugitive nobleman named Krishna Das. This gentleman was the son of the Ghaseta Begum's Hindu lover and not only had he succeeded in escaping with his wives and the balance of the Begum's treasure, but on the inexplicable recommendation of William Watts, the chief factor at Cossimbazar, he arrived in Calcutta and took up residence there with a local Sikh businessman named Amir Chund – more familiarly known to the British as Omichand. Whilst Amir Chund's considerable fortune was in part acquired through investments in the Company, his personal loyalties were obviously his own and he was not only thought with good reason to be in close contact with the Nawab, but would later be accused of encouraging the latter in his belief that the British were conspiring against him. As to Krishna Das, his true motives are also suspect, for when Calcutta was subsequently taken by the Nawab, far from meeting a terrible fate he was given a ceremonial robe and cheerfully sent on his way, raising a shrewd suspicion that the whole affair may have been a deliberate provocation. At any rate, loudly declaring his intention that 'unless the English consent to fill up their ditch, raze their fortifications, and trade upon the same terms they did in the time of Nawab Jafar Khan, I will totally expel them from the country',[7] the Nawab decided that Shaukat Jang could wait and instead turned his army against the all-too vulnerable Company factory at Cossimbazar.

When, on the morning of 20 May 1756, William Watts awoke to find the Company compound surrounded by a substantial detachment of the Nawab's troops, under an officer named Omar Beg, he at first saw no particular cause for alarm. The Bengalis had also surrounded the neighbouring Dutch and French compounds and while the movement of commercial goods was prevented, no attempt was being made to interfere with ordinary deliveries of provisions. Understandably enough, Watts assumed that the blockade was no more than one of those periodic exercises in extorting money from the Company, and was confident that he could afford to await events. After all, the compound was reasonably well defended and Captain Alexander Grant assured the Council down in Calcutta that there was nothing to fear:

> Cossimbuzar is an irregular square with solid bastions, each mounting 10 guns mostly 9 and 6 pounders with a saluting battery on the curtain to the river side of 24 guns from 2 to 4 pounders, and their carriages, when I left the place in October last, in pretty good order, besides 8 cohorn mortars 4 and 5 inches, with a store of shells and grenades. Their garrison consisted of 50 military under the command of Lieutenant Ellet, a Serjeant, corporal and 3 matrosses [gun handlers] of the artillery and 20 good lascars. The ramparts are overseen by two houses which lay within 20 yards of the walls, but as each is commanded by 5 guns from the bastions, the enemy could hardly keep possession of them.[8]

Ordinarily that ought indeed to have been sufficient to keep extortion at bay, but by 25 May the blockade had pointedly been lifted from the French and Dutch factories and only the British compound was still surrounded by the Bengalis. Food supplies were no longer permitted to come through the lines, and it was apparent that for some reason matters were growing more serious. Watts was also by now uneasily aware of just how comprehensively the compound was overlooked by those nearby houses.

Contradicting Grant's confident assertions, Watts flatly denied that there was any shot or shells for the guns and also petulantly complained that most of his fifty soldiers were 'black Portegueze', i.e. Eurasians. 'We might possibly,' he said afterwards, 'with this force have held out 3 or 4 days, which would not have prevented the consequences that have since happened.'[9] Therefore he had another letter smuggled out, this time requesting urgent reinforcements and forwarding an ultimatum from the Bengalis:

> We are informed by our vacqueel who had it from Golaum Shaw, that unless your Honour &c. will fill up the ditch and pull down the new works which he hears is begun upon, [at Calcutta] he is determined to attack us, therefore if your Honour &c. are

determined not to comply with his demand, we request you will
send us a supply of men, as our garrison is very weak, however we
think it adviseable for your Honour &c. to write a letter to the Nabob
immediately.[10]

This produced no result, for the Council correctly judged it impossible
to get any reinforcements since it was impractical to march them
overland and the river was too low to send them on by boat. As Grant
held to his opinion that the Cossimbazar factory was capable of holding
out until the expected rains, it was agreed on all hands that it was too
risky in the meantime to do more than advise Madras of what was
happening. Nothing therefore was done and a week later an
increasingly panicky Watts wrote of the Bengalis bringing up artillery.
He now wanted 100 men to be sent upriver at once, but it was already
too late for by then the Nawab himself had arrived and on the evening
of 2 June 1756, Watts came out of the compound, with an escort of just
two soldiers, to try and negotiate with him. Instead he was roughly
seized and his colleagues were forced to surrender the place without a
fight next day. This collapse was roundly denounced at the time as
cowardly by the other Companies, appalled by this blow to European
prestige. The Dutch factor in Cossimbazar even added the delicious
detail that Watts had rushed out of the compound to meet the Nawab
'like one distracted, in his nightshirt'.[11] Once the gates were opened the
Bengalis poured in. The Company's godowns or warehouses were very
promptly secured with the Nawab's seal, but no such protection was
extended to the staff's private quarters. An orgy of looting ensued over
the next few days with the Bengalis 'threatening the gentlemen to cut off
their ears, slit their noses and chabuck [whip] them'. For Lieutenant
John Elliot, who was commanding the garrison, the humiliation – or the
fear of worse – proved too much and he shot himself on 8 June.[12] In all
conscience, the surrender was inevitable and later acknowledged as
such by the French at least. Given a resolute commander and sufficient
provisions, the compound might well have been defended for longer,
but Watts was probably justified in complaining afterwards that if he
had not surrendered when he did, 'we undoubtedly should have been
blamed for having commenced a war with the Government'.

The Fort of Calcutta

At any rate the news of the seizure was not unnaturally received with
some dismay at Calcutta, especially as it was accompanied by reports
that the Nawab was already marching south towards Calcutta with an

estimated 50,000 men and a substantial train of artillery – including the best of the guns taken at Cossimbazar. What was more, notwithstanding the Nawab's fears of a mighty bastion being raised against him, the Council was uneasily aware that Calcutta's defences were in fact pretty well non-existent, and admirably described as such by Robert Orme:

> The river Ganges forms a crescent between two points, the one called Perrin's Garden, the other Surman's Garden. The distance between these, measured along the bank of the river, is about three miles and a half. In the deepest part of this crescent, about the middle between the two points is situated Fort William, a building which many an old house in this country [i.e. England] exceeds in its defences. It is situated a few paces from the riverside, on the banks of which runs a Line of guns the whole length of the Fort from north to south, and this is the only formidable part, as it is capable of annoying ships in the river. The ends of this line are joined to the two bastions of the Fort nearest the river by a garden wall and a gate in each, which would resist the shot of one six-pounder, but which would be forced by the second. Opposite to the two bastions mentioned are two others inland to the eastward, but within thirty yards to the north and forty yards to the south the bastions are commanded by large houses. To the eastward inland the top of the Church commands the whole of both the northern and eastern ramparts. Northward and southward for the length of a mile, and to the eastward about a quarter of a mile stand all the English houses, mostly separated from each other by large enclosures. Where the English habitations end to the northward commence those of the principal black merchants, which reach quite up to Perrin's Garden. To the southward down to Surman's Garden the houses, belonging to a lower class of the natives, are less conspicuous. Twelve years ago a ditch had been dug, beginning at Perrin's and carried inland of the town in a crescent, with an intent to end at Surman's, but only four miles of it are finished.[13]

That was in 1754 and two years later, as Captain Grant disgustedly elaborated, not only had nothing been done to improve the situation but if anything it had deteriorated, and that line of guns along the riverbank were still waiting to be mounted:[14]

> When we received the news of Cossimbuzar's being in the Nabob's possession, and of his intentions to march towards us with the artillery and ammunition of that place and with an army of 20,000

horse and 30,000 gunmen, who had been encouraged with the promise of the immense plunder expected in Calcutta, it was full time to enquire into the state of defence of a garrison, which had been neglected for so many years, and the managers of it lulled in so infatuate a security, that every rupee expended on military services was esteemed so much lost to the Company.

By last year's shipping there was positive orders from the Company to execute a plan sent home by Colonel Scot[15] for their approbation, but his death was thought too sufficient an excuse to postpone what they had so little inclination to have executed. By a later ship we were still further pressed by the Company to put our Settlement in the best state of defence possible, as there was great appearance of a French war. Captain [Jasper Leigh] Jones of the artillery, in September last, thinking it more particularly his duty to represent the defenceless state the garrison was in, and the situation of the cannon and ammunition, gave in a representation to the Governor and Council of what was immediately necessary for the defence of the place in case of a French war; such as making outworks, mounting the cannon which lay then useless for want of carriages, and putting their stores and ammunition in the best condition possible. The stile and form of this paper, and the manner of delivering it in, it seems gave offence, and Captain Jones was reprimanded for his irregularity in not delivering such representations first to the Commanding Officer of the troops.

However, though it contained many truths proper to be considered, there was no further notice taken of its contents, nor no orders given for any military preparations; trusting in the same kind fortune that had for so many years defended them in peace and security...

As Orme noted, away back in 1742 when Aliverdi Khan had been at war with the Maratha Confederation, the old Nawab readily authorised the construction by the British of a defensive ditch intended to circle the landward sides of the town. The threat receded before the ditch was completed, but nevertheless what was ever afterwards known as the Maratha Ditch effectively covered most of the town from the north and the east. In the years of neglect since then it had, naturally enough, deteriorated somewhat but it still provided a significant obstacle to the movement of troops and artillery, who could only get over it by means of a limited number of crossing points. Beyond that it was fairly useless as a defensive work since it was not only several miles in extent but by enclosing both the European core and the sprawling native and Eurasian suburbs it was also at its closest point well over a mile out from Fort William. There was absolutely no question of defending the four-mile-long perimeter, even if it had ever been completed. With the few troops actually available to serve as a garrison, the sensible course would have been to retire into the fort immediately. Instead, as Grant lamented, contrary to the advice of the military officers, the decision was taken to try and defend the White Town or European quarter as well as the fort:

> On receiving the unexpected news of the loss of a place, we thought capable to stand out against any numbers of a country enemy while they had provisions, and with such artillery and stores as they generally use. It was thought proper to join the military captains and Engineer to the Council in order to form a Council of war; they were afterwards desired to retire to consider of the properest methods for the defence of the inhabitants and Town of Calcutta in case of an irruption of the Moors. Accordingly we gave it as our oppinions, that batterys should be erected in all the roads leading to the fort at such distances as could be anywise defensible with the small number of troops we had; that the inhabitants should be immediately formed into a body of militia; all the carpenters and smiths in the place taken into the Fort to prepare carriages; the ammunition and stores put in the best order, and lascars and cooleys taken into pay for the use of the cannon and other works to be done, and likewise what sepoys and peons could be got to be formed into a body under the command of some European. It may be justly asked why we did not propose, the only method that as I thought then, and now do, could give us the least chance of defending the place, in case of a vigorous attack, the demolition of all the houses adjacent to the fort and surrounding it with a ditch and glacee; but so little credit was then given, and even to the very last day, that the Nabob would venture to attack us, or offer to force our lines, that it occasioned a generall grumbling and discontent to leave any of the European houses without them. Nay, the generallity wanted even to include every brick house in the place, Portuguese and Armenian, and thought it hard that any inhabitant should be deprived of protection against such an enemy. And should it be proposed by any person to demolish so many houses as would be necessary to make the fort defensible, his opinion would have been thought pusilanimous and ridiculous, had there been sufficient time to execute such a work as there was not, nor would it be possible to destroy half the number in triple the time, especially as we had not powder sufficient to blow them up.[16]

27

Fort William itself was in fact a curious hybrid kind of pseudo-fortress outwardly constructed in an outdated European style in the 1690s, but lacking the protective angled glacis and ditch calculated to keep an attacker at a distance and to 'sink' it into the ground as a protection against artillery fire. In fact it was primarily designed in the early days simply to provide secure storage for the Company's goods and to serve as a fortress only if need be. No-one contemplated that they would ever need to and in effect it was no more than a folly built on a grand scale. The Company were after all traders not soldiers. Outwardly it was laid out in the form of a rectangular trace with a long face fronting the river for 700 feet. The north face ran inland for 310 feet, while the south face stretched nearly 500 feet. There was a small bastion at each corner to provide flanking fire and on the landward side a projection covering the main gate, genteelly referred to as a ravelin. The high outer walls actually concealed a series of vaulted warehouses rising 18 feet above the surrounding ground level, over which the parade ground, and all the offices and other accommodation within the fort were built on a flat, stone-flagged *terreplein* or deck laid out on top of the vaults. Unfortunately, imposing as they were, even the outer walls suffered from a number of defects, as enumerated by Captain Rennie:

> The Fort of Calcutta stood near north and south parallel to the bank of the river, differing from a long square or paralelgram by having the north end not quite so wide as the south end. The curtain towards the land (or the east curtain) had six or eight windows through it, and each corner was a small bastion that flanked the curtains with two guns, and fronted three each way… About fifteen years ago the Company being in want of warehouses, Governor Bradyll built a very large one against the south end of the Fort; it was nearly square for it extended from the south-east to the south-west bastion and projected 60 or 80 feet beyond them; by these means these two bastions were rendered of very little use for defending the south end of the Fort, for the curtain between them was now the inner wall of a warehouse, and a large passage broke through it into the Fort by way of a door to this new warehouse, being now in place of the curtain was not stronger than a common house wall, it was also very full of very large windows, and by projecting beyond the bastions could not be flanked by their guns. It is true there was a terrace and a parapet with embrazures upon this warehouse, but the terrace could only bear a two-pounder, and the parapet was only three feet high.[17]

Nevertheless, notwithstanding these various deficiencies and the others noted by Orme, had the town been evacuated, the fort itself ought to have been defensible at least long enough for help to arrive from Madras. Instead a fatal overconfidence saw the Governor and Council opt to overstretch their already inadequate resources by trying to hold what ought to have been no more than an outpost line.

At the north end of the town, hard by the river at Perrin's Garden, was a crossing point over the Maratha Ditch known as the Chitpur Bridge. This opened first on to the Bagh (or Flower) Bazaar and then a long street, known as the Chitpur Road, which eventually traversed the length of Calcutta from north to south. This appeared to be the most likely avenue of approach by the Nawab's forces coming down from Hugli and was accordingly thought worth defending by converting the crossing into a drawbridge and constructing a little fort to cover it. Sometimes called Perrin's Redoubt by Imperial historians, but generally referred to at the time as the Bagh Bazaar Fort, this was a simple box-like structure made of pukka or mud bricks with embrasures for seven guns and a number of loopholes for muskets.[18]

Otherwise most of the hastily-improvised defences were constructed much closer in towards the centre and more or less corresponded to the irregular boundary of the European residential quarter. On the north side of the fort, at the far end of Cruttenden's Ghat or wharf, what was styled the North Battery was thrown up directly in front of the Saltpetre Godown in order to cover any approach along the river-bank.[19] Directly in front of the fort's main gate was a broad straight roadway which proceeded due eastwards, eventually crossing the Maratha Ditch by a causeway near to the oddly-named Bread and Cheese Bungalow.[20] Close to the fort the road was known as The Avenue, but once outside the European Quarter it became the Lal (or Red) Bazaar, and at that point an East Battery was erected squarely across the road, close by the court-house. Similarly, a South Battery was erected to cover a crossing point over the ditch between the burying ground and a Mr Wedderburn's house. Whilst on paper a defensive perimeter was sketched out linking the three batteries, this amounted to no more than a series of palisades and ditches – little better than barricades – hastily cut across the various streets. Otherwise it was a matter of relying upon the compound walls surrounding the individual houses. Inside the fort itself, efforts were made to build up the low parapets and close the over-wide embrasures with bags of cotton waste, as well as to repair gun carriages. Unfortunately, both this work and the ditching and palisading was greatly hampered by a dramatically spiralling shortage of labourers as the native inhabitants steadily drained away from Calcutta in the face of the Nawab's advance.

Manning the Walls

What was more, the garrison itself was seriously deficient. Not only had a considerable number of men been sent to Madras four years previously, but for some time now any recruits destined for the European companies in Bengal had been intercepted at Madras and diverted into that Presidency's forces, so that according to Rennie 'each of our five companys of soldiers had only five to seven Europeans, in all thirty-five, and the Train about as many, *viz.* in all seventy European soldiers, besides their officers, the others being all black Portuguze'.[21] He was not exaggerating. In theory each of the three captains in the garrison commanded a company but in fact their men had never paraded as such in living memory and Captain Grant therefore had great difficulty in establishing just how many men were actually present and fit for duty, since none of the garrison's officers had any idea. All too many men were lying in hospital or on detachment up-country or were simply unaccounted for, but after laboriously counting heads, Grant eventually reported that: 'Our military to defend it, exclusive of those at the subordinate Factory, amounted only to 180 infantry, of which number there were not 40 Europeans, and 36 men of the Artillery Company, sergeants and corporals included.'

The shortage of soldiers was at least something they could attempt to address. There were as yet no disciplined sepoy companies on the Bengal establishment to compare with those being raised in Madras, but this deficiency was partially erased by the hiring of some 700 *buxarries*, or native mercenary infantry armed with matchlocks.[22] Unfortunately, although they fought well at the very outset of the siege they all deserted after the first couple of days' fighting – and were strongly suspected of taking service under the Nawab instead. In addition, just as at Madras ten years earlier, a militia was hastily raised from amongst the younger civilians and when formally mustered on the morning of 8 June 1756, were reckoned to number upwards of 250; 'about one hundred of them were Europeans, part of whom were called off their duty in the shipping and could not well be reckoned as Militia. The remainder were country-born Portugueze and Armenians.' In all, by the time the siege opened the garrison numbered a notional total of 515 men.[23] The militia were initially formed into three companies, but, continued Drake, 'finding the Portugueze and Armenians extremely awkward at their arms it was judged proper that one company should consist entirely of Europeans and all the care possible was taken for disciplining those new troops that the time would allow of, they being constantly trained morning and evening in a body until it was found necessary to form the several dispositions at the three batteries. It is necessary to observe here that many Company's covenanted servants and young gentlemen in the Settlement entered as volunteers in the military, doing duty in every respect as common soldiers and always expressing a forwardness to be sent on command.'

The leadership structure of this enhanced force was by no means as complicated as might at first appear, and whilst the Governor, Roger Drake, was certainly not a military man, the criticism which he has attracted from historians is by no means fair. The regular garrison was at the time under the nominal charge of one George Minchin, who accordingly held the title of Captain-Commandant, along with Captain David Clayton as his second and a Captain John Buchannan. John Zephaniah Holwell's famous description of Minchin is particularly unflattering, but his opinion appears to have been shared by everyone who ever met him: 'Touching upon the military capacity of our Commandant', he wrote, 'I am a stranger. I can only say we are unhappy in his keeping it to himself, if he had any; as neither I, nor I believe anyone else, was witness to any part of his conduct that spoke or bore the appearance of his being the commanding military officer in the garrison.'[24] No such accusation of incompetence appears to have been levelled at Clayton, but then again no-one ever troubled to record any impressions of him at all, other than to note that he alone had not previously served in Europe or on the coast, which suggests he was something of a nonentity. Buchannan on the other hand was said to be brave and experienced and was to prove himself so in the days that followed.[25]

Now that the fit ones were properly mustered Lieutenant Smith was promoted captain-lieutenant in order to take day-to-day charge of Minchin's own company whilst the latter supposedly exercised command of the whole. Grant did not have a company (unless it was lost at Cossimbazar) but he was 'esteemed the best officer in the service, and in consequence thereof entrusted with the whole direction of the military as far as he could be, by the name of Adjutant General'.[26]

The militia, however, did not come under Minchin's command, either in theory or in practice. Just as in Britain itself at this period, rank in the militia corresponded to a man's rank in society, rather than any military qualifications or experience. Thus command of the militia was assumed by the two most senior members of the Council after the governor himself – Charles Manningham, the Export Warehouse Keeper, and

William Frankland, the Import Warehouse Keeper – simply because it was unthinkable that they should not be such great men in the militia as they were in civil life.

As to the Fort's artillery, Grant's survey discovered that there was

> hardly a gun on the ramports with a carriage fit for service. We had about three years ago 50 pieces of cannon, 18 and 24 pounders, with two mortars, 10 and 13 inches, with a good quantity of shells and balls for each; but they [had] been allowed to lay on the grass, where they were first landed ever since, without carriages or beds. Only the 10 inche mortars we made shift to get ready by the time we were attacked, but neither shells filled nor fuses prepared for mortars or cohorns, made as well as the rest of little use. Our grape were eat up by the worms, and in short all our amunition of all sorts, such as we had, [was] in the worst order; not a gun with a carriage fit be carried out of the Fort for any use, except the two field pieces, which was sent us from [Madras]. What powder we had ready, for want of care the greatest part was damp and the season of the year improper to dry it.

Part of the problem here was that while the Train of Artillery was unquestionably a part of the military, like the militia it also stood apart and just as in Britain a clear distinction was drawn between the Army proper and the Ordnance Department or Train, which was an independent body responsible for all matters pertaining to the artillery, ammunition and explosives. As of right, therefore, Captain Lawrence Witherington reported directly to the Governor and Council rather than going through Captain-Commandant Minchin. Unfortunately not only was Witherington engaged in an obscure feud of some kind with Minchin but he turned out to be curiously incapable of communicating with anyone else either, which despite Holwell's surprising endorsement of him, Grant no doubt correctly interpreted as covering up his incapacity:

> There happened unfortunately, a misunderstanding to subsist between the Commandant and Captain Witherington who commanded the Train, which prevented Captain Minchin's having the Returns he ought of the stores and ammunition; at least the latter did not exert himself properly in his command, which I imagine was owing to the Governor's giving too ready an ear to Witherington's complaints of Minchin, he happening at the same time to be but upon indifferent terms with the Governor. These animositys

amongst the persons who had the whole command and charge of the garrison in their hands did not contribute a little to our misfortunes.

Upon my being appointed Adjutant General I wrote down dayly what orders I thought might be necessary, and shewed them to the Governor for his approbation; They were afterwards issued out to the Adjutants of the military and militia, and by them carried to the commanding officer of each corps. Colonel Manningham, Lieutenant Colonel Frankland and Commandant Minchin for the more regular detail of duty were appointed Field Officers, to mount at the outworks dayly by rotation. I think amongst the first orders given on the news of the Nabob's approach. Captain Witherington was ordered to give in immediately a particular Return of the guns, ammunition and stores fit for service, as likewise of his company, volunteers entered, such as sea captains and Portuguese helmsmen and lascars, and everything else relating to the artillery. But the whole was never complyed with and only a return of the guns and ammunition given the night before the Governor retreated, being the 18th. I pressed dayly to the Governor the necessity there was of having his orders obeyed, and was sorry to receive no other answer, than that Witherington was a strange unaccountable man, and that he did not know what to do with him. Captain Minchin pressed likewise to have his orders complyed with in this respect, but in vain. From what motive or partiality to the man I cannot guess, without that his making a bustle and constant noise, recommended him as a very active man, who could not be supplyed was he suspended. I often repeated to the Governor the bad consequence that would ensue from trusting the safety of the garrison (as it chiefly depended on the state of our ammunition and stores) to the will and management of such a man, without giving any account or Return of his proceedings.

Such was the garrison that awaited Siraj-ud-Daula.

Chapter 3

Into the Black Hole

As a matter of course a letter was sent to Madras on 7 June requesting urgent assistance and in response the Council there hurriedly scraped some 200 men together by stripping all the garrisons along the coast and embarking them on the *Delaware* Indiaman under a redoubtable officer named Major James Killpatrick. Unfortunately there was no prospect of either him or his reinforcements arriving at any time soon and, with the Nawab's forces closing in, it was literally time to man the barricades.

On the morning of 12 June 1756, the Calcutta garrison was mustered and then deployed as follows: the Fort itself was assigned to the untrained rabble of Armenian and Eurasian militia, amounting to about 150 men, stiffened by just twenty-five regular soldiers. This uncertain band, some allegedly held to their posts at pistol-point, were commanded by Captain Minchin himself and it is very hard to avoid the impression that both assignments were carefully 'arranged' by Grant to keep the militia safely out of the way and to shuffle Minchin aside to where he could commit no blunders. Outside the Fort, the East, or Court House Battery was assigned to Captain David Clayton, assisted by Captain Holwell of the militia and three subaltern officers, including a Frenchman, Lieutenant Melchior Le Beaume.[1] Between them they commanded fifty 'military' and twenty volunteers, with twenty European militia and eight gunners together with an unknown number of *buxarries*. Another seventy-odd soldiers and volunteers, twenty militia and eight gunners were assigned to the South Battery under Captain John Buchannan and a militia officer named William Mackett. The North, or Saltpetre Godown Battery was more thinly manned by just thirty military and ten volunteers under Captain-lieutenant Smith together with the inevitable twenty European militia under the Rev.

William Mapletoft, and eight gunners. Each of the batteries had two pieces of cannon mounted. That to the north only had 12-pounders, but the other two had 18-pounders.

So far so good. Bengali boats passing up and down the river were also being stopped and rummaged by now and on 13 June an expedition was mounted against the Nawab's fort at Tanna, on the right bank of the Hoogli about 10 miles downstream from Calcutta:

> The *Prince George*, a ship belonging to [the] Madrass Establishment, in company with the *Dodley*, the *Lively* ketch, and *Neptune* snow, which were taken in the Company's service (as many other vessels were) were sent to Mucka Tanna, to demolish the fortifications there. About noon they sett sail, and in the evening landed what men they had, who entered the fort without opposition, and spiked seven guns they found there; six of which they threw in the river, but the 14th about eleven o'clock in the morning the enemy, about 3 or 4,000, advanced with great precipitation to the fort, which obliged what men we had landed to take to their boats; the enemy took immediate possession of the fort, and fired very smartly with their small arms from the parapets, as also from two field pieces they had planted behind some bushes to the northward of the fort, about 150 paces. The shipping returned the fire of the enemy the whole day, and in the evening dropt away with the ebb having done no visible execution. In this attack Captain Best of the *Lively* ketch received a wound across his belly with a shott, and one lascar was killed on board the *Dodley*.
>
> The next day being the 15th Lieutenant Bishop was detached with 30 men to reinforce the shipping, in order to drive the enemy from Mucka Tanna, upon which they were directed again to their stations under command of Captain David Rannie, who was appointed Commodore in this expedition; but whatever were the reasons the military returned the next day, without either they or the ships, making the least attempt against the enemy, indeed, 5 or 6 shot were fired by them, which were returned; in the evening the ships were ordered to return also.[2]

16 June 1756: The Battle begins

This was because the rest of the Nawab's army was coming on rather faster than expected and his arrival was now anticipated within hours rather than days. Accordingly, some of the ships were sent upstream to Perrin's Gardens to lie off the Bagh Bazaar Fort. There they were badly

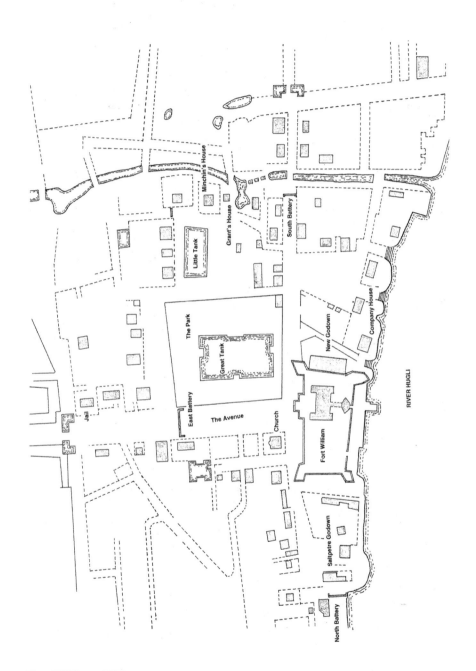

Fort William 1756

needed to support its isolated little garrison which was comprised of just twenty-five regulars and thirty *buxarries*, with two 3-pounder guns all under the command of Ensign John Francis Piccard.[3] As William Tooke continued:

> June 16th, advice was received early in the morning that the Nabob's forces had crossed the river a little above Hughley, and some at Chandernagore, and that they marched with surprizing expedition. About half past eleven the same day, the enemy appeared in great numbers at Chitpur, and their cannon arriving soon after, they began to fire briskly on the *Fortune* ketch and *Chance* sloop ... from a seven gun battery, one of which was an 18-pounder, the rest 6-pounders; however the vessels by keeping a quick fire maintained their stations; upon which the enemy turned their whole force upon the redoubt and accordingly brought up their cannon on elephants to the edge of a small wood, to the northward of the fossée. They then attempted several times to force a passage over the fossée under the fire of their cannon and small arms; but our little troop keeping a constant platoon fire on them, as likewise by playing smartly two three-pounders which they had there, and being reinforced with a detachment of 50 men under command of lieutenant Blagg, and the picquet under command of Captain Clayton advancing at about half past six, the enemy thought proper to retire. They must have sustained a considerable loss in this attack, for seventy nine of their dead were found the next morning, most of them killed with cannon shott at the corner of the wood where they had brought up their artillery.[4]

Grant, who was probably in a better position to know, told a slightly less dramatic story, relating that it was not until the afternoon that he received 'advice' from Piccard that he was coming under attack. In response the ensign was then 'immediately reinforced with an 18-pounder the 2 brass fieldpieces and 40 men under the command of Lieutenant Blagg, being resolved to give them a warm reception on their approach. They had got six pieces of cannon playing on the redoubt and sloop when the reinforcement arrived, but on our fieldpieces beginning to play they withdrew their cannon, and abandoned that post, inclining to the southward, where they had on the opposite side of the ditch got possession of a tope of wood from whence they killed one of our gentlemen volunteers and 4 of the military.'[5] Notwithstanding this, a sea captain named Mills asserted that the 18-pounder, which must have been a heavy beast, was not actually sent up until eight o'clock that evening, when it was exchanged for Blagg's two field guns. This would also tie in with Clayton also being sent out rather later than Tooke's account suggests and for a very different purpose:

> Before dark the whole body inclined to the southward, and crossed the ditch that surrounds the Black Town, the extent of it being so great, and passable in all parts, that it was impossible to do anything to interrupt them. Lieutenant Blagg about 8 at night demanded a further reinforcement to cover his retreat, as he was apprehensive of the enemys advancing through some of the lanes to cut off his communication. Captain Clayton was ordered with a party to that purpose, who returned safe with Lieutenant Blagg about 10 at night, and left Ensign Paccard in possession of the redoubt with his former detachment.[6]

At any rate both sides were agreed that it had been a serious repulse, and one which was comprehensively reinforced when Piccard resolved on a counter-attack that night.

> At midnight nothing was moving in the thickets; for every man, after eating his meal, had as usual betook himself to sleep; which Ensign Piccard, who had served on the coast of Coromandel, suspected from their silence, and crossing the rivulet at midnight with his party, seized and spiked the four pieces of cannon, beat up and drove all the troops out of the thicket, and returned without the loss of a man.[7]

It is not entirely clear why the Nawab had initially directed his general, Rai Durlabh, to tackle the Chitpur crossing head-on, rather than working his way around the Mahratta Ditch to find an undefended one, for the ditch at this point was effectively an inlet of the Hoogli and pretty impassable save by the bridge. There was some suggestion the Nawab was unaware of the alternatives, but this seems hard to believe. The most likely explanation is that having marched on Calcutta with the publicly expressed intention of destroying the British fortifications, he simply pitched on starting off with Kelsall's Octagon and the Bagh Bazaar Fort.[8]

17 June 1756: Lull before the Storm

> Next morning [continued Grant] being the 17th, Monsieur le Beaume (who was a French officer, and left Chandnagor on a point of honor) desired to be permitted to take possession of the Gaol

about 200 yards advanced before the battery, and where three roads terminates into the place.[9] He was accordingly ordered with 2 small cannon, 12 military and militia, and 40 buxeries or gunners; he broke embrasures through the Gaol House for the cannon, and made loopholes all round for the musquetry. All this day the enemy did not advance in sight of any of our batterys, but the plunderers annoyed the black inhabitants greatly which we could not possibly help without risquing our men to be shot at from behind houses and walls. Our peons[10] brought in severall of their people, but their reports were so different that we could not depend on it.

They informed us that they had all the Cossimbuzar cannon with some brought from Muxadavad [Murshidabad] of heavier mettall, about 25 Europeans and 80 Chittygong fringys[11] under the command of one who stiled himself Le Marquis de St. Jacque, a French renegaid,[12] for the management of their artillery, about 15,000 horse and 10,000 foot, but we found afterwards this to be short of their numbers. From the three grand batterys as many men as could be spared were detached to the breastworks thrown up in the small lanes, and such houses as most commanded our batterys taken possession with Serjeants and corporals' guards. This night all our peons deserted us, and in short every black fellow, who could make his escape, abandoned us. Upwards of 1,000 bearers left us in one night, on being ordered to carry the powder from the Magazeen into the Fort. And on the plunderers[13] advancing into the town, all the Portuguese familys crowded within our lines for protection to the number of some thousands.

18 June 1756: A Day of Dattle

The battle proper resumed next day. The enemy did indeed attempt to find a way through by the houses, but the little detachments scattered by Grant to hold the barricades and houses at first succeeded in preventing their infiltrating the perimeter. The defenders were obviously badly outnumbered but the Bengalis seem to have had trouble in bringing up sufficient men through the warrens of the 'Black Town' to overwhelm the individual outposts, far less co-ordinate their attacks. In fact at sunrise, Captain-lieutenant Smith, at the North Battery, having decided that the enemy was getting too close for comfort, 'detached Ensign Walcott with fifty men and a field piece, to hinder them from plundering the houses and to drive them to a greater distance, accordingly upon his advancing about 200 paces, forced the enemy from the houses they were possessed of, and obliged them to retire to a considerable distance with some loss, though without the loss of a single man on our side.'[14]

This was all well and good, but the discomfited would-be attackers merely drifted across to join in a much more serious attack shaping up against the crossroads where comparatively broad Lal Bazaar and Chitpur road met and by 8am the Bengalis were concentrating on Le Beaume's little garrison in the jail. Two cannon, 'one of them an 18 pounder by the size of the ball', as Grant wryly commented, were soon levelled against it and the pukka brick walls proved an ineffective defence. Clayton then reinforced Le Baume with a small reinforcement of a corporal and six volunteers under Ensign Peter Carstairs. Thus encouraged, the Frenchman ran out his two guns (mounted on ship or truck carriages) into the street, in order to return fire more effectively. Perhaps predictably however they were quickly driven back inside. Clayton at this point ordered Le Beaume to retreat before he was cut off, but at first he refused and demanded a further supply of ammunition instead. The argument continued until about 3pm, by which time three quarters of the gallant little band were wounded, including Carstairs and Le Beaume himself. Nor was it possible to get any ammunition through to the jail and so in obedience to Clayton's repeated orders Le Beaume at last spiked his original two guns and fell back with the field pieces.

Inevitably enough the Bengalis immediately took possession of the jail and the other adjacent buildings, bringing up cannon of their own and not only bombarding the East Battery but winkling out the various small detachments from the nearby houses. At first Clayton held on with the aid of his own artillery and some Coehorn mortars, but he and Holwell were becoming increasingly pessimistic about their chances and as the latter related:

> Thus circumstanced Captain Clayton ordered me (I think about 5 afternoon) to go down to the fort and represent the state of the battery, and receive orders, whether the post should be withdrawn or maintained … in an hour more not a man could have appeared on the battery, or stired in or out of the Court House, without being a dead mark to the enemy; to say nothing of our people having been needlessly fatigued and harassed to such a degree that I believe in two hours more not a man of us would have had strength enough to have walked to the fort.[15]

On the strength of this dismal report Drake authorised Clayton to spike his guns and withdraw. Holwell, however, was being somewhat disingenuous after the fact and as usual Captain Grant told a slightly different story. At the time Grant was trying to shore up the defensive perimeter along the south-eastern quadrant, where Captain Buchannan's South Battery was in some danger of being outflanked.

> They first broke into our lines through Mr. Nixon's house and fixed their collours (as is their custom every inch of ground they gain) at the corner of the Tank. We were now obliged to abandon the breastwork close to Mr. Putham's and all the houses of that Square, the enemy in multitudes taking possession of each of them. They brought some heavy pieces of cannon through the lane twixt Minchin's and Putham's houses and planted them at the corner of the Tank and door of Mr. Nixon's to play upon us as we passed and repassed to and from the batterys. Having thus lodged themselves in all the houses of the Square on which only two guns from the flank of the north-east bastion could bear, and that at too great a distance to annoy them much, they had a secure footing within our lines; and those houses (being most of them pucka with the multitudes that occupied them were too strong lodgements for us to pretend to dispossess them of; being at the same time attacked in some manner at each of the other posts.
>
> This situation of the enemy exposed the battery to have its communication cut off from the fort, as the enemy might surround them in the rear by advancing through the lane that passes by Captain Grant's and between Captains Buchanan's and Witherington's house; it was therefore thought necessary to order Captain Buchanan to retire with his cannon to the battery where 2 embrasures had been opened in expectation of such a retreat.

Afterwards he reckoned it was about 4pm when he delivered the order for Buchannan to retire to his fall-back position, about 200 metres further up the road, near the south-east bastion of the fort. From there Grant then proceeded to check how things were going at Clayton's position, where, as he explained, he learned to his dismay that:

> I think it was about 4 [in the] afternoon when I delivered this order and I then proceeded to Captain Clayton's battery at where they had the warmest part of the attack since our retreat from the Goal at 2, by the enemy's keeping possession of all the houses round it, and though we sent an 18 pounder (which by that time we had got mounted on a truck carriage, and were obliged to have drawen to the battery by the militia in the fort, all our lascars and cooleys having

abandoned us) in order to play upon the houses which the enemy possessed, they still not only maintained their ground but advanced apace through one house to another; this occasioned Captain Holwell to go in person to the Governor. Whether by a representation of the state they were in or at his own request he obtained an order to abandon that battery; which having been of the utmost consequence, ought not to have been done but by a determination of a council of war: especially as there was not such numbers killed, but it might have been easily maintained, at least till dark. On my arrivall at the battery I found all the guns spiked, except the two field pieces, with which they were then ready to retreat. I was not a little surprised to find things in this situation, and by the Governor's orders, as they informed me. I therefore requested their stay for a few minutes till I galloped to the fort for further orders. The Governor made me answer that the post was represented to him [by Holwell] as no longer tenible, and had accordingly ordered its being withdrawen.[16] Now the guns were spiked, there was nothing further to be done than to get them likewise withdrawen, as leaving them behind must have greatly encouraged the enemy, and convinced them of the pannick that seized us, which only could occasion such a precipitate retreat. As I was going back to the battery I found Captain Clayton and his command with the 2 fieldpieces half way towards the fort. I prevailed upon him to return with me, that, if possible we might not undergo the ignominy of leaving our guns behind us in such a precipitate manner. But when I ordered half the men to lay down their arms in order to draw first the 18-pounder while the other half stood with their arms for defence of the battery, not a man would stir or pull a rope. As nothing could be done I left Captain Clayton to make his retreat as regular as he could.

Grant's disgust at the premature and disorderly abandonment of the East Battery was amply justified by the even greater debacle that followed. Once the battery was gone the other detachments found themselves in imminent danger of being cut off. There was no alternative but to pull them back into the fort at once. Captain-lieutenant Smith, largely left undisturbed after his pre-emptive counter-attack that morning, effected his retreat expeditiously and in notably good order, briskly marching both guns and men safely back through the main gate. Unfortunately Buchannan's withdrawal went badly wrong. After Grant left him, he pulled his guns back to the so-called reserve battery. This movement was successfully covered by the various small parties and detachments posted in the adjacent houses.

Unfortunately, with the East battery out of action, the Bengalis were able to press forward and cut off the rearguard commanded by the intrepid Lieutenant Blagg. William Tooke was one of his party and grimly recounted how:

> Lieutenant Blagg and the volunteers under his command posted at the top of Captain Minchin's house were but in an indifferent situation, for about 3 o'clock in the afternoon Captain Clayton withdrew the serjeant and 16 men who defended the house next to them, and soon after the serjeant and 16 men, who defended the breastwork at Mrs Putham's, basely running away (on one of his men's being killed) left them greatly exposed to the enemy, who immediately took possession of all the houses round about, nay even of that house itself, and barricaded the dors up to the very top of the house, which passage to the top being very narrow they did not dare to attempt; in which situation they continued till near seven o'clock, received the fire of the enemy from every part, as likewise were in no small danger from our own guns at the factory, who were at that time playing very smartly on the enemy at that quarter; when, all their ammunition being expended, obliged them to take a resolution to force open the doors, and fight their way through with their bayonets, especially as by that time all the batterys were withdrawn and but one attempt made to relieve them, which party was repulsed by the enemy; so looking upon themselves as a forlorn hope were willing to extricate themselves the best they could. Accordingly the door was burst open, and upon endeavouring to retreat to a lane at the back of the house leading to the Rope Walk in hopes to get under shelter of our own guns, found the enemy so numerous as rendered that passage impracticable, and here Messrs. Smith and Wilkinson, two of the party, having imprudently advanced a little too far, were cut to pieces, though the first killed 4 or 5 of the enemy before he fell; the remainder by making good use of their bayonets (not having a single charge left) gained the front gate of the house. By this time the enemy were possessed of the whole square, so we were obliged to pass through all their fire, till they gained a field piece that was placed at the end of the park wall to cover Captain Buchannan's retreat, which playing upon the enemy drove them to a greater distance. The number of Moors killed by that party is almost incredible. The enemy acknowledge 173 killed, besides wounded, but the number was judged much greater as every shott must have taken place, the enemy being in such swarms, besides what were killed by bayonets in forcing a passage

through them. Those of the volunteers who remained were Messrs. Ellis, Tooke, Parker, Knapton, Law, Dodd, Drake, and McPherson, commanded by Lieutenant Blagg.[17]

There was to be no respite, and having made their escape Blagg and his remaining men were then assigned to defend the Company House, on the south side of the fort. Retention of this strongpoint was necessary to deny the Bengalis access to the riverside ghats or landing places at the back of the fort, but there was also another equally pressing need to hold on to it as Rennie explained: 'Three strong upper room brick houses, and the church [St. Anne's] all inclosed with a brick wall stood within pistol-shot of the Fort. These were Mr Cruttenden's at the north end; the Company's House at the south end; about the middle of the east curtain stood the church and Mr Eyre's house close to the north-east bastion.'[18] Unfortunately the Company House was itself overlooked by Rennie's and once it was occupied by the Bengalis, Blagg reckoned that by daylight his position would be untenable and also feared he was liable to be cut off 'by their being surrounded in the lane that leads to the waterside along the new godowns, where there was no guns to flank, so applied to the Governor and obtained leave to abandon it, in which situation it was left all night.' Similarly Piccard and his remaining men were evacuated from their lonely outpost by the Chitpur bridge and brought downriver by boat to the fort.

Inside Fort William, however, morale was on the point of collapse. Naturally enough the Eurasians and Armenians belonging to the garrison had insisted on their dependents being given shelter and now the fort was thronged with as many as 2,000 of them by some accounts, all packed into the warehouses below the parade and anywhere else they could find shelter. Yet at the same time all of the Bengali cooks and other servants had deserted and most of the survivors later complained of the impossibility of getting food prepared – seemingly no-one thought of employing the Eurasian refugees. Militarily too, the situation continued to deteriorate:

> Having withdrawn the batteries which defended the three principal avenues leading to the fort, the evening of the above day; the Company's House, Messrs. Cruttenden's and Eyre's, and the Church (all close to our walls) were taken possession of by the troops who retired from those batteries; and only the militia with 30 of the military continued for the defence of the fort. Till about eight at night I was employed in settling those outposts; in which time several resolutions had been taken in a council of war, of which I remained

for some time ignorant; such as permitting Messrs. Manningham and Frankland, our two Field Officers, to escort the [British] ladies on board the ships &c.[19] The guard settled in the Company's House was soon after, on application made by some of the young gentlemen to the Governor ordered to be with- drawn, and that advantageous post left to be taken possession of by the enemy; whereby they would not only have a total command of the two southerly bastions and curtain, but likewise of the wharf and gaut where all our boats lay, and consequently have it in their power to obstruct our communication with the river. Continual duty and want of refreshment so harrassed both military and militia that before 12 at night, not a man could be brought on the ramparts, till dragged from the different corners of the fort where they had retired to rest; and by the help of liquor, which several of them met with, numbers were rendered incapable of any duty. This with constant calls from the out- posts for provisions and water, and none ready dressed to supply them, occasioned a disorder and confusion in all quarters, not easy to be described.[20]

In the meantime, sensing that he was on the point of victory, the Nawab ordered a series of attacks to be mounted throughout the night. His men were unused to such tactics and do not appear to have pressed them very hard, but they were more than enough to wear out the exhausted defenders. As noted, Lieutenant Blagg was forced to evacuate the Company House at about 10pm and an hour or so later came reports that the enemy was preparing scaling ladders for a general assault from that direction. Orders were given to beat to arms but happily the attack when it did come was just as half-hearted and a shower of hand grenades dropped over the wall 'soon dislodged them', but then:

About one in the morning a second council of war was called, to consider of our then situation, and what in all probability we might expect it to be on the approach of day; as likewise, from every circumstance considered, for what time we might reasonably expect to maintain the fort. The Captain of the Artillery was first asked what quantity of ammunition we had then in store (you must observe the Governor never procured a return of it) and for what time he thought it would last according to the expences of the day past. His answer was, that at the same rate, it would not be sufficient for above three days, and even a part of that, he was affraid was damp. This of itself, but added to the other circumstances still more, made it the unanimous oppinion that a retreat on board the ships must be determined on in that time, should no circumstances intervene to make it sooner necessary; as nothing but the utmost barbarity was expected from our enemy in case of surrender, as by fatall experience we have found to be the case, with such as fell into his hands. The majority were of opinion that as such a retreat was already fixed on, the delay of it even untill next morning could be attended with no sort of advantage, but might on the contrary produce such consequences as would either make it impracticable, or attended with the greatest risque and precipitation. For instance, did the enemy get possession of the houses we then occupied and the Company's, there was but little to prevent their forcing oppen the two barriers that lead to the fort from the Company's House and Cruttenden's; and from those two houses they might keep such a fire on the gaut and wharff, as would make it impossible for a boat to lye there; either of which would have effectually prevented our retreat.

However, having taken the decision to retreat, an argument then arose as to the timing. Grant and Holwell were all for getting everybody out there and then under cover of darkness, but others disagreed 'first that it would be impossible to call the parties from the houses and get them shipped off before daylight, secondly as the flood [tide] was just set in they would be greatly exposed to the enemy's fire before they got on board of the ships. It was therefore agreed to continue in the fort until the next night and then to make a regular retreat if possible.'[21] Just at that moment, according to Tooke, a cannonball crashed through the room and although no-one was injured, the Council was immediately wound up 'with the utmost clamour, confusion, tumult and perplexity … without coming to any determination or resolution, but good-naturedly leaving every member to imagine his proposals would be followed and put into execution'.[22] Grant, for his part, sensibly retired to bed for an hour or two, but was soon on the ramparts again when he found the Bengalis 'warmly' attacking the last remaining outposts.

19 June 1756: Collapse

It was Saturday 19 June, the fourth day of the battle, and by now the Bengalis had brought up some heavy artillery of their own, including two 18-pounders which they planted in the Lal Bazaar. During the night Ensign Piccard and his men had also, bravely, re-occupied the Company House, but by 8 am he was brought back into the Fort badly wounded and within a couple of hours the officers in the other posts outside the walls were clamouring to be allowed to withdraw as well. The Nawab's troops were already able to get down to the riverbank and were now beginning to interfere with the disorderly evacuation of the Eurasian women and children which had begun at first light and as a result something of a panic started. Some of the small boats overturned, others were set on fire by burning arrows and then the big ships started to slip their moorings and drop down the river. It was the beginning of the end and Grant soon found himself caught up in the debacle:

> About 10 o'clock I received an alarm, when on the south east bastion, that the enemy had got possession of the Compound of the Company's House, and were forcing their way through the barrier that leads from thence to the fort; but when I came there, I found the report to be false. On my return towards the back gate, I saw the Governor standing on the stair head of the gaut beckoning to his servant, who was in a boat about 50 yards above.[23]
>
> I came up expecting he might have some commands for me, for I had not seen him before, since we broke up the council of war. When I addressed him, he pointed to me where the *Doddaley* and other vessells had fallen down below the Town, and numbers of boats full of Europeans were then proceeding on their way on board of them; saying that Messrs Manningham and Frankland, though sent for in the night, had still remained on board the *Doddaley* with the ladies; by which means they had so discouraged numbers of the gentlemen, as to induce them to provide for their own safety, in the same manner, and by their example. He then (without giving me time to make any answer) went down the stairs, up the waterside under the Line, and into the boat where his servant stood. I was somewhat amazed at his sudden departure being entirely ignorant of his intentions, and only supposed he had gone to give some particular orders to his servant: but finding he did not return soon, I thought it my duty to follow him, as I still remained unacquainted with his designs. When I came to the boat, and desired to know what he intended, he replied that he was resolved to provide for his own safety, as he found others were doing. I entreated him that if that was his resolution, he would wait till it was first intimated to Mr. Holwell and the rest of the garrison, and make as good a retreat as the situation of things would bear. He said it would be impracticable to make a regular retreat in the confusion things were then in; especially for want of boats, most of them being carried off by those who went before. That he therefore thought it would be in vain to

wait any longer; and supposed when the rest of the garrison saw him come off, such of them as could find conveyance would follow.

I had but little time for recollection in such a juncture, and was therefore the more readily determined by the circumstances which immediately ensued. Looking behind me at the stairs of the gaut I saw it crowded with people pressing to get away; and amongst the rest Commandant Minchin and Mr. Mackett going into a budjerow. This I concluded to be in consequence of their seeing the Governor first make his escape; and according to what he told me before had not then the least doubts remaining, but every other person who observed him and could find conveyance would think the example of their Governor and Commander- in-chief a sufficient sanction for them to abandon a place, already declared not tenible above two days, and then in the greatest confusion. I likewise foresaw that those who should be obliged to remain behind for want of boats, would be exposed to the mercy of a cruel enemy, unless relieved by having conveyances sent them from the ships. My station of Adjutant General had fixed me to no particular post in the fort, but more properly was to attend the Governor for his orders, and act in a manner as his aidecamp.

Looking behind, I perceived Mr. Macket and Captain Minchin setting off in their budgerow, and the stairs full of Europeans pressing to do the same. I concluded the retreat to be generall, and that everyone who could lay hold of a conveyance would choose to escape falling into the hands of a merciless ennemy, and so with Mr. O'Hara thought it justifyable to follow the Governor in a state of such apparent confusion and disorder, though greatly grieved to see how many of my friends and country-men were likely to fall a sacrifice for want of boats, as I believe there was not annother left at the gaut when the Governor came away.

Unsurprisingly, Tooke and those others left behind in the general collapse might be forgiven their anger and dismay. Pearkes declared that 'Captain Minchin's going occasioned not the least concern to anyone, but it was with great difficulty we could persuade ourselves Captain Grant had left us',[24] while Tooke rather more bitterly wrote that, 'Upon the Governour's going off, several muskets were fired at him, but none were lucky enough to take place.'[25]

At any rate, once aboard the *Dodaley*, Grant repeatedly urged that efforts should be made to bring off those still in the fort,[26] but her master, Captain Andrew Young flatly refused to risk his ship, and not only did Drake fail to back him up, but Manningham, who was a part-owner, sided with Young.[27] Only a small schooner named the *Hunter* made the attempt, but the lascars making up the greater part of the crew threatened to jump ship as it approached the shore and so her captain, Magnus Nicholson, was forced to sheer off.

Ashore, Holwell, whose own retreat was scuppered by his boat being stolen, made the best of a bad job by proclaiming himself the hero of the hour and assuming the presidency during a bizarrely formal Council meeting. The *Prince George* was still moored off Perrin's Garden and it was hoped that she would be able to drop down and use her boats to take the remaining Europeans off. Only about 170 of the defenders remained at this point and the decision was taken to evacuate the outposts and draw everyone into the fort. This was accomplished successfully but there was no let-up in the Bengali attacks and the ill-disciplined soldiers grew increasingly unmanageable. During the night many broke into the officers' quarters in search of alcohol and some fifty-six of the Dutch mercenaries deserted, led by a corporal.

20 June 1756: Surrender

Morning on Sunday 20 June 1756 brought further discouragement. The Bengalis had finally occupied the church and other buildings overlooking the defences and were soon pouring an increasingly destructive fire into the defenders. By midday, recalled Holwell, we had lost '25 killed and 70 or more of our best men wounded and our Train killed, wounded and deserted to all but 14 and not two hours ammunition left'.[28] And though they did not yet know it, the *Prince George* had gone aground and would later be plundered and burned.[29] There was no hope of escape and when round about 2 pm one of the Nawab's officers invited the British to stop fighting, Holwell ran up a white flag and told his men to stand down.

The cease-fire provided a welcome respite, but a couple of hours later he was engaged in a parley on the south-east bastion when word came that the Bengalis were already over the walls using bamboo scaling ladders and at the same time heard that Sergeant Hedleburg, a Dutch mercenary serving with the Train had also opened the west gate. As the Bengalis flooded into the fort which had defied them for so long, they not surprisingly at first ran amuck, 'killing anyone in a red coat', including the gallant Lieutenant Blagg, 'cut to pieces on a bastion'. Thereupon, Holwell and Buchannan, 'thinking that further opposition would not only be fruitless, but might be attended with bad consequences to the garrison', promptly 'delivered up their swords to a Jemmautdar that had scaled the walls and seemed to act with some authority' .

The battle was over, but one final act yet remained. The hours after the surrender were still casually chaotic. The victorious Bengalis naturally fell to looting and robbing, but otherwise at first no-one attempted to detain the erstwhile defenders, and a few of them simply walked quietly away amidst the confusion. As the evening wore on, however, some of the already drunk soldiers began to make a nuisance of themselves and the Nawab ordered the whole lot to be locked up. The garrison prison, referred to in traditional fashion as 'the black hole', offered itself and a number of the prisoners were crammed into a space measuring just five and a half by four metres. According to Holwell there were 146 of them in total, although he rather carelessly included a number of individuals who had been killed earlier. Nor did they represent all of the prisoners, for in early July, Watts wrote from Chandernagore that 'There are 79 of our serjeants, soldiers and others in the hospital here who escaped from Calcutta'.[30] The true figure still remains uncertain but whilst it was an unnecessary tragedy it was also recognised at the time (in India at least) as proceeding from indifference rather than malice. It was no more than the fortune of war and whatever the true death toll that night, it was soon to be surpassed.

Chapter 4

To Fulta and Back Again

Siraj-ud-Daula had not just won the battle and captured Calcutta, he had also convincingly demonstrated to all India that Bengal was not the Carnatic and that in Bengal, Europeans could not do as they pleased with impunity. A 'pair of slippers', he declared, was sufficient to keep the British in line and just to drive home the message, Calcutta was renamed Alinagar and Fort William itself was ordered to be rebuilt as a mosque. If the British displayed suitable contrition and wished to return and resume their trade they would do so on the Nawab's terms or not at all. The same went for the other European traders and by way of underlining the fact, both the French and Dutch were dunned for substantial 'contributions'.[1]

However, as it happens the British were not contrite and had not gone very far. The survivors of the debacle, that is to say those who had reached the ships by fair means or foul, first dropped a short distance downstream to a landing at Surman's Garden, where they waited just long enough to pick up some of the fugitives who got away from Calcutta after the surrender. Next morning, 21 June, they attempted to run past the Nawab's battery at Tanna, but lost the *Neptune* and *Calcutta*, both of which ran aground in the confusion and had to be abandoned. This necessitated a hasty retreat back to Surman's Garden, where they were joined by the *Speedwell* and the *Bombay*, which had both just come safely up the river! Thus encouraged and with a good following wind another attempt was made and this time they got through, albeit with the loss, again by grounding, of the *Diligence* and fetched up at Budge Budge on 24 June. There was still to be no respite there, for although another ship then arrived in the shape of the *Success* galley from Madras, the Nawab's men were already moving into the town and forbidding the local merchants to provide any supplies. By now conditions aboard the ships were becoming intolerable, 'not having a week's sustenance in the fleet of either food, wood or water, every vessel being crowded with men, women and children, country-born Portuguese'.[2] Ruthlessly, Drake put ashore all those refugees judged to have 'no connection with the Europeans' and left them to fend for themselves – or not. Everyone else was redistributed amongst the remaining ships and they all dropped downriver again, finally fetching up about 20 miles below Calcutta on the muddy and mosquito-infested island of Fulta. An appeal to the French for help was declined, but after some discussion the Dutch, who had a small pilot station on the island, arranged to have a shipload of supplies brought down from Hugli, in remembrance of old alliances. Thus sustained, the Calcutta people grimly held on there for the next six months, preserving a strict neutrality with the Dutch in order to avoid embarrassing their benefactors.

The stay at Fulta was by all accounts an unhappy experience, which in the end saw fully two-thirds of the men die of the inevitable fluxes and fevers – a far higher death toll than in the Black Hole as Robert Orme recounted in his contemporary history:

> The want of convenient shelter, as well as the dread of being surprised, obliged them all to sleep on board the vessels, which were so crowded that all lay promiscuously on the decks, without shelter from the rains of the season, and for some time without a change of raiment, for none had brought any store away, and these hardships, inconsiderable as they may seem, were grievous to persons of whom the greatest part had lived in the gentle ease of India.[3] Sickness likewise increased their sufferings, for the lower part of Bengal between the two arms of the Ganges is the most unhealthy country in the world, and many died of a malignant fever which infected all the vessels. But instead of alleviating their distresses by that spirit of mutual goodwill which is supposed to prevail amongst companions in misery, everyone turned his mind to invidious discussions of the causes which had produced their misfortune. All seemed to expect a day when they would be restored to Calcutta.[4]

And that was the point. Holwell, who was eventually released by the Nawab and had made his way to Fulta by 12 August, sourly claimed that Drake was only hanging on there until he could send a favourable account of the loss of Calcutta. Drake, on the other hand, countered with the indisputable fact that they lacked the supplies to evacuate everyone to Madras, but the truth was that none of them foresaw a future for themselves without Calcutta. Everything depended on its recovery and their return to it. In the meantime Fulta became a general rendezvous for stray East India Company personnel and their dependants from all over Bengal. Among them were the factors from Dacca and Jagdea who joined with the surviving Calcutta officials to form a governing Board or Agency. Predictably enough they were denounced as illegitimate by Holwell, who protested in particular against Drake's retention of authority in the face of his own specious claim to the governorship. However, finding that no-one was interested in his petulant complaints, he was eventually persuaded to sit on the Board and with that it smoothly transformed itself into a reconstituted council, which was itself soon subordinated to a smaller and much more manageable Select (or Secret) Committee comprising Roger Drake, John Zephania Holwell, William Watts and Richard Becher alone.[5] Thereafter, Roger Drake's authority was unchallenged and in the end distance and events saved him. It goes without saying that the Company's directors were dismayed by the disaster at Calcutta but a recall of the principals to face an inquiry in London was hardly going to be practical. Drake, for all the criticism of his handling of the affair, was at least tenacious and diligent in his efforts to recover both Calcutta and the Company's goods and although his name was omitted from the new council eventually nominated by Leadenhall Street in November 1757, he was otherwise 'continued' in the Company's service.[6]

The Bengal Military Reborn

The military position, on the other hand, remained difficult. When Major James Killpatrick eventually arrived from Madras with what had been intended as a reinforcement of 226 men for the Calcutta garrison on 28 July, he promptly reported back that he found 'neither men, guns, nor ammunition here ... The four field pieces you sent with me is all our Train: and the ammunition you sent with those is all we have got of the kind. Captain Winter [of the *Delaware*] spared us some powder and lead with which I have made up about fifty rounds a man.'[7]

Aside from the wretched and well-nigh invisible Minchin, the only regular officers to have escaped were Captain Grant, Lieutenant Le Beame and Ensign Carstairs, and the latter two were numbered among the survivors only because being badly wounded they had been evacuated the day before the debacle on the ghat.[8] In any case, once sufficiently recovered, Le Beaume was then sent on with Manningham in mid-July to explain matters to the Council at Madras. Grant, for his part, was also numbered among the sick for a time and the Council were in any case uncertain how to deal with him. There is some suggestion that, like Minchin, he had been dismissed, although there was no resolution on it, rather he was simply frozen out of military matters. Given the way Drake and Manningham smoothly resumed their positions despite being far more culpable than he in abandoning Calcutta, his real 'crime' was probably those heated exchanges on the quarterdeck of the *Dodaley* over the failure to go in and take off the rest of the garrison. Whatever the truth of the matter, Killpatrick needed him and so Grant submitted a letter to the Board on 20 August 1756 formally requesting that he be reinstated in command. For their part, on receiving it, they very hastily declared themselves 'well satisfied' with his behaviour at Calcutta and with rather more than just a hint of squirming embarrassment equally hurriedly added, 'that we have no objection to his acting in his rank of Captain in the military from which station they never suspended him, but only desired Lieutenants Keene and Muir to keep charge of their respective military to prevent any confusion'.[9]

Not that there were many soldiers left at that point to cause much confusion. Killpatrick's Madras contingent could only muster enough men for a single company.[10] Lieutenant William Keene (who soon died of fever) had turned up with the twenty-strong detachment which had been guarding the now abandoned factory at Jagdea while Lieutenant George Grainger Muir and a similar number of men came in from Balasore and John Cudmore likewise brought the Dacca detachment.[11]

There is no surviving accounting of the Bengal forces for this period and even as late as February of the following year there were just thirty-six European and ninety-one Eurasian rank and file fit for duty, and another thirty-three sick, besides the officers and NCOs.[12] They may have been sufficient in number to allow the commercial gentlemen to sleep more securely, but they were hardly going to retake Calcutta all by themselves.

Fortunately, Madras by now was alive to the seriousness of the situation, as a letter written on board HMS *Cumberland* relates:

> This accident [the capture of Calcutta] has given a great stroke to trade and a severe shock to all the merchants in India, which will be very sensibly felt, as Bengal was the very centre of trade, and loaded more ships than all their Factories in the Malabar and Coromandel Coast together. There were six ship loads of goods in the warehouses when it was taken. As soon as the news arrived, European goods fell 50 per cent, and chintz, muslin &c. rose 50 per cent. There are no goods to be bought here but at exorbitant prices: and at Bengal there

is not a piece of handkerchiefs, muslin or silk left. As Bengal supplied Madras with rice &c.there is almost a famine here: but we hope to make a good market with the commodities they want at Bengal from hence.[13]

Military force was needed but there were unexpected complications. The local naval commander, Vice Admiral Charles Watson, advised delay. His immediate concern was that due to the rains military operations would be impractical until the end of September and in the meantime he no doubt correctly reckoned 'one third of the men would fall sick before there would be an opportunity of their doing any service'. Even more importantly, he warned, there was a strong possibility of war with France and in such a case it would be unwise to strip Madras of the troops defending it.[14] The proposed expedition was stayed accordingly and it was not until 21 September 1756, by which time the full seriousness of the crisis in Bengal was properly appreciated, that the go-ahead was given, only for a fresh difficulty to arise. As we saw earlier, the capture of Madras by the French in 1746 compelled the Company to obtain the temporary assistance of regular troops in the form of twelve Independent Companies of Foot and a company of the Royal Artillery. At the war's end, those officers and men who declined the opportunity to enter the Company's service were shipped home again, but in 1754 with ongoing war in the Carnatic to all appearances spiralling out of control, a fresh contingent of regulars was sought. While the British Government's agreement to send some was welcome, it was not an entirely unmixed blessing.

This time the assistance took the form of His Majesty's 39th Regiment of Foot and three companies of the Royal Artillery, all under the overall command of Colonel John Adlercron of the 39th. Before deploying them to India the Government prudently secured a cost indemnity from the Company, but rather less happily at the same time passed a Mutiny Act for India.[15] This was accounted legally necessary since India was not then a part of His Majesty's dominions, but inter alia it asserted that King's officers were to take precedence over Company officers at all times. This was only a reflection of established precedent in Britain's North American and Caribbean colonies but while most officers were prepared to be sensible about it, Adlercron was not. His original instructions had defined his role as 'Commanding in Chief the [regular] Land Forces to be employed in the East Indies', which was straightforward enough, but it was also extended to include 'the Command of all the Forces belonging to the Company, on the Coast of Coromandel'.[16] The problem lay in the interpretation of the latter clause, which was intended to apply to operations in the field. Then and only then, the commander was to be a King's officer.

As it happens, however, Adlercron's arrival in India in October 1754 coincided with a truce, followed by a definitive peace treaty between the East India Company and the *Compagnie des Indes* in December. There was no need therefore for the colonel or for his regiment and certainly no immediate need for his leading an army in the field. Chagrined and frustrated, he responded by throwing his weight around and trying to assert his authority as commander-in-chief over all the forces in the region, belonging to both King and Company, demanding returns of unit strengths, ammunition and stores and so on as the traditional marks of subordination. Declining to give way to him, the East India Company for its part responded that it had consented that the colonel should command its forces in the field as and when required, but that was not the same thing as taking over its forts and its garrisons. In the end it took the Duke of Cumberland himself to settle the matter through the Secretary at War, who witheringly informed Adlercron that 'The India Company being Sovereign & answerable to His Majesty & Parliament for their Forts &c. The Command of those Forts are in the Company's Governors, & not in you, nor the Officers of His Majesty's Regiment under your Command.'[17] In the meantime, too, by way of quashing the pretensions of Adlercron and his second-in-command Samuel Bagshawe, the now-celebrated Robert Clive was given a King's commission as a Lieutenant Colonel of Foot, in the East Indies, shortly before his return to India in 1755.[18]

On learning that the Council was intending to give the command of the Bengal expedition to Clive,[19] whose new-found authority as a King's officer was *not* limited to the Coast of Coromandel, Adlercron flatly refused to release any of his men. Instead, he petulantly complained, 'Surely, gentlemen, you are not so unreasonable as to expect that I will send away any part of His Majesty's train or regiment (who are so immediately under my direction) and to leave to you the nomination [of command].' What was more, notwithstanding Clive's status as a regular, he refused to allow the Company to make use of the artillery and ammunition already embarked and insisted it be brought ashore again.

Admiral Watson, on the other hand, was much more accommodating. Having been appointed to command the expedition by sea, not only did he place five naval vessels at the Company's disposal,[20] but insisted that Adlercron furnish him with three companies of his regiment to serve on board as marines![21] All in all, once the Company's troops were embarked on Watson's ships and on five Company ones provided for the purpose, the expedition comprised 276 officers and men of HM 39th Foot, 616 Madras Europeans and 1,308 sepoys and lascars.[22]

The Expedition to Bengal

They sailed from Madras on 16 October 1756, straight into the north-west monsoon. In the first twelve days the fleet was blown as far south as Ceylon (Sri Lanka) and forced to beat right across the Bay of Bengal to what is now Burma, before creeping northwards again to the Hoogli. It was not until 5 December that Admiral Watson came to anchor off the mouth of the river and even then their troubles were not ended. They had only been provisioned in anticipation of a six-week voyage and so the ordinary discomforts of a cramped and tempestuous voyage had latterly seen rations cut by half and supplies of rice for the sepoys fail entirely. Yet the Hoogli itself provided no immediate relief, for such were the dangers of its uncharted shoals that it was necessary to wait for the spring tides on 8 December before Watson dared enter the river and consequently did not fetch up at Fulta until a week later. Even then the expeditionary force was incomplete, for the bad weather had not only delayed but scattered the fleet.

The *Marlborough* Indiaman sprang a leak and was diverted to Bombay (to get her safely out of the Bay of Bengal) and HMS *Cumberland* disappeared entirely for a time. Consequently, Clive complained; 'The absence of the *Cumberland* and *Marlborough* deprives me of about 250 Europeans and 430 sepoys with almost all the artillery and military stores.'[23] This loss was then compounded by the unwelcome discovery that the 'few effective Europeans at Fulta (volunteers included) did not amount to more than one hundred' – and even then only about thirty of them were actually fit for duty. It was fortunate indeed that Killpatrick had brought those four guns, but even they, as it would turn out, were of limited usefulness.[24]

It was also fortunate that in the meantime the Nawab himself had been distracted once again by his cousin and rival Shaukat Jang. The latter had not only defiantly disavowed his authority but had in fact stolen a march on him. While Siraj-ud-Daula was preoccupied with driving the British out of Calcutta, Shaukat Jang had craftily obtained a *firman* from the Moghul Emperor Alamgir in Delhi, confirming *him* to be the new Nawab of Bengal, Bihar and Orissa! Despite Siraj-ud-Daula's much-lauded success in taking Calcutta, Shaukat Jang's elevation was seemingly secured by the promise of a *crore* of rupees – 100 *lakhs* or something a little over £1 million. Whether the Moghul's vizier, Gaziuddin Imadul-Mulk, who facilitated the recognition of the would-be Nawab, actually fingered any of the money is questionable, for Shaukat Jang's 'reign' was to be a short one. By September, Siraj-ud-Daula had his army on the move again and settled the matter by accidentally blundering into a battle at Nawabgunj on 16 October 1756 – the very day Watson and Clive sailed from Madras. During the rather chaotic fighting, Shaukat Jang was shot through the head in dubious circumstances and his army incontinently fled. In time, the absence of a viable rival would, paradoxically, weaken Siraj-ud-Daula since it meant the British were seen as the only counterbalancing power which dissidents at the Bengali court might turn to, but for the moment his position was secure.

In the circumstances, although Clive and Watson were immediately co-opted on to the Select Committee, both pointedly declined to subordinate themselves to it, or even in Watson's case trouble himself to sit on it. What was more, the two equally pointedly demonstrated that this was no mere split between the military and civil departments by addressing the Nawab directly, without reference to the rest of the Committee. Predictably enough, having already defeated both the British and Shaukat Jang, the Nawab stoutly responded to their demands for satisfaction by assembling his army again and ordering Manik Chand to strengthen the defences of Calcutta and the other fortified posts along the river.

At a meeting on 22 December, an intelligence report on these defences was considered by the Select Committee and the decision taken to move on Calcutta,[25] but complaining of a violent cold and slight fever, Clive was initially forced to delegate the preparations to Killpatrick:

> The time now draws near for the quitting of Fulta, previous to which many necessary steps are to be taken, Boats, Sloops, etcetera, should be in readiness for the Embarkation of all our Military, Lascars and Seapoys, as likewise all our Stores, Provision etcetera. I think it would be a gaining of time, if all the Baggage, Stores, etc. were embarked immediately on large Boats, excepting what the Service on Shore absolutely requires. I would have all our Military and Seapoys supplied with 36 Rounds per man, and the rest of the Ammunition disposed of in such a manner as to be at hand when called for, I would have the two six pounders & two three pounders well supplyed with Ammunition and in readiness to Land at a Moments warning, for I take it for granted, we shall march from Budjee Budjee to Calcutta by Land, it would save us the Trouble of Embarking if we could do the same from Fulta, please to speak to the Governor to give orders that the Vessel which has the 100,000 Musket Cartridges on

Board to accompany the Squadron ... Dispose of the troops in such a manner that they may be in readiness to march over land to Calcutta, and, if necessary, to attack Bujee Budjee, Tana Fort, &c.[26]

Calcutta Regained

A few days afterwards the retaking of Calcutta got underway. There was a cunning plan that the ships should beat upriver to bombard the Nawab's fort at Budge Budge, while Clive marched overland from Moyapur with 500 men and two guns in order to ambush the garrison as it retreated. Setting off at four in the afternoon on 28 December 1756, they trekked for sixteen hours through swamps and a succession of deep rivulets, during which 'the men suffered hardships not to be described'.[27] Orme takes up the story thus, with a good deal more clarity than some of the principals involved:[28]

> The troops did not arrive until an hour after sunrise at the place of ambuscade. This was a large hollow, which in the rains might be a lake, sinking about ten feet below the level of the plain: it lay about a mile from the river, a mile and a half north-east of Buz-buzia, and half a mile to the east of a high road leading from this place to Calcutta. The eastern, and part of the southern bank of the hollow, were skirted by the huts and enclosures of a village, which seemed to have been abandoned some days before. The grenadiers and 300 Sepoys were detached from the hollow, to take possession of another village on the bank of the river adjoining to the northern wall of Buz-buzia; where, it was supposed, that their appearance would induce the garrison to mistake them for the whole of the English troops on shore; and that in consequence of this notion they would retreat along the high road, instead of the bank of the river. The company of volunteers[29] were detached, and posted themselves in some thickets near the high road, but on the farther side from the hollow, towards which it was intended that their fire should drive the fugitive garrison. The rest of the troops remained with Colonel Clive, and concealed themselves, some in the hollow, and others in the adjoining village, and the two field pieces were placed on the north side of the village. The troops being excessively fatigued were permitted to quit their arms, in order to get rest; every man laid himself down where he thought best, some in the village, others in the hollow; and from a security which no superiority or appearances in war could justify, the common precaution of stationing centinels was neglected.

This was more than a touch unfortunate, for Manik Chand, the governor of Calcutta, had marched down to save Budge Budge and the would-be ambushers were themselves about to be ambushed:

About an hour after the troops had lain down to sleep, they were awakened by the fire of small arms on the eastern side of the village into which at the same time, a multitude of matchlock men were discovered advancing with resolution. All the soldiers, wheresoever scattered, hurried on the alarm into the hollow, in which their arms were grounded, about 60 yards from the enclosures on the eastern bank; here they formed the line as fast as they could; but, unfortunately, the artillery-men, instead of repairing to the two field pieces which would have protected the whole, ran to seek protection themselves from the line. During this confusion the enemy, meeting no resistance, advanced and took possession of the eastern bank; from whence under the shelter of various covers, they kept up a continual, though irregular fire, wounding several and killing an ensign. Colonel Clive, apprehensive of a panic, should he order the troops to march out of the reach of the enemy's fire, commanded the line to stand firm, and detached two platoons, one from the right, the other from the center, opposite to which the enemy's fire was strongest. Of the platoon from the center eight men were killed by one volley before they gained the bank; the rest, nevertheless returned the fire, and then forced their way with their bayonets into the village; where they were joined by the other platoon, which had succeeded with the loss of only three men. This intrepidity quelled the enemy's courage, who no longer appeared in bodies but shifted in small parties from shelter to shelter, firing rarely and with little effect; however some officers on horseback exposed themselves with much resolution, endeavouring to rally their men, but in vain. In the mean-time, the company of volunteers, as soon as they heard the firing, marched back from the high road, and rescued the field pieces, of which some of the enemy had taken possession, but did not know how to use them. Upon this the artillerymen returned from the line to the field pieces and immediately began to fire them into the village, which soon drove all the enemy out of it, who fled as fast as they could to join a large body of horse, which was now discovered advancing from the south towards the hollow; but, on perceiving the fugitives coming from the village, this cavalry halted at a distance of half a mile. On this the English troops, with the field pieces, formed regularly on the plain, and advanced towards the enemy, who were commanded by Monickchund. They stood several shot from the field pieces, until one chanced to pass very near the turban of Monickchund, who immediately gave the signal of retreat by turning his elephant, and the whole body marched away to the north-east and returned to Calcutta.[30]

In the meantime Budge Budge remained to be taken, and by the Royal Navy at that. The Bengali gunners had opened fire on the ships at about half-past seven in the morning, but while they did some damage to the rigging they were soon overwhelmed by the sheer weight of naval gunfire. Nevertheless, some of the Bengalis gamely stuck it out and when their guns were silenced they still continued shooting with fire arrows. They were obviously not going to surrender, so preparations were made to land and storm the place. Captain Eyre Coote, having come ashore with his detachment of HM 39th as soon as Captain Pye's grenadiers appeared on the riverbank, was delighted to find that the Company troops were prepared to take orders from him and so promptly 'formed the King's troops into platoons … the Company's grenadiers in the rear of me, and divided the *seapoys* into the advanced and rear guards'. Finding a useful vantage point in an abandoned battery, he saw a possible covered approach leading to a flimsy-looking gate formed of wooden bars. Deciding it might be forced easily he had just ordered a march to be beaten by his drummers and was advancing to storm the place, when Captain Nicholas Weller of HM 39th, who was senior to him, turned up, ordered him to halt and insisted on marching to join Clive, who was unseen but evidently engaged in a furious firefight. No officer can be faulted for marching to the sound of the guns, and at that moment Weller's decision was absolutely correct, but by the time they came up with Clive they were too late to join in the fight and after hanging around for an hour or so they marched all the way back again. There Coote was consoled by the news that the admiral was going to land a body of 400 seamen, with the intention that the fort should be stormed that evening. Better still, Captain Weller returned on board sick, leaving Coote in sole charge again. Unfortunately, although the seamen were duly landed, Colonel Clive and Major Killpatrick, both exhausted by their own adventures, persuaded Watson that the attack should be postponed until the next day in order to rest their men first. When a disappointed Coote argued that the men would suffer if required to lie out all night, Clive, to get rid of him, sent him to ask the admiral whether the sailors should be re-embarked rather than have them lie out in the open all night. To Coote's chagrin, while he was still aboard the *Kent*, something as extraordinary as it was unpredictable occurred in the shape of an inebriated Scotsman:

One Strahan, a common sailor belonging to the *Kent*, having been just served with a quantity of grog had his spirits too much elated to think of taking any rest; he therefore strayed by himself towards the fort, and imperceptibly got under the walls; being advanced thus far without interruption, he took it into his head to scale at a breach that had been made by the cannon of the ships; and having luckily gotten upon the bastion, he there discovered several Moor-men sitting on the platform, at whom he flourished his cutlass, and fired his pistol, and then, after having given three loud huzzas, cried out, 'the place is mine'.[31]

A number of his shipmates straggled after him, probably at first with the intention of dragging him back to safety before he got into too much trouble, but once up there they too were infected by the madness of the moment and were soon followed by others. They all tumbled in disorderly-like and the fort was carried happy-go-lucky, without, as a disgusted Coote recorded, 'the least honour to anyone'.[32] Just four soldiers were wounded and Captain Dugald Campbell of the Company's forces was shot and killed by one of his own men in the confusion.[33] By way of consolation, Coote 'had the honour to command it that night' but the emptiness of the honour was underlined by the decision to demolish the place next morning.

Next it was the turn of Tanna. The earlier intelligence report revealed there were now two forts, one on each side of the river, but when the fleet went up there on 1 January 1757, they were both found to be deserted. Instead of the fifteen guns identified in the report, a quite improbable number of 'about forty guns' was claimed instead. However, three of the captured vessels previously used as targets were now stuffed with combustibles to serve as fireships and so the admiral manned and sent up his boats to deal with them, and then early next morning, confident that the river was clear, the advance on Calcutta began.

Once again it was to be assaulted both by land and by water, and to that end Clive and the Company's Europeans were landed to join with the sepoys and march north to intercept the Bengalis as they withdrew. A formal minute made by Admiral Watson's secretary very matter-of-factly recounted what happened next:

At half past 7 a.m. Colonel Clive and the Company's troops were landed opposite Tanau ... At three quarters past 8 the *Tyger* and *Kent* weighed and came to sail for Calcutta. The *Bridgewater* and *Kingfisher* sloop followed and the *Salisbury* was left behind as a guardship at

Tanau. At 40 minutes past 9 the enemy first fired at the *Tyger*. At 42 minutes she returned a shot, at 45 several more, and continued a fire with her starboard broadside. At 48 minutes they fired on the *Kent*. The *Tyger* being stern to Calcutta she fired her stern chace, and afterwards as she brought guns to bear on the Fort. At 15 minutes past 10 she engaged with her larboard broadside. At 20 minutes the *Tyger* anchored. At 25 minutes the *Kent* began to fire with one of her lower tier, which struck the Fort, and immediately after several more. At 28 minutes made the signal for engaging, and engaged with our whole starboard broadside, as every gun bore upon the Fort. At 30 minutes past 10 the *Kent* anchored, in swinging fired her stern chace and small arms from the tops. Brought our larboard broadside to bear and engaged with it. Veerd away to a whole cable [185 metres], the enemy having abandoned their guns abreast of us. At 45 minutes past 10 sent a message to Captain Latham, for the *Tyger* to veer what cable she could. At 46 minutes the enemy waved from the shore and shewed English colours. Sent a boat on shore to the Fort with Captain King. At 55 minutes past 10 Captain Coote with the King's troops and an officer from the *Kent* were sent on shore to take possession of the Fort, and at 11 o'clock they hoisted English colours.[34]

By way of putting a period to the action, ten minutes later another boat from the *Kent* was manned and sent to seize and rummage a French sloop which had been innocently watching the proceedings. Unfortunately this complacent narrative masked a furious row entirely in keeping with the rest of this eccentric campaign. Calcutta had already been evacuated by Manik Chand long before Clive marched up, let alone being in a position to intercept his retreat. All that remained for him to do was march in and reclaim the East India Company's premises. Instead, to his astonishment and fury he was refused admittance!

The admiral, in ordering Coote to take possession of the fort had directed that he was 'to garrison the Fort of Calcutta with His Majesty's troops you have now on shore, and take care to post your sentinels and guards so as not to be surprised by the enemy. In the evening I shall be on shore, and you are not to quit your post, or deliver up your command till further orders from me.'[35] Of itself this instruction was unremarkable, but while no-one doubted Coote's courage, the virtues of tact and occasionally common sense were not numbered among his accomplishments. When a hot and footsore Clive turned up at the gates at the head of the East India Company troops, the sentries barred his way and told him 'that there were orders that none of the Company's officers or troops should have entrance. This, I own, enraged me to such a degree, that I was resolved to enter if possible, which I did, though not in the manner maliciously reported, by forcing the sentries; for they suffered us to pass very patiently upon being informed who I was.'[36] Coote, confronted, presented his orders from the admiral, appointing him Governor of the Fort. Clive was unimpressed and immediately retorted that he denied any authority Admiral Watson had to appoint 'an inferior officer in the King's service' to be Governor of the Fort, and told Coote that if he disobeyed his orders he would be arrested. Coote stiffly gave way but in turn appealed to the admiral, who sent his Flag Captain, Charles Speke, to find out what on earth was going on. In the eighteenth century, military officers quite literally carried their commissions in their pocket and Clive testily responded that he had taken command of the Fort 'By the authority of His Majesty's Commission, as Lieutenant-Colonel, and being Commander-in-Chief of the land forces.' Given his otherwise cordial relationship with Clive it is unlikely Watson had intended Coote to behave quite as he did, but his own authority was now at stake and so he fired off a thundering response:

> Sir, – after what I said to Major Kilpatrick, I am extremely surprised to find you have not withdrawn the Company's troops, which puts me under a necessity of acquainting you, if you still persist in the continuing the fort, you will force me to take such measures as will be disagreeable to me, as they possibly can be to you. I hope yet, after you have prudently considered this affair, you will not drive me to the extremities I should be sorry to be urged to, for the plea you make of being the commanding officer of the land forces, gives you not the least authority to enter a place (forcibly) conquered by me, and garrisoned by troops under my immediate command.
> Your most obedient humble servant, CHAS. WATSON.[37]

This was allegedly underlined by a verbal message that if Clive did not quit the fort he 'should be fired out'. For his part, Clive was equally unintimidated. 'In answer he said he would not answer for the consequences, but that he would not abandon the Fort, upon which Captain Latham [of the *Tyger*] was sent; and when the matter was talked over coolly, it was soon settled; for he told Captain Speke and Captain Latham repeatedly that if Admiral Watson would come and command himself he had no manner of objection.'[38] The compromise was successful, for upon the admiral coming ashore Clive politely surrendered Fort William to him and then Watson in turn handed it back to the East India Company in the person of Roger Drake, in his official capacity as President of the Bengal Council.

Thus ended a curious contretemps, which was then hastily glossed over by all those involved, including Coote. Indeed the only surviving accounts of it appear to be contained in Clive's private letter to Pigot of a week later and in his evidence to a Parliamentary committee in 1772. It would be easy therefore to dismiss it as an ill-tempered exchange over nothing, which was an all-too typical symptom of the climate, were it not for hints that Clive was attempting a coup.

He himself alluded to the accusation in his 8 January letter to Pigot when he bitterly wrote how Coote 'presented me with a commission from Admiral Watson, appointing him Governor of Fort William, which I knew not a syllable of before; and it seems this dirty underhand contrivance was carried on in the most secret manner, under a pretence that I intended the same thing, which, I declare, never once entered my thoughts'.[39] He probably had his tongue firmly pressed in his cheek when making that declaration, for he was already embroiled in an acrimonious dispute with the Bengal Council. As he admitted in 1772, 'The Governor and Council of Madrass looked on the Government of Bengal as annihilated', hence his instruction that he should not allow himself to be subordinated to the Bengal lot.[40] They, naturally, resented this and would continue to resent it for some time to come. Rightly or wrongly it may well be the case that Clive was being deliberately forestalled in order to ensure that Calcutta was restored to its rightful owners, the Company's government of Bengal, rather than be seized by its rivals in Madras.

Be that as it may, the East India Company was back in Calcutta and on 3 January 1756 both Roger Drake and his Committee on behalf of the Company and Admiral Watson, on behalf of the King, formally declared war on Siraj-ud-Daula.

Chapter 5

Drums along the Hoogli

Having formally declared war on the Nawab, both admiral and Company immediately demonstrated that they meant business by launching a punitive expedition up the river to the old port of Hugli. There were sound reasons for this. There were understood to be large stocks of grain and rice accumulated in the town which might sustain his army, and yet more enticingly it was also believed that a substantial quantity of the East India Company's own goods, earlier seized by the Nawab, was now stored up there.

Accordingly, on the night of 7 January 1757, some 170 Regulars of HM 39th Foot, Captain William Pye's Madras grenadier company, and 300 Madras sepoys, all under Major James Killpatrick, were loaded on to the twenty-gun *Bridgewater*, 'and all the sloops and vessels that could be got together', and sent up the river. Unfortunately the expedition got off to a bad start when the *Bridgewater* demonstrated the necessity of a Hoogli pilot by running aground. With no British ones to be had, Captain Henry Smith pressed a quartermaster from a Dutch brigantine, the *De Ryder*,[1] lying off Barnagore. Despite that remembrance of old alliances which had moved them to assist the refugees at Fulta, the Dutch were now finding themselves in an increasingly difficult position. It was not their fight and they had far more to lose from a vengeful Siraj-ud-Daula than they might grudgingly gain from their British rivals, yet it was being made plain to them by Admiral Watson that if they did not offer their active support they would be regarded as hostile.

Piloted by the un-named Dutch quartermaster, the expedition eventually came abreast of Hugli by 8 am on 10 January 1756, and promptly fired some cannon into the town, to which the Bengalis could only reply with musketry, and so according to the *Bridgewater*'s log:

66

At noon Lieutenant Morgan was sent with Lieutenant Lutwich, four boats and 50 men under his command, to prevent Monychong's crossing with his army abreast of the Fort, in which he succeeded having only two men wounded in the boat that he was in with musket balls; at 3 in the afternoon the troops were landed, Major Killpatrick with 200 battalion men and 500 *seapoys*, Captain King, Lieutenant Morgan, of the *Tyger*, Lieutenant Lutwich of the *Salisbury*, Lieutenant Clark of the *Kent*, and Lieutenant Hayter of the *Kingfisher* with 200 seamen; the *Bridgewater*, *Kingfisher* and *Thunder* bomb weighed and went up the river abreast the Fort; at 4 they began to fire and bombard the Fort, the ships and Fort kept a constant fire on each other till 2 in the morning of Tuesday the 11th when they found we had made a breach in the wall; the seamen marched down to the water side with scaling ladders on their shoulders, the army in the rear; they hailed the ships to cease firing, clapt their ladders to, and mounted the wall; the enemy were deceived by a false attack which was made at the land post gate with our *seapoys*; they entered the Fort where some of our seamen had a small skermidge with the rear of the enemy in their retreating out of the north-west gate.[2]

Coote, naturally enough, told it a little differently, relating that he was sent by Major Killpatrick to reconnoitre the breach and that upon his pronouncing it practicable it was the soldiers who stormed the fort while the sailors helpfully 'put up our scaling ladders and assisted in getting us in, which we did without any loss'. Nor was any mention made of Bengali losses, although he rather optimistically reckoned the garrison to have been some 2,000 strong![3] Next day he and Captain Pye were set to carrying out a sweep through the town, but on the following day, 12 January, he nearly came to grief when ordered to destroy a large granary outside the town:

I was detached with 50 soldiers and 100 *seapoys* to burn a village about three miles from the Fort, and was to be joined by some sailors on my march. I took possession of a Portuguese convent, where I was informed that between 3 and 4,000 of the enemy were encamped behind the village that I was going to burn; however as it was a very great granary I knew it must be of very great service could I succeed: I therefore marched into the village about a mile and a half, and then ordered the *seapoys* and sailors to set fire in the rear of me as I marched back again, which I did but before I had got halfway back some of my advanced guard came running in, and told me the enemy, consisting both of horse and foot, were marching up the street, and had taken possession of several houses, and also the men-of-war's boats. As my rear was well secured by the houses being all on fire, I made no doubt but I should give a good account of them that attacked me in the front; as I could see they were all horse my 50 men were formed into three platoons, but the street was so narrow I was obliged to march by files, I therefore made every platoon into two firings and advanced by street firing very briskly upon them, but found them not so eager as they seemed to be at first. Upon our first fire we killed their chief officer and four or five of their men, upon which all their horse went away, but I found they fired up the lanes upon my right flank as I marched by, I therefore ordered some of the men to fire down as we passed; as soon as I had got out of the village, I drew up the men and halted, and formed an advance and rear guard of *seapoys,* whom I found had not continued burning in my rear as I ordered them. I found the men-of-war boats all safe. In this skirmish we killed ten of the enemy and had but one sergeant wounded. Major Kilpatrick upon hearing our firing but had marched out of the garrison to support me, but the affair was over before he joined us.[4]

For his part, Killpatrick raided the nearby Dutch settlement at Chinsura. Benefiting from the delay caused by the grounding of the *Bridgewater*, a quantity of Company merchandise was said to have been spirited out of Hugli and secreted there. It is unclear whether much if any of it was actually recovered but it sparked another furious row with the hapless Dutch.[5] By 16 January their work in Hugli was done and having demolished the fortifications they re-embarked and dropped down the river to Calcutta. There was some thought of next mounting a similar expedition to Dacca but this was set aside on receiving news that the Nawab was once more approaching from the north.

Clive had in the meantime been trying to put Calcutta into a proper state of defence. Fort William was at long last provided with a proper ditch and glacis and an 'esplanade' cleared for out to 150 metres in front of it.[6] However, neither he nor Watson had any thought of standing a siege. On the contrary, rather than run the risk of being trapped in the town, Clive moved his forces out to a camp on Barnagul Plain on the north side of the town, covered by the Chitpur tank, which was turned into a strongpoint 'for the reception of our bazar, cooleys and baggage'.[7] Yet if he was to fight a war of manoeuvre he needed far more men and so he wrote to the Admiral on 20 January 1757, confessing his plight:

Sir – I have the honour to send you a return of our present strength in camp, to which if the Grenadier company be added[8] to our whole military force, rank and file, will not exceed 300 Europeans. You are very sensible, Sir, that with sickness and other accidents how far this force falls short of what was intended to act offensively against the Nabob of Bengal; indeed at present nothing but our strong situation can enable us to act against him at all. I must therefore request the favour of you, Sir, to land the King's forces and to lay your commands on the officer who commands them to put himself under my orders; assuring you at the same time that whenever you think it for the good of the service to recall them, upon signification thereof to me by letter, they shall be returned.[9]

Watson responded positively the next day, generously saying that, 'I cannot help thinking of the number of your own troops are too few even to act defensively against the Nabob, therefore I have given orders to the captains of the several ships to discharge their troops, and have directed Captain Weller to join you, and put himself under your command until further orders.' Of itself this was welcome, although Clive grumbled privately to Pigot that, 'It had been better for the service had they never come and I had the like number of Company's in their room.'[10] Even they were still not enough and so he set about raising a battalion of sepoys for the Bengal Establishment. This was accomplished quickly enough by recruiting Buxarries, exchanging their matchlocks for European firelocks and training them as regulars. Regimental tradition holds that from the outset they were dressed in red jackets, hence their nickname, the *Lal Pultan* (Red Platoon), and for once the legend may be true since a short time earlier Clive had talked of insisting on a quantity of broadcloth belonging to the Company being handed over to the military.[11]

The argument over the broadcloth was symptomatic of a growing estrangement between Clive and the Bengal Select Committee at this time. Roger Drake and his colleagues considered, with a great deal of justice, that they were the legitimate representatives of the Company in Bengal. It naturally followed, they argued, that Clive and the troops he brought with him from Madras were only a reinforcement for their own depleted military and entirely subject to their authority. Clive, as we have already seen in the row at the gates of Fort William, begged to differ. When the Committee finally took its courage in its hands and demanded in writing that he acknowledge his subordination, he flatly refused, but nevertheless professed his willingness to co-operate – on his own terms.[12]

And there perforce the matter rested, for on 3 February, disdaining attempts to negotiate, the Nawab's advance guard once again entered Calcutta:

> About noon hearing that small parties of the enemy were got into the skirts of the town, Captain De la Beaume was detached with 80 Europeans, 15 *seapoys*, and two pieces of cannon, to the redoubt at Bogbuzar, from thence to defend that part of the town, and prevent the enemy's plunderers from annoying the inhabitants, which he effected having killed a good number and taken between thirty and forty prisoners. At 5 in the afternoon the major part of the battalion and *seapoys* with four field pieces advanced towards the enemy in order to harass them on their march and to discover whether they were not making some lodgement in a wood within reach of our camp; as soon as we came abreast of this place, they began a brisk fire upon us from nine pieces of cannon, some of them thirty two pounders, which they had placed to cover their march; on this we immediately formed and returned the cannonadement which continued but a short time, it being near sunset when we began: we soon discovered the enemy draw off their cannon and proceeding on their march to their encampment; at the same time the [British] forces returned to camp. The loss was inconsiderable on both sides; one *matross* and three *seapoys* killed and Captain Weller and Fraser slightly wounded, eight of the enemy's horse were killed and as many men.[13]

The following day the main body of the Nawab's army arrived and settled into a camp estimated at being five miles long, on the east side of Calcutta. Two envoys, Messrs Walsh and Scrafton, were sent off on a last attempt to negotiate with the Nawab, but on their being fobbed off, the soldierly decision was taken to attack him at once.

Still short of men, Clive once again begged Admiral Watson for assistance and accordingly 500–600 seamen were landed under Captain Thomas Warwick of the *Thunder*.[14] Half of them were to be employed in pulling the six field pieces and the howitzer, and carrying ammunition, while the rest served as infantry. This gave Clive a total of 500 regular European infantry and 300 seamen, 800 sepoys and 70 gunners, of which 'a few Europeans with 200 new raised *bucksaries*' were necessary to guard the camp.[15]

With the forces at his disposal Clive was very properly wary of taking on Siraj-ud-Daula in open battle and instead aimed on a surprise attack on his headquarters in Amir Chand's garden or summer residence, out

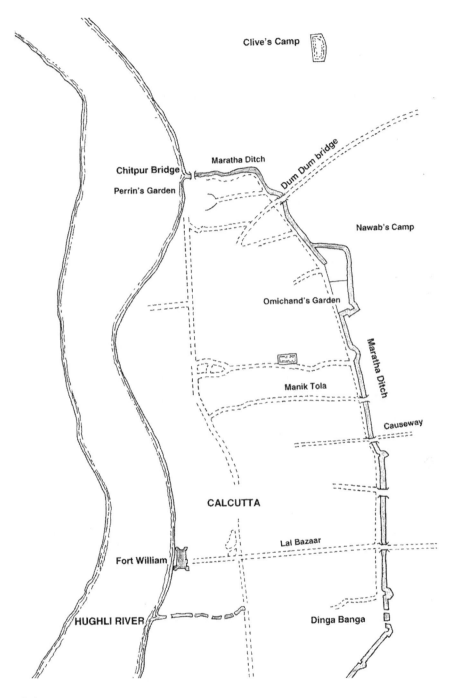

Calcutta

by the Mahratta Ditch in the early hours of 5 February 1757. Robert Orme's masterly account cannot be bettered:

> The order of march was a line advancing in half-files, that is three men abreast: half the Sepoys marched before, and half behind the battalion of Europeans; in the rear were the field-pieces with the artillerymen and Lascars and all the sailors. To lessen the incumbrance of carriages, there being no bullocks to draw them, the Lascars carried the ammunition of the field-pieces on their heads; and to deter them from flinging away their loads and taking flight, they were guarded on all sides by a party of the sailors; other sailors were allotted to draw the field-pieces, and the rest of them marched as they could, immediately behind the rear division of Sepoys; Colonel Clive kept in the middle of the battalion.
>
> Of the Nabob's army a part, with the general Meer Jaffier, were within the Morattoe ditch; and most of these encamped near Omichund's garden, as a protection to the Nabob, who lay there; but much the greatest part encamped between this ditch and the lake, overspeading all the ground between, without method or order. A little before the dawn of day, the English line came upon their advanced guards, stationed in the ditches of that part of the high road which leads from the bridge at the head of the lake, to the Morattoe ditch. These guards, after firing their matchlocks, and discharging some rockets, ran away: but one of the rockets striking the cartouch-box of one of the Sepoys, set fire to the charges, which blowing up, communicated the mischief to several others, and the dread of catching this fire threw the whole division into confusion:[16] fortunately none of the enemy were at hand to take advantage of it, and Captain Coote, who marched at the head of the grenadiers, immediately in the rear of the Sepoys, rallied them and restored the line of march. By this time it was daylight, when a very thick fog, peculiar to the mornings of this season of the year in Bengal, began to overspread the ground. The line proceeded without farther interruption, until they came opposite to Omichund's garden, when they heard the sound of horses coming upon them on the full gallop from the right; on which they halted.
>
> This cavalry was a body of Persians excellently mounted, and stationed as an outguard to the Nabob, under that part of the Morattoe ditch, which encloses Omichund's garden: they were suffered to come within thirty yards before the line gave fire, which fell heavy, and killing many of them, the rest instantly dispersed in great confusion.[17] The line then proceeded slowly, platoons

constantly firing on either hand; whilst the field-pieces in the rear fired single balls forward, but obliquely outward, on each side of the line; but all without any immediate object; for the fog prevented any man from seeing beyond the ground on which he trod. About a mile to the south of the garden is a narrow causeway, raised several feet above the level of the country, with a ditch on either side; it leads from the east to the Morattoe ditch, and across it into the company's territory. The enemy had barricaded the passage; which it was intended to force, and from thence to proceed, as it were, back again, along the high road adjoining to and on the inside of the rampart, in order to attack the Nabob's quarters at the garden: but as soon as the first division of Sepoys changed their former direction and began to march along the causeway, the field-pieces in the rear, on the right of the line, continuing to fire foreward, killed several of them: upon which the whole division sought their safety in the ditch on the other side of the causeway, and the troops who succeeded them crossed it likewise, not knowing what to do.

As soon as this was reported to Colonel Clive, he ordered the whole line to continue crossing the causeway, but to halt immediately after they had passed it, intending to form them into some disposition proper to storm the pass; this brought the whole together into one irregular heap, and whilst Colonel Clive was waiting for the return of two or three officers whom he had sent to examine the barricade, the troops were unexpectedly assailed by a discharge from two pieces of heavy cannon, loaded with langrain [langridge or grapeshot] and mounted within 200 yards upon a small bastion of the Morattoe ditch, to the right of the barricade, which killed and disabled 22 Europeans; another discharge soon followed, with less, but however with some effect. This annoyance instantly overset the resolution of storming the pass; and the line immediately began to extend itself again, as well to present the fewest bodies to the cannonade, as to gain without delay a broad high road, which about half a mile to the south of the causeway, crosses the Morattoe ditch into the Company's territory, and then joins the avenue leading to the fort of Calcutta.

But their progress was now continually retarded by the excessive labour and difficulty of transporting the field-pieces; for the ground between the causeway and the road was laid out in small rice fields, each of which was enclosed by a separate bank, so that the field-pieces could only be drawn along the ditches between the banks, and were therefore at every field in a different direction: sometimes, likewise, it was necessary to raise them over the banks into the field, in order to repulse the enemy's cavalry; who after nine o'clock, when the fog cleared, were discovered threatening the left; ever and anon advancing so near, that it was necessary to detach platoons from the line to repulse them.

In the mean-time the fire of the enemy's two cannon continued, and a querter of a mile to the south of these two other pieces began likewise to annoy the line from the same rampart.

At ten, after much fatigue and action, the troops having abandoned two of the field pieces, which had broken down, arrived and formed in the high road leading to the avenue, where a body of horse and foot were posted in front to defend the passage across the Morattoe ditch. Several large bodies of cavalry likewise assembled in the rear, acting with more courage than those in front, and pressed hard upon one of the field-pieces, which was gallantly rescued by Ensign Yorke, with a platoon of Adlercron's regiment [HM 39th]. The fire of a few other platoons dispersed the enemy in front; and the troops now being within the Company's territory, might have proceeded along the road on the inside of the ditch, quite up to Omichund's garden, where the Nabob still remained, surrounded by a large body of cavalry; but Colonel Clive thinking that they had already endured too much fatigue, continued marching straight along the avenue to the fort, where they arrived about noon.

Twenty-seven of the battalion, 12 sailors, and 18 Sepoys were killed, and 70 of the battalion, with 12 sailors, and 35 Sepoys, were wounded; two captains of the company's troops, Pye and Bridges,[18] and Mr Belcher, the secretary of Colonel Clive, were killed; Mr. Ellis, a factor, who with several other young men in the mercantile service of the company, served as a volunteer, lost his leg by a cannon ball.[19]

All in all it was an unhappy affair, which at first resulted in some considerable murmuring among the troops as to Clive's mismanagement of it. Certainly he did not cover himself with glory in what he would later admit was the hottest fight he was ever engaged in. Yet whilst it was a tactical defeat which came perilously close to utter disaster, it also turned out to be the victory which decided the campaign. It seems improbable that they had inflicted anything like 1,300 killed and wounded as claimed afterwards, but the very fact that the British had boldly marched into the midst of the Bengali camp, comprehensively shot it up and then marched safely away again made a wonderful impression.

The Nawab remained where he was, tensely awaiting another visit, but then the next day, 6 February, he commenced a general retreat and re-opened negotiations. This time they were carried through and three days later a peace treaty was signed, whose terms left no doubt that the British had not only won the brief war but gained everything they had fought for.[20]

All the parties concerned now entered upon a period of uncertainty which may be summarised thus: first, Siraj-ud-Daula had been defeated on the battlefield and forced to make humiliating and expensive concessions to the East India Company. He quite naturally resented this and had no reason to trust the British who had twice provoked him into going to war and who now seemed intent on going to war with their

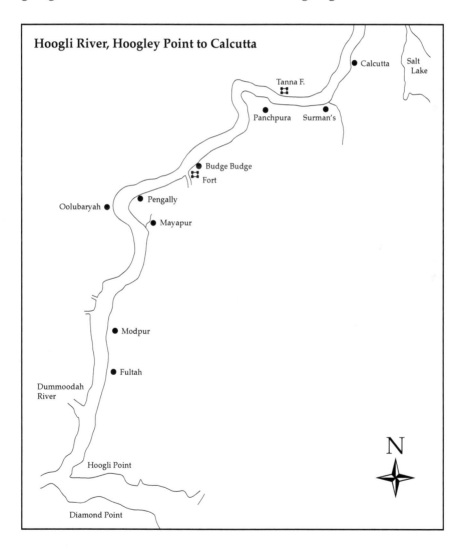

Hoogli River, Hoogley Point to Calcutta

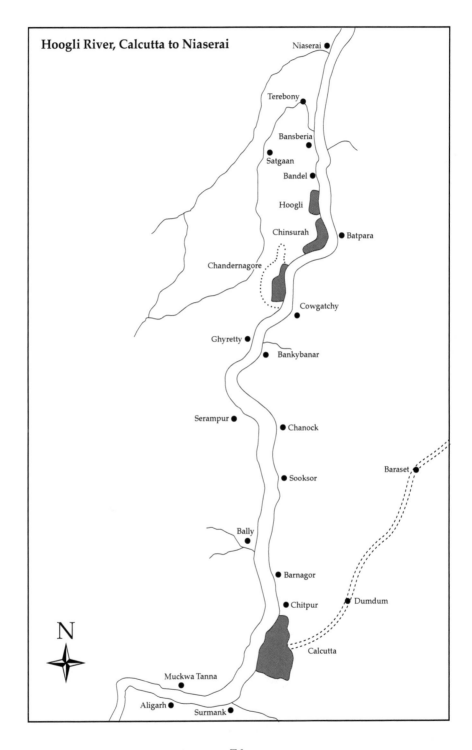

Hoogli River, Calcutta to Niaserai

Niaserai

Terebony

Bansberia

Satgaan

Bandel

Hoogli

Chinsurah

Batpara

Chandernagore

Cowgatchy

Ghyretty

Bankybanar

Serampur

Chanock

Sooksor

Baraset

Bally

Barnagor

Chitpur

Dumdum

Calcutta

N

Muckwa Tanna

Aligarh

Surmank

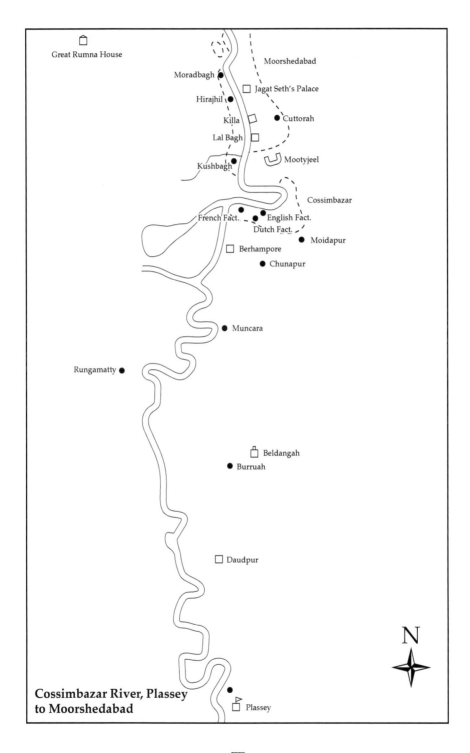

Great Rumna House

Moorshedabad

Moradbagh

Jagat Seth's Palace

Hirajhil

Killa

Cuttorah

Lal Bagh

Kushbagh

Mootyjeel

Cossimbazar

French Fact.

English Fact.

Dutch Fact.

Moidapur

Berhampore

Chunapur

Muncara

Rungamatty

Beldangah

Burruah

Daudpur

N

**Cossimbazar River, Plassey
to Moorshedabad**

Plassey

French neighbours. While he had no particular reason to love the French, he feared that their defeat would remove a vital counterweight to British power. For that reason he returned a *lakh* of rupees to Pierre Renault, the chief there and rather more provocatively accorded the French exactly the same privileges he had just been forced to grant to the British. In this he was being pointedly even-handed, but at the same time, he was also engaged in secret negotiations with the French as potential allies. General de Bussy was still active in the Northern Circars and the Nawab pleaded with him for '2,000 soldiers and musketry under the command of one or two trusty chiefs'.[21] Had Bussy been willing to send them, the arrival of 2,000 properly-disciplined troops – even if most were sepoys – would have completely upset the fragile truce.

Nor were the British satisfied with the outcome of the campaign, for militarily little had been decided. Calcutta had been recovered but the Nawab had only been driven off, not defeated. As we have seen, Drake and the rest of the Bengal Select Committee were extremely unhappy about Clive's refusal to subordinate himself to them, largely through the well-founded fear that he and his men might at any time return to Madras if the situation there required, leaving them in the lurch once more. Clive was quite open about this particular possibility and indeed his eagerness to go, but notwithstanding his initial bombast he was well aware that a garrison of some 300 Europeans would be required to hold Calcutta, let alone secure the outlying stations. As this number approximated to his own field force, exclusive of sepoys, there was clearly a dilemma. The few Bengal Europeans and the newly-recruited sepoys were not yet sufficient to do the job themselves, even if the Madras sepoys were to be left behind as a reinforcement. A treaty of neutrality with the French would at least frustrate a potentially fatal alliance with the Nawab.

Similarly, Watson was uncomfortably aware that far from cruising the high seas to take, burn and sink any ships belonging to his King's enemies, as admirals are traditionally expected to do, he and his warships were all of 70 miles inland at the behest of a company of tradesmen – and therefore not best placed to meet an anticipated French fleet coming from Europe. On the one hand, he was alive to the possibility that without a treaty Chandernagore would have to be taken and might need his heavy guns to do it, yet on the other he was equally aware he could not move his big ships upriver to Chandernagore until the next spring tides. That meant a delay he probably could not afford if he was to be back at sea when the French fleet arrived. Therefore he was at first willing enough to heed the

Nawab's insistence that the British should refrain from hostilities against the French.

Such an agreement was therefore desired by all three parties. For the French it removed the immediate threat to Chandernagore. By offering a degree of security to Calcutta it justified the withdrawal of Clive's troops and the Royal Navy, and lastly it offered a face-saving restoration of the Nawab's authority. At the last moment, however, having finally received official confirmation that war was declared in Europe, Watson scuppered the talks by enquiring as to whether Renault, the French chief at Chandernagore, actually had the authority to enter into such a treaty. Renault was forced to confess that he did not. Any treaty would need to be ratified by his superiors in Pondicherry. Now only the Nawab's insistence that peace should be maintained prevented a British attack, but it could not be long delayed.

Meanwhile the Nawab, Siraj-ud-Daula, was now facing a quite different threat from a totally unexpected direction. An Afghan army had taken the imperial capital of Delhi and was marching eastwards, threatening the neighbouring province of Oudh and ultimately Bengal itself. The Nawab was hoping that the British would help him fight off the Afghans, and indeed when William Watts was sent to Murshidabad to ensure the terms of the treaty were complied with, the Nawab requested of Clive that 'you will send me 25 artillery soldiers with him, and write upon a separate paper their monthly allowance which they shall duly receive from my Treasury with an additional gratuity when I give them their demission'.[22] The British professed themselves willing to help, not least because, as Clive advised Pigot:

> I have already acquainted you of the revolution which has happened at Dilly [Delhi], since when the Nabob writes me he has received advices that the Afghans are marching towards his Provinces. He has desired me in the strongest terms to join him, and has offered to pay a lack of rupees per month for the maintenance of the forces. The Gentlemen here as well as myself are of the opinion the offers are too advantageous to be refused; indeed our late treaty binds us to assist him and I need not represent that if this plunderer got into the Province there will be an end to the Company's affairs for some time. Part of the Nabob's army are already marched for Patna, and he himself will leave Muxadabad very soon with the rest.
>
> I began my march on the 8th, and am close to Chandernagore. The Nawab testifies some reluctance at our attacking this place; however I am in hopes we shall not leave it behind us ...[23]

Meanwhile, a fierce diplomatic battle was being waged in the Nawab's court between the British representative, William Watts, and his French counterpart, Jean Law,[24] which ended abruptly with an ambiguous letter capable of being interpreted as permission to attack the French.[25] That was all Clive and Watson required.

As at Calcutta, the French settlement was largely open and had grown outwards from a fortified citadel. The difference in this case was that Fort d'Orleans was no 'deserted and ruined Moorish fort' (as one officer had unkindly but accurately described Fort William) but a far more modern affair, as described by Renault himself:

> The Fort of Orleans, situated almost in the middle and surrounded by houses which command it, was a square of 100 fathoms, built of bricks, flanked with four bastions of 16 guns, without outworks, ramparts or glacis. The south curtain, which was about 4 feet thick, raised only to the cordon, was provided only with a platform for three guns; it also had to the west a platform for three guns, but the rest of this curtain, as well as that of the north, was only a wall of earth and brick, a foot and a half thick; and warehouses lined the east curtain which faces the Ganges and which we were still working at. All this side had no ditch and that which surrounded the other sides was dry, about four feet deep, and properly speaking nothing but a ravine. The fortifications of the Fort up to the cordon were 15 feet high, and the houses which commanded it from the edge of the counterscarp within musket range, had a height of 30 feet.
>
> I had the good fortune, nevertheless, in spite of all obstacles, the Nawab's prohibition of all work on any fortifications and the emptiness of our cash chest, to finish the west curtain with a great warehouse behind, the parapet of the south curtain and a part of an inner wall intended to hold up the earth with which I intended to terrace it, and to finish building the curtain facing the Ganges.[26]

In 1756 its garrison had comprised seven officers, 105 European soldiers and 141 Eurasians.[27] By March of the following year, when the British came knocking, Renault discovered himself to have a total of 794 men to defence the place, comprising 237 European soldiers (including a company of fifty grenadiers formed from the East India Company's deserters), 100 Eurasian artillerymen and 167 sepoys, 120 sailors and 170 militia. There were also some 2,000 of the Nawab's men, although their reliability was dubious to say the least and they withdrew before any fighting began. Taking Chandernagore was not going to be easy and the key to doing so was going to be Admiral Watson's ships and Admiral Watson's guns.

In prudent anticipation of a British attack, Renault therefore had 'two ships, a ketch, a scow, a hulk and a vessel without masts'[28] scuttled to block the channel and prevent the warships coming abreast of his walls. Clive therefore assured Watson that he could supply all the necessary planks and other materials to raise batteries against the walls, if the admiral would land some heavy guns. First, though, he needed to secure the town, as Coote related:

March 14th. – Read His Majesty's Declaration of War against the French King; the 3rd division of the Bombay troops consisting of 100 men, joined us; Colonel Clive ordered the picquets with the Company's grenadiers to march into the French Bounds, which is encompassed with an old ditch, the entrance into it a gateway with embrasures on top, but no cannon, which the French evacuated on our people's advancing; as soon as Captain Lynn (who commanded the party) had taken possession, he acquainted the Colonel, who ordered Major Kilpatrick and me, with my company of grenadiers to join Captain Lynn, and send him word after we had reconnoitred the place; on our arrival there we found a party of French was in possession of a road leading to a redoubt that they had thrown up close up under their Fort, where they had a battery of cannon, and upon our advancing down the road, they fired some shot at us; we detached some parties through a wood and drove them from the road into their batteries with the loss of some men; we then sent for the Colonel, who as soon as he joined us, sent to the camp for more troops; we continued firing at each other; in an irregular manner till about noon, at which time the Colonel ordered me to continue with my grenadier company and about 200 *seapoys* at the advance post, and that he would go with the rest of our troops to the entrance which was about a mile back. About 2 o'clock word was brought to me that the French were making a sortie; soon after I perceived the *seapoys* retiring from their post, upon which I sent to the Colonel to let him know the French were coming out. I was then obliged to divide my company which consisted or about fifty men into two or three parties (very much against my inclination) to take possession of the ground the *seapoys* had quitted; we fired pretty warmly for a quarter of an hour from the different parties at each other, when the French retreated again into their battery; on this occasion I had a gentleman (Mr. Tooke) who was a volunteer, killed, and two of my men wounded; the enemy lost five or six Europeans and some blacks; by their retiring I got close under their battery and was tolerably well sheltered by an old house, where I continued firing until about 7 o'clock, at which time I was relieved and marched back to camp; this night the Colonel sent a party to take possession of the southward of the town.[29]

Next day, it was discovered that under cover of darkness the French had 'evacuated the battery we attacked the preceeding night, and had spiked their guns, and that he was in possession of it; we were likewise informed during our march that the French had evacuated all their batteries to the southward and had retired to the Fort; the chief of which was a half-moon battery newly erected in order to defend a narrow part of the river where they had sunk some ships in order to hinder the passage of our men-of-war. The others (three in number) were thrown up at the end of the three principal streets of the town, all which batteries we took possession of before 12 o'clock at noon, which made us masters of the town, and brought us within half a musket shot of the Fort.'

Thereafter the pace slowed dramatically. Musketry was exchanged in a suitably desultory fashion and on 17 March some light Coehorn mortars and a slightly heavier 13in one were brought into play. This, in contemporary parlance, was by way of amusing the enemy because two days later work began on building two proper batteries opposite the south face of the south-east or St. Joseph bastion; in one of which it was intended to mount five 24-pounders while the other was intended for three. The former was cunningly hidden behind the walls of houses, but the French soon realised what was happening and on 20 March Coote recorded that, 'The enemy began to play upon our three-gun battery, which we returned, but they soon silenced it and almost demolished the work.' Next day the work continued and the three-gun battery was almost completed when the French began 'firing warmly again at it and knocked down a veranda close by the battery, the rubbish of which choked up one of our guns, very much bruised two artillery officers, and buried several men in the ruins'. Nor did matters improve and Coote's diary notes: '*March 22nd.* – Finished our 5 gun battery, but got no more than 4 guns in it; the enemy in the evening found out where we were making our battery and fired very warmly on it; the detachment of the King's troops were ordered on board His Majesty's ships *Kent, Tyger* and *Salisbury*.'[30]

HM 39th Foot was going into action again, but this time as marines. Admiral Watson arrived off Chandernagore on the morning of 19 March and on the following day sent in his own formal summons to surrender.

In the best traditions of the service he sent it by way of a lieutenant in a boat under cover of a flag of truce, rather than simply knock on the door. Not being blindfolded, the lieutenant shamelessly took the opportunity to note the positions of the blockships and reported back to the admiral that there was still a clear channel which would allow his warships to close with the fort. That same night the channel was buoyed but it was not until 23 March that the tide was sufficient to carry the ships up the river. 'At 6 o'clock in the morning' noted Coote, 'signal was made for weighing; soon after the Colonel marched with the Company's troops from camp into the town, opened the four gun battery and began to fire from the three gun battery which was tolerably well repaired; the Colonel had likewise placed musketry on several houses, who kept a continual fire on the south east bastion; at half past six the *Tyger* was under sail and stood up the river for the Fort, the *Kent* following her, and the *Salisbury* bringing up the rear; the enemy had a mud battery of six guns close to the water's edge, from which they kept a continual fire on the *Kent* and *Tyger*, as well as from the south-east and north-east bastions, which did the *Tyger* some damage, but on her coming abreast of the mud battery, the enemy spiked up their guns and retired into the Fort; at 7 o'clock the *Tyger* came to an anchor opposite the south-east, both of which bastions consisted of five guns in face and three in flank; they fired very warmly and with a good deal of success; the *Kent* very unfortunately dragging her anchor exposed her quarter to the fire of the flank of the south-west bastion; the *Salisbury* brought up in the rear.'[31]

Coote's bare narrative disguises a very hard-fought battle of near-unparalleled ferocity as fort and ships battered each other at murderously close range. It was intended that all three ships should bombard the fort, but in the event the *Kent* dragged her anchor and fell back downstream sufficiently to prevent the *Salisbury* coming into action. Nevertheless, as Renault admitted, the two ships were enough, for he only had fouteen guns, of 8, 12 and 18 pounds, with which to oppose them:

> I immediately sent the company of grenadiers with a detachment of the artillery as a reinforcement to the south bastion and the bastion du Pavillon, which face the Ganges; but these troops under the fire of the ships joined to that of the land batteries rebuilt the same night and of more than three thousand men placed on the roofs of the houses which overlooked the Fort, almost all took flight, leaving two of their officers behind, one dead and the other wounded. I was obliged to send there, immediately and in succession, all the Marine and the inhabitants from the other posts.

The attack was maintained with vigour from 6am to 10.30 when all the batteries were covered with dead and wounded, the guns dismounted and merlons destroyed in spite of their being strengthened within by bales of goods. No one could appear on the bastions which were devastated by the fire of more than a hundred guns; the troops were terrified during this attack by the loss of the gunners and of nearly 200 men; the bastions having been undermined threatened at each discharge to crumble away.

Worse, he could see Clive's infantry lying down, ready to storm the place and knowing that 'in the condition in which the place was, I could not with prudence expose it to an assault. Accordingly I ordered the drum to beat a parley.'[32]

Rather to Clive's understandable annoyance, as soon as the white flag was hung out the admiral sent a boat racing ashore and not only secured Renault's surrender but tried to conclude matters all by himself. In fairness he may have felt he had earned that right, for as Coote, who as usual was aboard the *Kent*, recorded:

During the engagement the *Kent* had three of her 32-pounders dismounted, 19 men killed and 74 wounded; among the former was Mr Perreau First Lieutenant, and among the latter Captain Speke, Mr Hay Third Lieutenant, Captain Speke's son and four or five petty officers, my detachment consisting of 30 rank and file, had nine men killed and five wounded; the larboard side (which was the side we engaged with) was hulled in 138 places, besides three or four shot through our main mast, and as many through the mizzen;[33] the *Tyger* had 14 men killed and 56 wounded, the master being the only person of rank among the former; among the latter Admiral Pocock slightly hurt; of the King's detachment under Captain [Archibald] Grant one man killed and two wounded; the *Salisbury* had none killed or wounded, and the enemy were so much employed against the ships that the army ashore under Colonel Clive had but one man killed and ten wounded.[34]

As for the French, their actual losses amounted to forty dead and seventy-four wounded, besides those already sick in hospital. In all, 215 prisoners were taken.[35] The terms of the capitulation as dictated by the admiral required the substantial body of deserters from the Company's forces to be delivered up to justice, but those not already killed or wounded, about sixty in number, made their escape as soon as the white flag appeared.[36] Ominously, they did so in a body and remained fully armed.

Chapter 6

The Battle of Plassey

Once again, victory ushered in a period of uncertainty. Having bought the promise of British assistance against the Afghans by reluctantly allowing them to attack Chandernagore, the Nawab was appalled by the result. On the one hand he congratulated Clive on his triumph while at one and the same time hastily reaching an accommodation with the Afghans and desperately trying to obtain assistance from the French. Over the next couple of months a furious diplomatic battle raged in Murshidabad as William Watts and Jean Law, his French counterpart, each attempted to dish the other. Still only 20 years old and sadly lacking in maturity, experience and good advice, Siraj-ud-Daula was constantly vacillating. At one stage towards the end of April it looked as if he might actually arrest Law, but the Frenchman had prudently brought an escort of grenadiers and the Nawab backed down, allowing Law to take his leave and withdraw to Patna.

Contrarily, Siraj-ud-Daula still rightly distrusted the British and remained in correspondence with Law in continuing his efforts to secure French assistance. That of course only confirmed the Company in its belief that there could be no lasting peace while he ruled Bengal. Consequently, the happy realisation that various parties were conspiring to effect a revolution in Murshidabad provided the convenient opportunity which the Company needed. It is unlikely that Watts or any other Company agent actually initiated the plotting; the Bengali court was sufficiently Byzantine to create its own opportunities, and in this case the real prime movers were apparently not the nobles themselves but the powerful Seth banking family.

In view of the developing situation, Clive wrote to Collet, who had taken charge at Cossimbazar, instructing that the Company's garrison and its 'treasure' were to be withdrawn from the station as soon as possible 'in consideration of the uncertainty of the Nabob's disposition'.[1] Collet's men were mostly deserters from the French service who had been enlisted after the fall of Chandernagore and were considered to be unreliable. Accordingly, Captain Alexander Grant was sent off to carry out the evacuation. In addition to an escort of twenty sepoys, he was given some spare arms and ammunition as Clive was also unsure as to whether Collet's men were properly armed in the first place. The Nawab, hearing of this, not unreasonably assumed that the Company was in fact *strengthening* its garrison and sent orders that Captain Grant be intercepted. There were blood-curdling threats that if any ammunition was found in his boats those carrying it would have their noses cut off, but in the event Grant was stopped in his palenkeen by Bengali troops encamped at Plassey, and politely turned back by Rai Durlabh.[2]

At the same time Clive found himself under the necessity of justifying the continued presence of the Company's forces at Chandernagore, despite being advised by the Nawab it was no longer necessary for the British to go up to Patna. In order to allay his suspicions, the artillery and the Bengal and Bombay detachments under Major Killpatrick were returned to Calcutta on 2 May, but the rest remained. 'Calcutta is become a place of such misery since your army has almost destroyed it,' Clive disingenuously explained, 'that there is not much room for more soldiers without endangering their lives by sickness.'[3] The Nawab rightly remained suspicious, for the move was mere play-acting and Killpatrick was under orders from Clive to re-embark the lot 'at a minute's warning'.

A chronicling of the various intrigues then ongoing need not detain us long, for the story of the plotting and the various betrayals has been well covered by numerous scholars since Robert Orme wrote his history of the 'fighting, tricks, chicanery, intrigues, politics and the Lord knows what'.[4] It is sufficient to note that by the end of May all appeared to be in place and a Bengali nobleman named Mir Jafar (who as it happens was an uncle of Siraj-ud-Daula) was ready to sign his name to a treaty with the British. It was a treaty which promised the East India Company's support for the revolution in return for all manner of concessions and privileges, which might be accounted legitimate, but also required the payment of quite massive sums of money. This was not just by way of compensation to the Company for its losses to date, and its efforts yet to be made; but also encompassed substantial 'gifts' to all concerned, from Lieutenant Colonel Robert Clive all the way down to each of the common soldiers and sepoys. The riches promised made some of those involved quite giddy at the prospect. They may not yet have lost their heads but some of them were prepared to do quite absurd things. Central to the conspiracy as agent, go-between and advisor was the omnipresent figure of Amir Chund, once again in good odour with the Company and seemingly working in its interest to such good effect that Watts was at first unstinting in his praise. Inevitably it soon became apparent that, like everyone else, the Sikh businessman was playing his own game and was not to be trusted. Whilst the famous affair of the two treaties, one written on red paper which allowed Amir Chund a substantial share of the Nawab's treasure and the real one written on white is well-known, the fact of the matter is that from the outset all of the parties concerned were each of them intent on betraying the other for their own advantage – and that included Mir Jafar and the other far from enthusiastic conspirators.

Approach March

On 28 May, Clive was confident enough to once again request practical assistance from Admiral Watson. This time it was to be in the form of some 200 of his seamen, half of whom were wanted to form a garrison for Chandernagore while the rest were needed to accompany the army.[5] He also requested that the navy provide any additional boats which might be needed for transporting Major Killpatrick's detachment up the river. Notwithstanding the arrival of the Bombay detachments, the last of HM 39th Foot, and even some additional Madras sepoys, Clive was painfully aware that he still lacked a comfortable sufficiency of troops. Calcutta was therefore to be left guarded only by a handful of gunners and invalids.[6] Otherwise he wanted every soldier who could march to be out with him in the field. Killpatrick duly came up on 12 June and next morning, after formally delivering the fort of Chandernagore into the care of Lieutenant John Clerke RN, the expedition set off upriver to Niaserray. A rendezvous had been once proposed there with Mir Jafar. He was nowhere in sight, however, and the following day saw another long and fatiguing move further upstream to Culnah. As on previous operations, the European troops and the artillery were carried in boats while the sepoys marched overland along the river bank.[7] This was not entirely a happy arrangement and Coote recorded that the movement to Culnah was so fatiguing that 'one *jamadar* [junior officer], one *hauvildar* [sergeant], and about twenty-nine of the Madrass *seapoys* deserted on the march'.[8] Nevertheless there was no real alternative and had the European troops also been required to march overland the pace would have been slower and the stragglers far greater in number.

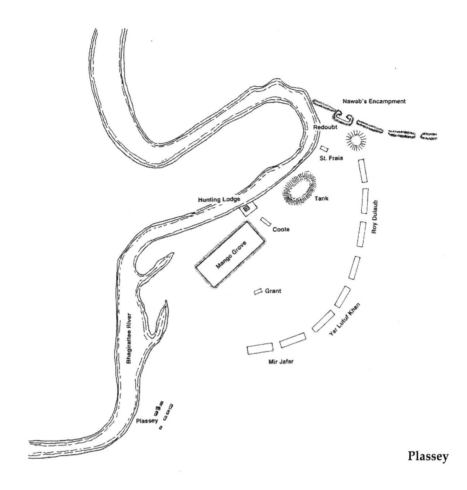

Plassey

At any rate, it was there at Culnah, after making a dramatic escape from Murshidabad, that Mr Watts turned up together with thirty soldiers from Cossimbazar.[9] Watts brought gloomy news. The Nawab for his part was well aware something was going on and suspicious of everyone, including Mir Jafar. The conspiracy was not yet unravelling but all of those concerned were getting cold feet and whilst they might still be prepared to join in a revolution, no-one was prepared to start it.

Wariness, therefore, on the Company's part was also prudent and so the army halted at Culnah for most of 15 June while the 704 European infantry were formed into a brigade of two battalions, each with its own integral artillery assets. To ensure that both battalions were equal in size, HM 39th Foot was combined with the Bengal Europeans to form the 1st

Battalion under Major James Killpatrick, while the Madras Europeans and Bombay Europeans became the 2nd Battalion.[10] To command the latter, Captain Archibald Grant, the senior officer present with HM 39th Foot, was made up to major – to Eyre Coote's palpable disgust.[11]

Despite little being heard from Mir Jafar, and all of it a succession of excuses for inaction, Clive then resolved to continue his cautious march upriver by way of Mirzapore and Tantesaul and by 17 June the army was at Pattlee. There they halted again, and a newly-promoted Major Eyre Coote was ordered to go forward to seize the fort at Cutwa, some 12 miles away. The *killadar* or governor was supposedly sympathetic and willing to surrender after the barest show of resistance. Coote accordingly set off next day at noon with a mixed detachment of 200 Europeans and 500 sepoys. As usual, the latter walked while the Europeans and two guns – a howitzer[12] and a 6-pounder field piece – were carried by boat.

About 10 o'clock on the night of 18 June 1757, they halted three miles short of the fort and Coote quietly disembarked his infantry while the artillery remained aboard the boats and continued upstream, with the intention that a convenient landing place would be found for it closer to their objective. At first all went well. Coote arrived undetected outside Cutwa at about midnight and secured three prisoners who told him that the garrison had withdrawn from the town into the fort, but that Manik Chund was expected in the morning with a reinforcement of 10,000 cavalry.

They were exaggerating, obviously, but, notwithstanding, Coote had to move without delay. Unfortunately, having identified a suitable landing place for the guns, it all went ridiculously wrong. As he ruefully recounted, he went off with a small party to reconnoitre the fort,[13] but 'about this time one of the King's soldiers being suddenly taken ill grew delirious, and whilst in the agonies of death made so great a noise as to discover to the enemy where we were drawn up, on which they began firing at us pretty briskly'.[14] A hasty retreat ensued and Coote ensconced his people in one of the bastions forming part of the town's defences, where he would at least be safe from the rumoured cavalry. At that point, word came from his artillery officer, advising that most of the boats were aground well short of the landing place, so an increasingly irritated Coote ordered him to land the guns where he was. Then came the last straw: 'At daybreak he himself came and informed me, he could not find the limber of the 6 pounder nor the wheels of the hobit [howitzer] carriage.'[15]

Thoroughly frustrated at 'finding no dependence on the artillery' (and still apprehensive of Manik Chund turning up), Coote next tried diplomacy and more than a little bluff, by sending forward a *jemadar* named Mirza Shah Abbasbeg with a flag of truce:

> To acquaint the Governor of the Fort, that, being invited by the principal men of the country, we came as friends to assist them against the tyranny of the Nabob, and notwithstanding his continual firing upon me, I had resolved not to return it (though in my power, my batteries being all ready) until I received his answer with regard to delivering up the place, which if he refused I would immediately storm and give no quarter; to which he sent me answer that as he had received the command of the Fort from the Nabob he could not deliver it up without his orders, and was resolved to defend it to the last; the *jemadar* likewise informed me that he had not been permitted to cross the river, which divides the town from the Fort, but that the Governor had come down to the waterside to him. I then formed the whole into two divisions, the Europeans making one, and the seapoys the other, and gave orders to Mootenbeg,[16] who commanded the seapoys, to march on very briskly, cross the river, and lodge himself under the opposite bank which was about thirty yards from the Fort, and from thence to keep up a continual fire whilst the Europeans crost the river a little higher up. On our advancing the enemy fired some shot without effect, and I could perceive them running out of the Fort, which we immediately entered and found fourteen pieces of cannon of different calibers and a quantity of ammunition ... As soon as I had made myself master of the place, dispatched a letter to the Colonel acquainting him with it, and receiving a congratulatory letter in answer, about 2 in the afternoon he joined me.[17]

Next morning it rained – hard – and so the army remained in Cutwa for two days, still waiting in vain to hear something positive from Mir Jafar and the other conspirators. By 21 June, Clive felt compelled to call a council of war and put to it the proposition he had been mulling for some days, that, 'Whether in our present situation without assistance and on our own bottom it would be prudent to attack the Nabob, or whether we should wait till joined by some Country power.' According to Coote, who recorded the only surviving account of the discussion:

> The Colonel informed the Council that he found he could not depend on Meer Jaffier for anything more than his standing neuter in case we came to an action with the Nabob, the Monsieur Law with a body of French was then within three days march of joining the

Nabob, whose army (by the best intelligence we could get) consisted of about 50,000 men, and that he called us together, to desire our opinions, whether in those circumstances it would be prudent to come to immediate action with the Nabob, or fortify ourselves where we were and remain till the *monsoon* was over, and the Morattoes could be brought into the country to join us.[18] The question being put began with the President and eldest members, whose opinions are opposite their names; and I being the first that dissented, thought it necessary to give my reasons for doing so, which were, that as we had hitherto met with nothing but success which consequently had given great spirits to our men, I was of opinion that any delay might cast damp; secondly, that the arrival of Mr. Law would not only strengthen the Nabob's army and add vigour to their councils, but likewise weaken our force considerably, as the number of Frenchmen we had entered into our service, after the capture of Chandernagore, would undoubtedly desert to him upon every opportunity; thirdly, that our distance from Calcutta was so great, that all communication from thence would certainly be cut off, and therefore gave us no room to hope for supplies, and consequently that we must be soon reduced to the greatest distress; therefore gave it as my opinion that we should come to an immediate action, or if that was thought intirely impracticable, that we should return to Calcutta, the consequence of which must be our own disgrace and the inevitable destruction of the Company's affairs.[19]

Contrary to the long-established custom of the service, instead of beginning by asking the opinion of the most junior officer present, Clive then immediately cast his vote in favour of remaining at Cutwa, and thereby no doubt influenced most of the others to follow suit. Of the twenty officers present, thirteen of them, headed by Clive, voted to sit tight and await events. Coote, obviously, voted instead for immediate action and significantly the other six dissenters lining up behind him included all but one of the Bengal officers.[20]

That of course was not the end of the matter. Both Orme and Coote related that a bare hour after the council broke up, Clive changed his mind and announced his intention of crossing the river next morning. Years later in his evidence before the Select Commission, Lord Clive, as he then was, proved surprisingly evasive about this, claiming to have been misunderstood by Coote and pointing to the fact that the army did not cross the river (at this point called by its true name, the Baghirathi), until the evening of 22 June. And even then that was only after he had received a letter from Mir Jafar, at last promising to join him. There are contradictions here in that Coote claims the army crossed at 6 am and then halted in a large *tope*, or grove of trees, some two miles off, until 4 pm.[21] Clive's contemporary headquarters journal, on the other hand, explicitly states the army crossed the river 'at 5 in the evening'. As there is otherwise no reason to question either journal, the most likely explanation as confirmed by Orme is that the advance guard crossed in the morning to secure a bridgehead, but Clive delayed bringing the main body over until he had heard from Mir Jafar later in the day.[22]

Be that as it may, the Company forces were actually marching into a trap. Marching through heavy rain and flooded fields, Clive arrived at the little village of Palasi or Plassey sometime around midnight, and there he realised he had been betrayed. As Orme put it: 'To their great surprize, the continual sound of drums, clarions, and cymbals, which always accompany the night watches of an Indian camp, convinced them that they were within a mile of the Nabob's army.' Rai Durlabh, the officer who intercepted Grant in April, was still occupying his fortified camp in a bend of the river just north of the village. Worse still, contrary to Mir Jafar's assurances the Nawab was indeed present with an army said to number some 35,000 infantry, 15,000 cavalry and no fewer than fifty-three guns, most of them heavies, albeit a Dutch report next day stressed that it was only the 12,000-strong vanguard under Mir Madan which actually engaged in the battle.[23] In either event, Clive might well have reflected that taking on heavy odds and trusting to pluck and European discipline to carry the day was one thing, but this was ridiculous.

Be that as it may, there was nothing to be done until daylight so Clive established himself with his own advance guard in a substantial walled compound surrounding a large hunting lodge, afterwards known as Plassey House. The rest of the army, as it came up, was directed to bivouac in a nearby large grove or orchard. It was three in the morning before his rearguard arrived and all he could do in the meantime was hope that a messenger would after all come in the night with words of assurance from Mir Jafar or any of the other conspirators.

The Day of Battle

The battlefield which Clive viewed from the top of the hunting lodge at about 6 am on the morning of 23 June 1757 was admirably described afterwards in Robert Orme's history:

> The grove of Plassy extended north and south about 800 yards in length, and 300 in breadth, and was planted with mango-trees, in

92

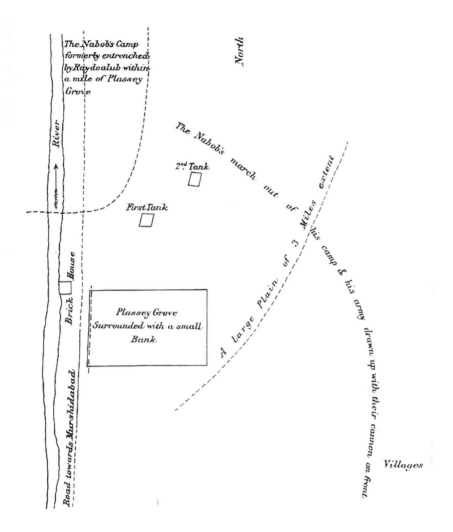

The Nabob's Camp formerly entrenched by Roydoalub within a mile of Plassey Grove

North

River

The Nabob's march out of

2ⁿᵈ Tank

First Tank

his camp & his army drawn up with their cannon on front

Brick House

Miles extent

Plassey Grove Surrounded with a small Bank

A Large Plain of 3

Road towards Murshidabad

Villages

PLAN OF THE PLASSEY GROVE (Ascribed to Clive).

Stanford's Geog¹ Estab¹. London.

regular rows. It was inclosed by a slight bank and ditch, but the ditch was choaked with coarse weeds and brambles. The angle to the south-west was 200 yards from the river, but that to the north-west not more than 50. A little to the north of the grove, and on the bank of the river, stood a hunting-house of the Nabob's, encompassed by a garden-wall. The river, a mile before it reaches this house, curves to the south-west nearly in the shape of an horse-shoe, including a peninsula about three miles in circumference, of which the neck, from the stream to the stream again, is not more than a quarter of a mile across. About 300 yards to the south of the peninsula, began an entrenchment, which Roydoolub had thrown up to secure his camp: the southern face, fronting the grove of Plassy, extended nearly in a straight line, about 200 yards inland from the bank of the river; and then turning to the north-east by an obtuse angle, continued nearly in this direction about three miles. Within this entrenchment encamped the whole army, of which a part likewise occupied the peninsula. In the angle [where the line crossed the Murshidabad road] was raised a redoubt, on which cannon were mounted. About 300 yards to the east of this redoubt, but without The camp, was a hillock covered with trees; and 800 yards to the south of this hillock and the redoubt, was a small tank or pond; and 100 yards farther to the south was another, but much larger tank: both, as all such public reservoirs of water in Bengal, were surrounded by a large mound of earth at the distance of some yards from the margin of the water.[24]

As the sun rose the Nawab's mighty host began filing out of their entrenchments and deploying on to the plain in three large columns or divisions, commanded by Rai Durlabh, Yar Lutuf Khan, and Mir Jafar respectively. All three men were supposedly party to the conspiracy, but clearly not now to be depended upon. The first took up a position with his right flank resting on the wooded hillock to the east of the Murshidabad road and from there all three divisions, interspersed with artillery, curled in a vast crescent, with the left of Mir Jafar's column eventually resting just 800 metres from the south-east angle of the grove, outflanking and indeed almost encircling the East India Company forces. The gap between Rai Durlabh's right flank and the river was then filled by the Nawab's advance guard, said to comprise 5,000 cavalry and 7,000 infantry commanded by a general named Mir Madan. Unlike the others, he was unquestionably loyal to the Nawab and could be counted upon to fight.

Clive, reckoning that remaining where he was would be taken as a sign of timidity, decided to respond by bringing his own little army out on to the plain and forming them opposite Mir Madan's division, with his left resting on the hunting lodge and his right extending out beyond the grove. In regard to the deployment of the East India Company forces, Captain John Corneille of HM 39th Foot helpfully relates that, 'The Europeans from the time we set out had been divided into two battalions and were now drawn up accordingly, the first on the right (in which was the detachment of our regiment) and the second on the left.'[25] In actual fact they were thus deployed as a single battalion divided into four grand divisions.

Coote recorded that 'the first division was commanded by Major Kilpatrick, the second by Major Grant, the third by Major Coote, and the fourth by Captain Guapp'. It needs to be appreciated, however, that Coote was not counting them off from right to left or vice versa. By custom, by practice and latterly by the teachings of General Humphrey Bland,[26] Killpatrick's first division, comprised of the detachment of HM 39th Foot, was indeed very properly standing on the right of the line, but Archy Grant, as second in seniority, did not stand next to him but instead stood on the opposite flank commanding the Madras division; while the third division, the Bengal Europeans under Coote, formed the right centre and Captain Guapp's fourth division, comprised of the Bombay detachment and the remainder of the Madras detachment formed the left centre.[27]

As for the sepoys, in April the Madras companies mustered 1,399 men fit for duty, exclusive of officers and *havildars* or sergeants, while the Bengal companies on the other hand had only 515 men present at that time, although they were still busy recruiting. At the outset of the campaign Clive's journal records there were then 2,200 sepoys, while Coote offers a comparable 2,100. However, 500 men were of course detached from that total on the day before to serve as a garrison for Cutwa, so the sepoy battalions formed on either flank of the Europeans at Plassey probably amounted to about 800 men apiece. Seniority ought to have placed the Madras sepoys on the right and the Bengal sepoys on the left, but there is no certainty of this. About 200 metres north of the hunting lodge were some brick kilns and there Clive planted a small battery of two 6-pounders and his howitzer, escorted by some seamen, while the rest of the guns were planted on the outer flanks of the European brigade.

An anonymous but detailed eyewitness account then makes the curious assertion that they 'were informed that the body of the enemy which was in sight, had no cannon with them'. However, as he then dryly goes on to relate, 'We were scarcely drawn up in this manner, when a 24lb shott from their camp, bounding along, and carrying off the arm of one of the King's grenadiers, convinced us that their cannon was come up.'[28] They were indeed, as Orme vividly relates:

> The greatest part of the foot were armed with matchlocks, the rest with various arms, pikes, swords, arrows, rockets.[29] The cavalry, both men and horses, drawn from the northern regions, were much

stouter than any which serve in the armies of Coromandel. The cannon were mostly of the largest calibres, 24 and 32 pounders; and these were mounted on the middle of a large stage, raised six feet from the ground, carrying besides the cannon, all the ammunition belonging to it, and the gunners themselves who managed the cannon, on the stage itself. These machines were drawn by 40 or 50 yoke of white oxen, of the largest size, bred in the country of Purnea; and behind each cannon walked an elephant, trained to assist at difficult tugs, by shoving with his forehead against the hinder part of the carriage. The infantry and cavalry marched in many separate and compact bodies. Forty vagabond Frenchmen under the command of one Sinfray,[30] appeared at the larger tank, that nearest the grove, with four pieces of light cannon. Two larger pieces advanced and halted on a line with this tank, close to the bank of the river.[31]

In the course of half an hour, another ten Europeans and twenty sepoys were killed and wounded, while the Company's short 6-pounders could make no effective reply at such long range. For the moment at least, Clive decided to retire and place his infantry and guns back under cover behind the bank and ditch surrounding the grove. Contrary to his earlier fear, the Bengalis did not immediately go over to the attack but very sensibly contented themselves with intensifying their bombardment, as Orme continues:

The enemy, elated by this retreat, advanced their heavy artillery nearer, and fired with greater vivacity than before; but their shot only struck the trees; for the troops were ordered to sit down, whilst the field-pieces alone answered the enemy's cannon from behind the bank. Explosions of powder were frequently observed amongst their artillery. At eleven o'clock Colonel Clive consulted his officers at the drum Head; and it was resolved to maintain the cannonade during the day, but at midnight to attack the Nabob's camp.[32]

Instead, the complexion of the battle abruptly changed. A sudden thunderstorm blanketed the battlefield for about half an hour and there was real concern in the British ranks that under cover of the rain the Nawab's cavalry would attack.[33] Instead, it remained standing where it was, for unbeknown to them, Mir Madan had been fatally wounded by a shell-splinter. His then bleeding to death on the floor of the Nawab's tent was hardly calculated to stiffen the latter's resolve, and instead of riding out to rally his troops in a soldier-like fashion, he supposedly sent for Mir Jafar and ordered him to take command of the army. How far later accounts of their meeting (if it ever took place) are to be trusted cannot be determined, although Orme followed the general's own account in writing that as soon as Mir Jafar entered the tent, Siraj-ud-Daula 'flung his turban on the ground, saying, "Jaffier, that turban you must defend".'[34] At that, supposedly, the general agreed to take up the reins, but counselled standing fast behind the entrenchments. As we shall see there are grounds for doubting Jafar's version but the one indisputable fact of the matter was that the temporary leadership crisis caused by the death of Mir Madan created a temporary but untimely vacuum in the Bengali army's high command, which was immediately and ruthlessly exploited by the gallant Major Killpatrick.

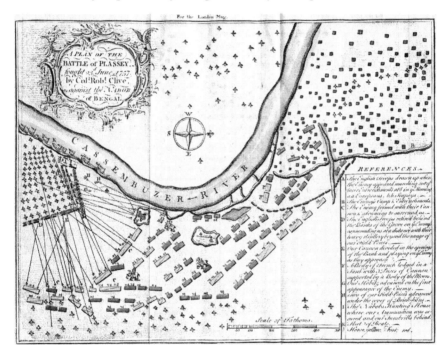

Plassey 1757

Bereft of its general, Mir Madan's division began retiring at about 2 pm. First the guns went back and then the infantry and cavalry, all in good order and covered by St. Frais and his French gunners. Then the other divisions began following suit, shuffling to their right in order to draw behind the entrenchment. Given that Mir Jafar remained with his division on the left, this movement was more than likely a spontaneous one following the death of Mir Madan, and Jafar's claiming the credit for it more opportunistic than truthful.

At any rate Killpatrick seized what Corneille calls the lucky moment and went forward with both the grenadier company of HM 39th and at least one sepoy company,[35] to seize the smaller tank. As it had already been abandoned, he succeeded in doing so without loss and promptly opened fire with a couple of guns.[36] Clive at this point was nowhere to be seen, but Killpatrick very properly:

> Sent information of his intention, and the reason of it, to his commander, who chanced at this time to be lying down in the hunting-house. Some say he was asleep; which is not improbable, considering how little rest he had had for so many hours before; but this is no imputation either against his courage or conduct. Starting up, he ran immediately to the detachment, reprimanded Kilpatrick sharply for making such a motion without his orders, commanded him to return to the grove, and bring up the rest of the army; and then proceeded himself with the detachment to the tank, which Sinfray, seeing his party left without support, abandoned; and retreated to the redoubt of the intrenchment, where he planted his field-pieces ready to act again.[37]

Getting the rest of the army out of the trees and deployed into a battle-line was going to take time, so as soon as Killpatrick regained the grove, he despatched Cote with four more platoons from the 1st battalion as an immediate reinforcement for the badly exposed detachment out at the tank.[38] Just for good measure, Coote took a couple of guns with him and although unremarked, Killpatrick must also have sent forward some more of the Bengal sepoys, for both the part they were to play in the fight and the casualties they were to suffer up there clearly point to more than just the grenadier company being involved.

However, the hasty reinforcement did not go quite according to plan. Orme explained that as soon as the detachment went forward, Mir Jafar's division advanced, as if to intercept it. Accordingly, 'Three platoons of the line, whilst in march, and a field-piece, were detached to oppose them under the command of Captain [Alexander] Grant and Lieutenant Rumbold; and Mr. John Johnstone, a volunteer, managed the field-piece, the fire of which soon stopped the approach of the supposed enemy.'[39]

As for the rest of the army, in response to the same threat, Killpatrick initially halted it where it was by the grove, for as Corneille dryly put it, 'it was considered that all our ammunition was there and that the enemy's party of horse seemed to be tending that way, so the orders were countermanded except for four platoons of the second battalion and two more guns.'[40] There they were left undisturbed either because Mir Jafar, as he afterwards piously insisted, had no real intention of falling upon his putative allies, or more likely because the semi-fortified grove, not to mention Johnstone's gun, had an ugly look to it and was best left alone. Prudence was called for.

However, if all was quiet by Plassey Grove itself, the fighting up by the tanks was increasing in intensity. Once Coote's men (less Grant's detachment) were up, 'Clive posted half his troops and artillery at the lesser tank, and the other half at a rising ground about 200 yards to the left of it. From these stations the cannonade was renewed with more efficacy than before, and killed many of the oxen which were drawing the artillery, which threw all the trains that were approaching into disorder'. On the other hand, the 'Frenchmen with Sinfray plied their field-pieces from the redoubt; and matchlocks from the intrenchments, from ditches, hollows, and every hole or shelter, as also from the bushes on the hillock east of the redoubt, kept up a constant although irregular fire, whilst the cavalry advanced several times threatening to charge sword in hand, but were always stopped and repulsed by the quick firing of the English field-pieces.'[41]

Contrary to Mir Jafar's assertion that the Nawab had begged *him* to take command of the army, Siraj-ud-Daula had actually found a more worthy successor to Mir Madan in Mohun Lal's son-in-law, Bahadur Ali Khan.[42] The new general was made of sterner stuff altogether, but was hampered by being unable to get his heavy artillery up. It had earlier been withdrawn into the camp and while it was no doubt possible for the *berkanduz* (or matchlock men) to scramble over the entrenchment, the only way out for the guns was through that single opening where the Murshidabad road passed through. Clive's gunners quickly realised their opportunity and switched to the all-too tempting target offered by those white oxen. Their Bengali counterparts were nothing if determined and no sooner were the dead and injured animals from one gun dragged out of the way, than they tried to get another gun pushed through the gap, but all to no avail for each time the teams were shot down in bloody ruin.

After nearly two hours of this heavy firing on both sides, and ammunition no doubt running low, Clive decided it was time to resume the offensive and having again called forward the main body at about 4 pm he sent the sepoys and grenadiers to storm the other tank and the small wooded hill. Both were carried with little or no loss for by now Bahadur Ali Khan was also dead and the charge immediately precipitated a general retreat, headed by none other than Siraj-ud-Daula himself, mounted on a fast camel.[43] 'From that moment,' recalled Corneille, 'they never more made head against us. We immediately pursued them into their camp and they as fast fled from it. Here we found most of their heavy cannon, some with upwards of a hundred oxen yolked to them, others dismounted, and all in the utmost confusion.'[44]

With no cavalry, Clive could not mount a proper pursuit, but conscious that he was still very much outnumbered, he decided to hustle them along, kept his own men firmly in hand and pushed straight through the camp. 'The English soldiers being told,' said Orme, 'that they should receive a donation of money, received the orders to march on to Daudpore with acclamations, nor shewed any desire to stop for the plunder which lay spread around them. They halted, however, until the commissaries had taken possession of as many oxen as sufficed for all the artillery and carriages of the army; their own being much inferior to the Nabob's. A detachment was sent forward, under Major Coote, to pursue, or rather to observe if the enemy rallied; and the whole army arrived at eight o'clock, and rested at Daudpore.'

'Twas a famous victory – and a cheaply bought one at that. In all, the 1st Battalion had only ten wounded, while the 2nd Battalion had one killed and four wounded. The sepoys suffered more with three dead and ninteen wounded in the Madras Battalion and thirteen dead and twenty wounded in the Bengal Battalion. Proportionately, the artillery suffered most with three dead and two officers and six men wounded, all seemingly in the close-range firefight up at the tank.[45] Bengali losses are unknown, although Mir Jafar's report of 500 killed, despite being accepted without question at the time and endlessly repeated ever since, is almost certainly as unreliable as estimates of their strength at the outset of the battle.[46]

Epilogue:

Patna

When the last loyal troops broke and ran, and Siraj-ud-Daula fled, the three principal conspirators, Rai Durlabh, Yar Lutuf Khan and Mir Jafar, carefully stood aside from the rout and the latter at least hastened to assure Clive of his good intentions; protesting his fulsome regrets at not being able to join with him on the battlefield.

'In the morning' [wrote Orme], 'Colonel Clive deputed Mr. Scrafton and Omarbeg to conduct Meer Jaffier to Daudpore, who received them with reserve, and an air of anxiety, as if he apprehended that the English refented his conduct, in not having joined them, conformably to his promises; he, however, immediately proceeded with them to Daudpore, accompanied by his son, Meirum, and his usual retinue. On entering the English camp, he alighted from his elephant, and the guard drew out, and rested their arms, to receive him with the usual honours. Not knowing the meaning of this compliment, he started back, as if he thought it a preparation to his destruction but Colonel Clive advancing hastily, embraced, and saluted him Nabob of Bengal, Behar, and Orixa, which removed his fears.'[1]

Mir Jafar had reason enough for his guilty conscience, for messengers allegedly going astray was no excuse for his equivocal behaviour before and during the battle. While Clive for his part was under no doubts that their supposed neutrality during the battle had been at best precarious, he was sufficient of a realist to know that he needed Mir Jafar and the other conspirators, for the present at least, and that the affair was not yet over. Siraj-ud-Daula was still at large and might yet bring in the French. As a first step, therefore, Mir Jafar had to be proclaimed Nawab in his place as soon as possible, even if it took British bayonets to do it. And then the vast sums of money promised to the Company and to the soldiers carrying those bayonets, had to be collected and handed over;[2] and of course Siraj-ud-Daula himself had to be accounted for. The first and last were quickly accomplished, the new Nawab was conducted to the *Musneed* or throne by Clive himself and the old one captured within a few days and brutally murdered. His demise was squalid but necessary, for the regime change was by no means universally popular. There was an abortive plot to assassinate Clive (supposedly led by Rai Durlabh) and the fact of Mir Jafar's standing aside from the battle as they fought hard and died at Plassey was remembered and bitterly resented by many of the surviving Bengali soldiers.

This then presented a problem when it was realised that the campaign was not quite over, for Siraj-ud-Daula's deputy in Bihar, a gentleman named Ram Narain, was one of those not yet reconciled to the new regime, especially as he and Rai Durlabh were bitter enemies. Of itself this ought to have been of little concern to Clive, but complicating matters enormously was the continued presence of Jean Law and his little army. Notwithstanding his earlier falling out with Siraj-ud-Daula, the Frenchman, had responded to the latter's call for assistance with some 140 Europeans and ninety sepoys,[3] but he was still several days march away when the Battle of Plassey was lost and won, and afterwards barely an hour away from rescuing the former Nawab when his flight ended at Rajmahal on 30 June. Now, in need of an employer, it was feared that Law might join with Ram Narain. As Orme delicately put it:

> The new regency at Muxadavad had, therefore, no reason to expect his [Ram Narain's] willing acquiescence to the revolution, or not to suspect that he would not entertain the party with Mr. Law, and even strengthen himself still more by alliances with the neighbouring powers to the westward. The best means of averting these consequences consisted in sending a detachment expedite and strong enough to destroy the French party before they reached Patna, or a force sufficient to deter Ramnarain from taking them into his pay when they should arrive there.
>
> Meer Jaffier, notwithstanding the seeming acquiescence of the soldiery to his accession, was afraid to trust any considerable body of them at a distance, and especially in the precarious province of Behar; but was ashamed to acknowledge his mistrust, which Clive penetrated, and determined to undertake the expedition with the English troops alone.[4]

Eyre Coote eventually got given the job[5] and two sepoy grenadier companies were sent off as an advance guard on 4 July, under *Subadar* Moideen Saib, but it was not until two days later that the rest were ready to go, comprising three more companies of sepoys and two European companies under Captain Alexander Grant of the Bengal service,[6] namely the Madras grenadier company and another ad hoc company made up of volunteer detachments from the Bengal and Bombay Europeans. There were also two of the ubiquitous short 6-pounders, under Lieutenant John Kinch of the Bombay Artillery. According to Ives they amounted to 223 European officers and men, but the real total according to the 3 August return was just 156 Europeans.

The expedition, alas, was doomed from the start. By the time Coote set off on 6 July, Law was already halfway to Patna and the boats provided were too leaky and too slow to carry them up the river in what ought to have been a close pursuit. What was more, as is often the case with mixed detachments, the soldiers themselves were more than a little demob-happy and consequently frequently drunk and ill-disciplined. At more than one stage, Coote was forced to leave the Europeans and the artillery behind under Grant to have the boats patched up while he pressed ahead with the five sepoy companies. Mir Jafar's brother, Daoud Khan, promised to provide a large body of cavalry but in the event only 120 turned up and even they refused to march without an advance of pay which Coote was unable to provide. Nevertheless, he pressed on up the Ganges, only to receive a letter from Mr Pearkes, now the East India Company's chief at Patna, advising that Law had passed the city on 16 July with 100 Europeans, 165 sepoys and no less than eight guns, and was marching hard for the safety of the neighbouring province of Oudh. Nevertheless, Coote stubbornly kept going until first his European troops mutinied and then the sepoys. At last he and his four captains[7] held a council of war on 4 August, where it was unanimously agreed that as the French were out of reach and they themselves were out of arrack, they should return to Murshidabad.

And so quietly ended one of the most remarkable of campaigns. A year earlier the East India Company was no more than a trading concern; now it was indisputably the strongest power in Bengal, and the Nawab was its puppet. When Mir Jafar grew restive and sought Dutch aid to free himself of the British, he was promptly deposed and replaced by his son-in-law, and so on it went as the Company extracted yet more concessions, yet more gold and above all more land and revenues. Clive effectively became Nawab of Bengal in 1765, and it was possession of Bengal, the richest province of the Mughal Empire that enabled the East India Company to slowly take over the subcontinent, until in 1784 an India Act placed the Company under the oversight of a British government-appointed Board of Control. The Battle of Plassey was won by the mercenary soldiers of a commercial undertaking, but the governance of an empire was too serious a matter to be left to that Company's shareholders.

Appendix 1

East India Company Forces in Bengal 1756–1757

Elements of the military forces of all three East India Company presidencies took part in the campaigns culminating in the Battle of Plassey on 23 June 1757. Initially the various 'Military' or European companies were consolidated into a single infantry battalion, but the arrival of a substantial Bombay contingent in March 1757 made it possible to re-organise them into two separate battalions shortly after setting off on the Plassey campaign.

The 1st Battalion comprised the Bengal Europeans and a three-company detachment of HM 39th Foot – while the 2nd Battalion was formed by combining the Madras Europeans with the newly-arrived Bombay Europeans.[1] In due course HM 39th was recalled to England shortly after the end of the campaign. The Madras and Bombay contingents, however, contrary to the strict understanding that they were only on loan, did not return to their home stations but were instead permanently absorbed into the Bengal European Regiment under Major James Killpatrick.

Bengal Europeans

The East India Company's military establishment in Bengal at the outset of the troubles in 1756 comprised five companies of infantry and one of artillery with a total strength of 647 officers and men as, enumerated in a return dated 29 February 1756.[2]

At Calcutta

Officers and soldiers,	Europeans	260
	Eurasians	225
	'Company's servants'	45
		485[3]

At Cossimbazar

Officers and soldiers,	Europeans	24
	Eurasians	16
		40

At Dacca

Officers and soldiers,	Europeans	31
	Eurasians	15
		46

At Luckipore

Officers and soldiers,	Europeans	20
	Eurasians	11
		31
	Total	647

Of those men, the garrisons of Cossimbazar and Calcutta were of course lost at the fall of those places. Many of the survivors of the Calcutta garrison subsequently appear to have fetched up at the French settlement of Chandernagore and eventually for the most part re-enlisted into the French service. A party of twenty-five men from Balasore under Lieutenant William Keene and twenty more from Luckipore, or rather Jagdea, under Lieutenant George Grainger Muir, evacuated their posts safely and made their way to Fulta at some time in July. Similarly, the garrison of the factory at Dacca, then comprising twenty-five military under Lieutenant John Cudmore (presumably exclusive of the Eurasians) was captured by the Bengalis, but subsequently released. Cudmore then made his way to Fulta at the end of August and presumably brought his men with him.

By that time, a contingent of European troops from Madras had also arrived at Fulta. On 14 July 1756 the Council at Fort St. George had resolved to send two companies of infantry and a detachment of artillery to Bengal under Major Killpatrick. There is fairly general agreement that they numbered about 200 men, and William Tooke provides a precise figure of 226 men when they arrived on board the *Delaware* on 31 July. The following officers are recorded in the ship's log:[4]

Major James Killpatrick
Captain Dugald Campbell[5]

Captain Godwin, Train of Artillery, died 12 September 1756
Captain Sampson, died 1 September 1756
Lieutenant Bogar, died 12 September
Lieutenant Herdman, died 10 September 1756.[6]

Unfortunately, as illustrated by the mortality among the officers, they proved extremely sickly, having already contracted some form of malignant fever during the voyage. The official headquarters journal records that only thirty men were still fit for duty when Clive arrived in December 1756. By that time Major Killpatrick had amalgamated the survivors of his detachment with the remaining Bengal military and a number of volunteers enlisted at Fulta, to form a new Bengal European detachment.

The earliest surviving returns appear to come after the recovery of Calcutta. The first set of figures appears as part of a general return of Clive's forces dated 22 February, which shows a raw total of 211 officers and men (exclusive of artillery) on the Bengal establishment, i.e.:[7]

1 major [Killpatrick], 4 captains, 1 captain-lieutenant, 2 lieutenants, 3 ensigns,[8] 12 serjeants, 12 corporals, 2 drummers and 127 Centinels fit for duty.

NB: Of those centinels fit for duty no fewer than ninety-one were Eurasians.

In addition a further one captain, one ensign, six serjeants, two corporals, four drummers and thirty-three men were returned as sick, and since the campaign began four men were recorded as having been killed in action (presumably in the fight outside Budge Budge), four others died from unspecified causes and eight were wounded, although these casualties are not broken down by rank.

A subsequent return six days later on 28 February provided a more detailed breakdown in a *General Muster of the Troops near Calcutta under Command of Major James Killpatrick*, which covered only the Bengal troops and found 199 officers and men organised in three companies, listed as was customary in order of their captains' seniority.[9] Other than simply listing all the rank and file as Europeans, rather than differentiating between Europeans and Eurasians as the earlier muster does, the two sets of figures agree tolerably well, although this time only three rather than five captains are listed. It needs to be emphasised, however, that those mustered under Killpatrick belonged to the field army and evidently did not include at least one company of Bengal troops providing a garrison for Fort William and this was presumably where Captains Grant and Cudmore were to be found.

Captain George Muir's Company:
This was presumably the company he had brought in from Jagdea, although his only subaltern had joined at Fulta.

Captain George Grainger Muir
Captain Lieutenant Peter Carstairs[10]
5 serjeants, 6 corporals, 2 drummers and 15 centinels.

Captain Melchior Le Beaume's Company:
Le Beaume's company, surprisingly enough, was considerably larger than the other two. Orme, however, refers to 'a company of seventy volunteers, who embodied themselves at Fulta', and presumably they were placed under the command of Le Beaume, who had made a name for himself in the earlier defence of Calcutta. Subsequently Le Beaume himself was rather arbitrarily cashiered by Clive following the capture of Chandernagore and his company was then broken up and the personnel distributed between Muir's and Frazer's companies.[11] Encouragingly, the aggregate increase of 110 men in the size of both companies between 28 February and the next muster at Chinsura on 7 April 1757 corresponds almost exactly with the 116 men recorded as serving under Le Beaume in the earlier muster.

Captain Melchior Le Beaume
Lieutenant John Dyer
Ensign De Lubers[12]
6 serjeants, 3 corporals, 2 drummers and 105 centinels.

Captain John Fraser's Company:
Fraser's company represented the remnants of Killpatrick's detachment brought from Madras, but again at least one of his officers joined at Fulta. Contrary to later regimental legend there is no evidence that Fraser's company was designated as grenadiers.

Captain John Fraser[13]
Lieutenant Charles Keir (or Kerr)
Adjutant William Gibbons
Ensign Pritchard
Ensign William Rider[14]
7 serjeants, 3 corporals, 3 drummers and 32 centinels.

The fall of Chandernagore rendered the maintenance of a proper garrison in Calcutta unnecessary. Therefore, by the time the 7 April muster took place the two Bengal European companies which had been serving in Calcutta were called forward to join the field army – if indeed they had not already come up for the attack on Chandernagore.

Captain Alexander Grant's Company:
Captain Alexander Grant's company appears to have been newly raised at this time and its officers included Lieutenant Dyer and Ensign De Lubers, who had earlier served under Le Beaume before his company was broken.

> Captain Alexander Grant
> Lieutenant John Dyer
> Ensign De Lubers
> Ensign Harry [?] Verelst
> 3 volunteers, 3 serjeants and 2 corporals, 1 drummer and 38 centinels
> (9 Europeans and 29 Eurasians).

Captain George Muir's Company:
> Captain George Grainger Muir
> Captain Lieutenant Peter Carstairs
> Ensign Maclean
> Ensign William Ellis
> 3 volunteers, 3 serjeants and 5 corporals, 2 drummers and 50 centinels (half Eurasians).

Captain John Cudmore's Company:
Captain Cudmore had been the commandant at Dacca and had arrived with his men at Fulta as early as 26 August 1756.[15] As noted above his company was probably in the Calcutta garrison at the time of the February muster.

> Captain John Cudmore
> Ensign Demee David
> Ensign Pritchard[16]
> Ensign Champion[17]
> 3 volunteers, 3 serjeants and 1 corporal, 1 drummer and 63 centinels (20 Europeans and 43 Eurasians).

Captain John Fraser's Company:
> Captain John Fraser
> Lieutenant Archibald Keir

Adjutant and Ensign William Gibbons
Ensign Barnes
1 Quartermaster, 3 volunteers, 9 serjeants and 6 corporals, 6
drummers and 107 centinels (51 Europeans and 66 Eurasians).

A subsequent abstract dated 10 April and presumably based on the 7
April muster then summarised the strength of the Bengal detachment as
twenty-five officers and volunteers doing duty and seven sick with 299
non-commissioned officers and centinels doing duty and thirty sick.[18]

The last return compiled before the Battle of Plassey was compiled by
Captain John Fraser a week before on 15 June. At that time the Bengal
detachment formed part of the newly created 1st European Battalion and
comprised a total of twenty-one officers, three volunteers, twenty-one
NCOs, eleven drummers, 120 European centinels and forty-eight
Eurasians; all of them presumably fit for duty.[19] The final return dated at
Sydabad (the former French factory outside Murshidabad) on 3 August
1757, at the conclusion of the campaign, found the Bengal Establishment
expanded to its original five companies, thanks to the addition of a new
one commanded by the now reinstated Captain Le Beaume:[20]

Captain Alexander Grant's Company:
 Captain Alexander Grant; 'on command'[21]
 Lieutenant John Dyer
 Lieutenant De Lubers[22]
 Lieutenant Harry [?] Verelst
 2 volunteers, 3 serjeants and 4 corporals, 2 drummers and 33
 centinels (all Europeans!).[23]

Captain George Muir's Company:
 Captain George Grainger Muir
 Captain Lieutenant Peter Carstairs
 Ensign Maclean
 Ensign William Ellis[24]
 2 serjeants, 2 corporals and 2 drummers; 34 centinels (18
 Europeans and 16 Eurasians).

Captain John Cudmore's Company:
The only officer present was an un-named ensign; both Cudmore
himself and a second ensign being 'on command'.

 1 serjeant, 1 corporal and 2 drummers; 31 centinels
 (19 Europeans and 12 Eurasians).

Captain Melchior Le Beaume's Company:

Captain Melchior le Beaume
2 ensigns present, with 1 lieutenant sick
2 serjeants and 1 drummer; 26 centinels
(14 Europeans and 12 Eurasians).

Captain John Fraser's Company:

Captain John Fraser
Lieutenant Archibald Keir
Lieutenant Barnes
Adjutant and Ensign William Gibbons
1 quartermaster, 3 serjeants, 1 corporal and 3 drummers; 32
centinels (of whom only 7 were Eurasians).

A. Bengal Artillery

Grant's return of the Calcutta garrison on 11 June 1756 found thirty-five
European artillerymen there, most of whom appear to have been Dutch,
and all or most of them were subsequently killed, captured or deserted
when the place fell.

Major Killpatrick then brought a small train of artillery from Madras,
but as noted above, both officers died at Fulta in September 1756, along
with at least some of the personnel. His four guns were therefore taken
over by Bengal volunteers. The 22 February 1757 return does not
distinguish between Madras and Bengal gunners, but the more detailed
list of Killpatrick's men on 28 February evidences only two officers,
Lieutenant John Johnstone[25] and Lieutenant Thomas Lewis, both Fulta
refugees; four serjeants, one corporal and one drummer; eight
bombardiers, ten gunners and twelve matrosses.[26] There may in
addition have been other gunners in the Calcutta garrison, but this is
unclear.

At any rate, at Chinsura on 7 April, the Bengal Artillery mustered:

Lieutenant John Johnstone
Lieutenant Thomas Lewis
2 serjeants
2 corporals
1 drummer
6 bombardiers
10 gunners
41 matrosses, for a total of 62 personnel.

The 3 August muster at Sydabad found both lieutenants were still present but otherwise there were only three sergeants, three bombardiers, three gunners and nine matrosses.

B. Bengal Sepoys

Other than the ad hoc recruitment of mercenary *berkanduz* or *buxarries* during the defence of Calcutta, there were no native infantry carried on the Bengal establishment prior to the arrival of Colonel Clive. As noted in the text, when faced with a shortage of troops, he duly set about recruiting *berkanduz* and having them armed and disciplined in European fashion. With plenty of hard cash available (another source of resentment to the Bengal Committee) he was able to carry this out relatively quickly and raise what was initially a strong four-company battalion.

The 22 February return cites: four *subadars* or company commanders; thirty *jemadars* or junior officers; twenty-five *havildars* or serjeants; thirty-two *naiks* or corporals; twelve coulourmen and one trumpeter, leading 371 sepoys. None of them were returned as sick, but six had been killed and six wounded.

Killpatrick's 28 February return however cites only five *jemadars*, four *havildars* and three *naiks*, with a tom-tom, and a total of 265 sepoys present with the field army at Chitpur. The remaining officers and NCOs and the balance of 106 sepoys must in the meantime have been assigned to the Calcutta garrison, before rejoining the field army in time for the Chinsura return of 7 April, at which time the battalion once again mustered four companies as set out below.[27]

> *Subadar* **Shaik Emaun's Company:**
> 1 *subadar*, 4 *jemadars*, 8 *havildars*, 9 *naiks*, 3 coulourmen and 79 sepoys
> *Subadar* **Condojee's Company:**
> 1 *subadar*, 3 *jemadars*, 7 *havildars*, 7 *naiks*, 3 coulourmen and 96 sepoys
> *Subadar* **Syed Hassan's Company:**
> 1 *subadar*, 4 *jemadars*, 7 *havildars*, 9 *naiks*, 3 coulourmen and 98 sepoys
> *Subadar* **Moideen Saib's Company:**
> 1 *subadar*, 4 *jemadars*, 5 *havildars*, 7 *naiks*, 3 coulourmen and 95 sepoys.

In addition there were noted to be a further two *jemadars*, one *havildar* and ninety-nine men described as 'New *Seapoys* entertained', i.e. newly enlisted. All in all, according to the subsequent abstract dated 10 April and presumably based on this one, there were a total of 515 sepoys (including those 'new entertained') doing duty and twenty-one sick.[28]

Eventually there were seven companies recorded in the 3 August return at Sydabad, totalling:[29]

7 *subadars*
28 *jemadars*
56 *havildars*
61 *naiks*
21 colourmen
13 tom-toms
3 trumpeters
886 sepoys.

C. Madras Contingent

Establishing the composition of the troops brought by Colonel Clive from Madras is far from straightforward in that not only do the reported numbers of those embarked vary, but even then not all of them actually reached Bengal, while those who did so came ashore at different times.

The starting point therefore is a return dated 8 October 1756 listing the European officers and men then at Fort St. George, Madras, earmarked to go to Bengal.[30]

	Lieutenant Colonel	Captains	Capt. Lieuts.	Lieutenants	Ensigns	Volunteers	Sergeants	Corporals	Drummers	Centinels	Bombardiers	Gunners	Matrosses	Total
Fort. St. George 8 October 1756														
Train of Artillery		1	5				5	5	3		21	21	48	103
Grenadiers[31]	1		1	2	2		8	6	3	94				112
Captain Maskelyne's	1		1	2	2		6	6	4	73				89
Captain Gauppe's[32]	1		2	1	2		4	6	4	77				91
Captain Campbell's[33]	1		1	2	1		6	6	4	73				89
Captain Callendar's	1		3	1			6	6	4	73				89
Total	5	1	10	10	8		35	35	22	390	21	21	48	573

N.B. 2 captains, 2 lieutenants   4[34]
      2 sergeant-majors, 1 quartermaster sergeant,
      1 corporal   4
      And 12 camp colourmen not returned in the
      body of the Return   12   20   593
              ROBERT CLIVE, Lieutenant Colonel

On 13 October 1756, the Council at Fort St. George, Madras, then advised Clive that; 'We have embarked on the several ships of the squadron [i.e. the Royal Navy], all officers included, 528 military and 109 Train, and on the Company's ships *Walpole* and *Marlborough* with the *Boneta* ketch and those on board His Majesty's ships 940 sepoys and 160 lascars with twelve field pieces, one haubitzer, and a necessary quantity of ammunition, and reposing full confidence in your abilities we have appointed you to be Commander-in-Chief of the land forces to be employed on the present expedition.'[35]

However, Clive himself came up with a rather different figure in his own embarkation return as included in his official military journal, compiled by his brother-in-law, Captain Neville Maskelyne:[36]

	King's Troops	Company's Troops	Sepoys and Lascars
King's ships:			
Kent	65	77	59
Cumberland	97	150	67
Tyger	56	146	70
Salisbury	58	147	57
Bridgewater	–	96	–
Company's ships			
Walpole	–	–	413
Marlborough	–	–	360
Protector	–	–	132
Lapwing snow	–	–	90
Bonetta ketch	–	–	60
	276	616	1,308

Unfortunately, as we have seen, the fleet was battered and somewhat scattered by the monsoon and consequently arrived in Bengal in a piecemeal fashion, as recorded in the headquarters journal.[37]

> *Dec. 16th.* – The Company's troops and *seapoys* on the *Kent, Tyger* and *Walpole* landed at Fulta, where they joined the detachment under Major James Kilpatrick; the military encamped in a plain to the eastward of the town, and the seapoys were posted at the avenues leading to it.
> *Dec.* 22nd. – The Grenadier and Artillery companies from the *Salisbury* and *Bridgewater* joined the battalion in camp where the whole continued till the 27th.

This gave him a disposable force of 466 European officers and men, of which ninety-six would have been the artillerymen carried on the *Bridgewater*. No distinction is made between sepoys and lascars, so the total of the former is uncertain.

The sepoys carried on the smaller ships arrived later, but unfortunately, none of the 150 Madras Europeans on board HMS *Cumberland* ever reached Bengal. Some 100 officers and men were landed at Vizagapatnam in time to discourage an attack by De Bussy, and the remainder set ashore at Madras in exchange for naval personnel discharged from the hospital there.

D. Madras Europeans

As a result, the 22 February return (compiled subsequent to the fighting at Budge Budge and Calcutta) listed the Madras infantry as below. It will be noted that unlike their counterparts in Bengal and later from Bombay, the Madras European companies apparently did not include any Eurasian personnel. Indeed, Orme notes with apparent surprise that at Plassey 'the *Topasses* were blended in the battalion with the Europeans', which strongly suggests that in the Madras service the two were strictly segregated and that if they were enlisted at all, Eurasians were being employed in non-combatant roles.[38]

1 lieutenant colonel (Clive)
3 captains present and fit for duty and 3 more wounded
4 lieutenants present and 1 sick
6 ensigns
1 adjutant
1 quartermaster
7 volunteers
35 serjeants present and fit for duty and 4 more sick or wounded
23 corporals present and fit for duty and 6 more sick or wounded
14 drummers present and another sick or wounded
242 centinels present and fit for duty and 58 more sick or wounded.

Of the whole, no fewer than forty-three had died from various causes since their arrival in Bengal, twenty-six were killed in action and fifty-one wounded.

The 7 April muster at Chinsura therefore discovered the Madras battalion somewhat reduced in numbers and evidently in some need of reorganising:

Grenadier Company:
Originally this was Captain William Pye's company, but it passed to Linn after Pye was killed in action outside Calcutta on 5 February 1757.

> Captain William Lin[39]
> Lieutenant Campbell as Lieutenant and Quartermaster[40]
> Lieutenant Robert L. Knox
> Lieutenant Tuite
> 2 volunteers, 6 serjeants and 5 corporals, 2 drummers and 65 centinels.

Major James Killpatrick's Company:
> Major James Killpatrick[41]
> 4 serjeants, 3 corporals and 2 drummers; 26 centinels.

Captain Neville Maskelyne's Company:
> Lieutenant Scotney as Lieutenant and Adjutant[42]
> Ensign Stringer
> 3 volunteers, 3 serjeants, 5 corporals and 3 drummers; 60 centinels.

Captain Callendar's Company:
> Ensign Tabby
> 3 serjeants, 3 corporals and 32 centinels.

Vacant Company:
Probably a part of Captain Robert Campbell's Company – see 3 August entry below.

> No officers listed
> 3 serjeants, 3 corporals, 2 drummers and 17 centinels.

Captain George Guapp's Company:
This was one of the Swiss companies hired by the East India Company in 1751.

> Captain George Frederick Guapp[43]
> Lieutenant Joecher
> Ensign Oswald
> Ensign Wiecks
> 7 serjeants, 6 corporals, 4 drummers; 60 centinels.

Supernumeraries:
>Captain Thomas Rumbold[44]
>Captain Rudolf Wagner[45]
>Captain Christian Fischer[46]
>Captain John Fraser as Adjutant[47]
>15 serjeants, 1 corporal, 1 drummer and 11 centinels.

The abstract dated 10 April and presumably based on this one summarised the overall strength of the Madras detachment as twenty-four officers and volunteers doing duty and just one sick, with 294 non-commissioned officers and centinels doing duty and fifty-two sick.[48]

Fraser's abstract of 15 June then found the Madras detachment comprising a total of nineteen officers, seven volunteers, forty NCOs, fourteen drummers, and 218 centinels; all of them Europeans, forming the major part of the newly created 2nd Battalion.[49]

By 3 August, the six companies had therefore been consolidated into four, although this probably took place at the time of the 15 June re-organisation, when the Madras and Bombay detachments were joined together as the 2nd Battalion. Once again there were as a result a surprising number of supernumeraries:

Grenadier Company:
Vacant at this time due to the death of Captain Linn in June.

>Lieutenant Campbell as Lieutenant and Quartermaster
>2 serjeants and 9 centinels present and fit for duty.
>Lieutenant Tuite, 3 volunteers, 4 serjeants, 3 corporals and 52 sentinels 'on command'.[50]

Captain George Guapp's Company:
>Captain George Frederick Guapp
>Lieutenant Joecher
>Ensign Oswald
>Ensign Wiecks
>6 serjeants, 4 corporals and 3 drummers; 32 centinels present and fit for duty
>1 corporal and 7 centinels 'on command'.

Captain Thomas Rumbold's Company:
This had been Captain Maskelyne's Company before being taken over by Rumbold after Maskelyne returned to Madras in March, due to ill-health.

Captain Thomas Rumbold; 2 ensigns, 3 serjeants, 1 corporal, 1 drummer and 14 centinels were returned as being 'on command'. Lieutenant Bryan Scotney present as Lieutenant and Adjutant 3 volunteers, 3 serjeants, 3 corporals, 2 drummers and 50 centinels present and fit for duty.

Captain Robert Campbell's Company:

Campbell appears to have been embarked on HMS *Cumberland* in October 1756 and having been diverted by way of Vizagapatam did not arrive until after the taking of Chandernagore. There he appears to have taken over Captain Callendar's company as well as the remnant of his own – identified in the previous return as 'vacant'.

Captain Robert Campbell; 2 drummers and 8 centinels 'on command'
Ensign Tabby
5 serjeants, 7 corporals, 2 drummers and 32 centinels present and fit for duty.

Supernumeraries:

2 captains (Wagner and Fischer), 1 ensign, 1 volunteer, 12 serjeants, 1 drummer and 6 centinels present and fit for duty
1 lieutenant and 7 serjeants 'on command'.[51]

E. Madras Artillery

As to the artillery, the 22 February 1757 return evidenced a total of six officers, six sergeants, seven corporals, three drummers and ninety-nine men present and fit for duty, with a further two sergeants and fourteen men in hospital. As noted above however no distinction is drawn between artillerymen on the Madras Establishment and those of the Bengal Establishment, but deducting the latter as set out in Killpatrick's return of 28 February, leaves approximately:

4 serjeants
6 corporals
14 drummers [4?]
16 bombardiers
13 gunners
39 matrosses.

Very similarly, the 6 April return evidences:

Captain Robert Barker[52]
Captain-lieutenant John Francis Paschoud[53]
Captain-lieutenant William Jennings
Lieutenant Bonjour
Lieutenant Ford
Lieutenant Charles de Torriano[54]

4 serjeants
5 corporals
2 drummers
16 bombardiers
18 gunners
37 matrosses.

Memorandum (relating to all three artillery detachments)

There are sick 2 Captain-Lieutenants, 2 Lieutenants, and 22 of the Train (being 1 Serjeant, 5 Bombardiers, 8 Gunners, 8 Mattrosses) who are sick in the Hospital and returned in the above Muster. Pay Rolls exact with the above Muster.

There are on Command at Cossimbazar, 1 Lieutenant (Mr Cassells) and 14 of the Train who are drawn pay for, but not returned as above.

As to the 3 August muster at Sydabad after most of the fighting was over, there were then present:

Captain-lieutenant John Francis Paschoud
Captain-lieutenant William Jennings
Lieutenant Bonjour
Lieutenant Ford
Lieutenant Charles de Torriano
1 adjutant
5 serjeants
2 corporals
1 drummer
14 bombardiers
6 gunners and 26 matrosses present and fit for duty.

In addition Lieutenants Cassells and Holts were still on the sick list after having been wounded at Plassey.

F. Madras Sepoys

As noted above the sepoys, commanded by *Subadar* Kezar Singh, arrived at various times between late December 1756 and the end of March 1757, and are not differentiated from lascars in the embarkation returns, hence the variation in numbers.

At any rate 22 February 1757 (after the fighting at Budge Budge and Calcutta] found:

9 *subedars*
29 *jemadars*
63 *havildars*
64 *naiks*
21 colourmen
16 tom-toms
713 sepoys.

Two *jemadars*, six *havildars*, four *naiks* and sisxty-seven sepoys were returned as sick, for a total of 1,002 all ranks.

In addition twelve men were returned as killed and fourteen more dead from non-combat causes, while forty-nine were wounded, although as always it is unclear whether they were included within the overall sick list.

The Chinsura return of 7 April, after a further contingent had arrived in Bengal, is the most informative, listing no fewer than sixteen companies:

Subadar **Kezar Singh's Company:**
1 *subadar*, 3 *jemadars*, 7 *havildars*, 8 *naiks*, 2 colourmen, 3 tom-toms and trumpeters and 79 sepoys
Subadar **Vurdarauze's Company:**
1 *subadar*, 4 *jemadars*, 8 *havildars*, 9 *naiks*, 2 colourmen, 3 tom-toms and trumpeters and 76 sepoys
Subadar **Bawan Singh's Company:**
1 *subadar*, 4 *jemadars*, 7 *havildars*, 7 *naiks*, 2 colourmen, 2 tom-toms and trumpeters and 81 sepoys
Subadar **Comrapah's Company:**
1 *subadar*, 4 *jemadars*, 8 *havildars*, 8 *naiks*, 3 colourmen, 2 tom-toms and trumpeters and 75 sepoys
Subadar **Peer Mahomed's Company:**
1 *subadar*, 3 *jemadars*, 8 *havildars*, 9 *naiks*, 2 colourmen, 3 tom-toms and trumpeters and 79 sepoys
Subadar **Rasool Khan's Company:**

1 *subadar*, 4 *jemadars*, 7 *havildars*, 7 *naiks*, 1 colourman, 3 tom-toms and trumpeters and 76 sepoys

Subadar Mahomed Khan's Company:
1 *subadar*, 4 *jemadars*, 8 *havildars*, 9 *naiks*, 3 colourmen, 4 tom-toms and trumpets and 74 sepoys

Subadar Raganaigne's Company:
1 *subadar*, 4 *jemadars*, 6 *havildars*, 9 *naiks*, 3 colourmen, 3 tom-toms and trumpeters and 71 sepoys

Subadar Hyder Saib's Company:
3 *jemadars*, 7 *havildars*, 7 *naiks*, 3 colourmen, 3 tom-toms and trumpeters and 77 sepoys

Subadar Survian's Company:
1 *subadar*, 3 *jemadars*, 7 *havildars*, 5 *naiks*, 2 colourman, 2 tom-toms and trumpeters and 79 sepoys

Subadar Shaik Daoud's Company:
1 *subadar*, 4 *jemadars*, 10 *havildars*, 9 *naiks*, 1 colourman, 1 tom-tom or trumpeters and 83 sepoys

Subadar Tim Naik's Company:
1 *subadar*, 4 *jemadars*, 8 *havildars*, 8 *naiks*, 2 colourmen, 3 tom-toms and trumpeters and 71 sepoys

Subadar Vengana's Company:
1 *subadar*, 4 *jemadars*, 9 *havildars*, 9 *naiks*, 2 colourmen, 3 tom-toms and trumpets and 69 sepoys

Subadar Jaffer Mahomed's Company:
1 *subadar*, 4 *jemadars*, 9 *havildars*, 8 *naiks*, 2 colourmen, 1 tom-tom or trumpeter and 55 sepoys.

Memorandum:

> There have been killed of the Madrass seapoys at Charnagore – 1 Subadar [presumably Hyder Saib], 3 Jemadars, 3 Havildars, 1 Naik, and 7 Seapoys. The four last companies of the Madrass arrived here from thence last month, [23 March 1757] the sick being 1 Jemadar, 3 Havildars, 2 Naiks, and 47 Seapoys returned in this Muster.[55]

In total, according to the 10 April abstract, there were no fewer than 1,399 Madras sepoys on duty and thirty-two sick.[56]

G. Bombay Europeans
The piecemeal arrival of the Bombay contingent was chronicled thus in Clive's military journal:[57]

March 5th. – Lieutenant Molitur with 8 sergeants, 8 corporals, 2 drums and 53 privates besides 43 *topasses*, in all 114, arrived at camp from Bombay

March 12th. – Captain Buchannan with 11 sergeants, 11 corporals, 3 drums, and 61 privates, besides 28 *topasses*, from Bombay, joined the troops at camp

March *14th* – Captain-Lieutenant Edgerton with 4 sergeants, 4 corporals, 1 drum, 9 privates and 24 *topasses* from Bombay arrived at camp.

The 7 April muster at Chinsura then recorded them as below:

Captain Andrew Buchanan's Company:
Captain Andrew Buchanan
Lieutenant Villars Walsh
Ensign Robertson
Mr. McLean, quartermaster
2 volunteers, 12 serjeants and 10 corporals, 3 drummers and 122 centinels
(66 Europeans and 56 Eurasians).

Captain Andrew Armstrong's Company:
Captain Andrew Armstrong
Lieutenant Charles Palmer
Ensign Tottingham
9 serjeants and 9 corporals, 3 drummers and 125 centinels
(64 Europeans and 61 Eurasians).

As summarised in the subsequent abstract dated 10 April the strength of the Bombay detachment was then nine officers and volunteers doing duty and none sick with a total of 263 non-commissioned officers and centinels doing duty and thirty-one sick.[58]

Fraser's pre-Plassey abstract of 15 June then found the Bombay detachment, forming part of the 2nd Battalion, comprising a total of eight officers, one volunteer, seventeen NCOs, four drummers, eighty-one European centinels and forty-three Eurasians.[59]

The 3 August muster at Sydabad found both companies present but reduced in numbers. Captain Buchanan had died on 5 June[60] (hence Armstrong now being the senior officer) and his company was commanded at Plassey by Charles Palmer, who had formerly been lieutenant to Armstrong. It will be noted that Mr. McLean, the battalion's quartermaster, had at the same time transferred to Armstrong's company.

Captain Andrew Armstrong's Company:

Captain Andrew Armstrong
1 lieutenant
2 ensigns
Mr. McLean, quartermaster
5 serjeants and 1 corporal, 1 drummer and 63 centinels present and fit for duty (35 Europeans and 28 Eurasians).

In addition two corporals, one drummer and thirteen men were returned as 'on command' and 1 ensign, 2 sergeants and a Eurasian centinel sick.

Captain Charles Palmer's Company:

Ensign Robertson [sick]
2 serjeants and 4 corporals, 2 drummers and 42 centinels present.
(23 Europeans and 19 Eurasians)

Captain Charles Palmer
Lieutenant Villars Walsh
1 volunteer, 1 sergeant and 13 men were returned as 'on command'.

H. Bombay Artillery

At Chinsura on 6 April, the Bombay train comprised:

Captain-lieutenant Egerton
Lieutenant Molitore
Lieutenant Turner
Lieutenant John Kinch
2 serjeants
2 corporals
1 drummer
6 bombardiers
10 gunners
41 matrosses.

The muster at Sydabad on 3 August, however, found only:

Captain-lieutenant Molitore
2 serjeants
1 drummers
5 bombardiers
7 gunners and 15 matrosses

In addition, however, one lieutenant (John Kinch), one drummer, one bombardier, two gunners and eleven matrosses were recorded as being 'on command' as part of Coote's expedition up the Ganges.

NB: It should be noted that notwithstanding statements in some secondary sources, there were no Bombay sepoy units engaged in the campaign. The error may arise from the *Topasses* or Eurasians being counted separately despite not being segregated into discrete units.

I. HM 39th Foot

According to Clive's embarkation return, a total of 276 officers and men of HM 39th Foot were placed aboard four ships of the line, supposedly to serve as marines.[61] Admiral Watson certainly employed them as such, landing them at need for specific operations but then embarking them again as soon as possible afterwards, until on 21 January 1757, he agreed to place them under Clive's command as part of the land forces.

At this point the contingent of ninety-seven officers and men serving on board HMS *Cumberland* had not yet arrived, so a month later on 22 February the total present still amounted to just two captains, three lieutenants, three ensigns, five serjeants, six corporals, five drummers and 123 rank and file, with another fourteen rank and file returned as sick. During his account of the battle outside Calcutta on 5 February, Eyre Coote refers to his 'having had a company of grenadiers formed out of the King's troops' and thereafter there are frequent references to these grenadiers. It should be emphasised however that this designation was a conceit of Coote's and his men should not be confused with the regimental grenadier company which remained with Colonel Adlercron in Madras.

March 24th. – Lieutenant Corneille with the detachment of the King's troops from the Cumberland arrived at Chandernagore.

In the meantime, the 7 April muster discovered the whole to be numbered as follows:

Captain Archibald Grant's Company:
Captain Archibald (Archy) Grant

Lieutenant John Corneille
Ensign Joseph Adnett
Ensign Blair
3 serjeants and 3 corporals, 2 drummers and 72 centinels.

Captain Nicholas Weller's Company:

Captain Nicholas Weller[62]
Lieutenant Pierson as adjutant
Ensign Martin Yorke
Ensign Balfour
3 serjeants, 3 corporals and 2 drummers and 71 centinels.

Captain Eyre Coote's Company:

Captain Eyre Coote
Lieutenant Bush as quartermaster
Lieutenant Caleb Powell
Ensign Fenton
2 serjeants, 4 corporals and 3 drummers and 70 centinels.

This, according to the 10 April abstract, produced a total of seven officers and doing duty and four sick with 199 non-commissioned officers and centinels doing duty and thirty-nine sick.[63]

Fraser's abstract of 15 June then found the detachment of HM 39th comprising a total of nine officers, fifteen NCOs, six drummers, and 194 centinels.[64]

> *June 15th.* – The Colonel thought proper to appoint Captain Archibald Grant a Major.[65]
> *June 16th.* – ... this day the Colonel appointed Captain Eyre Coote a Major.

As with the other units, the muster at Sydabad found all three companies reduced in numbers. Most of the officers and men, moreover, were returned as being 'on command', although not engaged in Coote's pursuit of Law.

Captain Archibald Grant's Company:

Captain Archibald Grant
Lieutenant John Corneille[66]
Lieutenant Bush as quartermaster
Quartermaster
2 serjeants and 3 corporals, 1 drummers and 57 centinels.

Of the above Lieutenant Bush, with a serjeant, corporal and four centinels were present in the camp at Sydabad, together with an additional ten sick. The rest of the company was 'on command'.

Captain Nicholas Weller's Company:
Captain Nicholas Weller
Lieutenant Pierson as adjutant
Lieutenant Joseph Adnett
Ensign Martin Yorke
3 serjeants, 3 corporals and 3 drummers; 64 centinels.

Of the above only Lieutenant Pierson, with two corporals, two drummers and twelve centinels were present in the camp at Sydabad, together with an additional four centinels on the sick list.

Captain Eyre Coote's Company:
Captain Eyre Coote
Lieutenant Caleb Powell (sick)
2 ensigns
1 serjeant, 4 corporals and 3 drummers; 56 centinels.

Of whom only one serjeant and ten sentinels were left in the camp, together with Lieutenant Powell and one ensign, one sergeant and ten centinels sick – four of whom may actually have been wounded from Plassey.

Uniforms

Notwithstanding a plethora of Victorian (and subsequent) illustrations depicting the East India Company's European soldiers being dressed exactly as their counterparts in Europe, with heavy coats, tight gaiters and so on, their clothing was in fact much more practical. Soldiers serving in Madras in the 1740s were ordered to be 'new cloathed once in two years with English cloth out of the Company's warehouses'. That English cloth was probably only used for the soldiers' red coats. In June 1748 Stringer Lawrence's orders laid down that whilst each captain was to be responsible for clothing his company, 'for regularity the Major or Officer commanding the Companys shall appoint a pattern coat and hat or cap suitable to the climate to be approved of by the Governor, and to which every Captain will conform at the first making of the new cloathes'. As the red woollen coat was to be 'suitable to the climate' it was presumably lined with cotton gingham, rather than wool as at home, and probably cropped short as well.

The troops sent from Madras will have been distinguished by the buff-coloured facings of Stringer Lawrence's old regiment, HM 14th Foot, which he had introduced in 1748 and displayed on the turned-back cuffs and probably on turned-back lapels as well. Whether the military companies of the other presidencies had the same is at best questionable as they each had their own distinctive facing colours later on in the century.

The hat appears from a slightly later illustration of a Madras artilleryman to have been a conical affair made of white cotton or linen stretched over a rattan framework, with a narrow brim. The cap was no doubt worn by the grenadier company and will have followed the traditional 'mitre' style; red at the rear with a buff-coloured front. A near contemporary caricature of a Company grenadier depicts a teapot on the front but real ones presumably bore the arms of the East India Company: a red cross on a white shield, and for a crest a gold lion rampant carrying a crown, and gold lions for supporters, each carrying a flag of St. George. Underneath was a scroll with the motto AUSPICIO REGIS:ET:SENATUS ANGLIAE. On the cap this motto may have appeared on the little flap or brim, but it is worth noting that in the caricature this simply bore the initials E.I.C. As to other clothing, a list of 'necessaries' issued to troops in Trichinopoly in 1755 included Pariar (or native) shoes, gingham breeches and waistcoats, with coarse shirts and stockings, but never a mention of gaiters.

The caveat needs to be added at this point that whilst the Madras and Bombay military were certainly properly uniformed during the 1757 campaigns, the same may not have been true of the Bengal Europeans. The survivors of the original garrisons. those rank and file who had escaped from Dacca, Jagdea and Balasore, would still have had their red coats and so too would Fraser's Company which came from Madras. Otherwise, apart from that single clue offered by Clive's reference to the Company's broadcloth, there is no evidence of new clothing being made up and some of the 'Bengal Vol.unteers' who filled up the thinned ranks may not have had uniforms at all. Accoutrements at this time appear to have been made of tanned leather (presumably blackened) rather than the buff leather used by regulars, and followed what was then a common style used by colonial troops comprising a narrow girdle or waist-belt supporting a six- or eight-round belly-box and a bayonet suspended vertically in a frog.

Officers wore scarlet frock coats (originally a brighter red than that worn by the rank and file, although no doubt much faded and stained by the time they reached Plassey) and to judge by a portrait and a surviving coat belonging to a Swiss officer in the Madras service named

Daniel Frischmann, were cut much more in a European style, with a large quantity of silver lace. However this was very much a formal uniform topped off by a silver-laced tricorne hat, and on active service much lighter and plainer coats were preferred and 'round' or wide-brimmed hats.

Artillery uniforms are unrecorded at this period but presumably followed the same style and were distinguished by the traditional gunners' colours of a blue coat with red facings, as was certainly the case later. Although the gunners on the Bengal establishment who helped defend Calcutta in 1756 will have been so dressed, it is possible that no uniforms were worn by the newly-raised Bengal Artillery which served in the 1757 campaigns.

Madras Sepoys were first persuaded to wear red coats in 1756, and those raised in Bengal the following year had them too, and so were known as the *Lal* (Red) *Pultan* as a result. The earliest known illustration of a Sepoy – from Bombay – in the early 1770s depicts a soldier wearing a very simple red jacket, but is otherwise entirely clothed in ordinary native dress. No facing colours are recorded prior to 1759, and they were very much subject to change thereafter.

As regulars, HM 39th Foot wore the ordinary British uniform of the day; a red coat, which in this case had green facings on the lapels and cuffs. Ordinarily these facings would also have been displayed on the turned-back linings to the skirts, but regiments serving in hot climates normally had their coats lined with brown linen. Similarly white linen waistcoats and breeches replaced the red woollen ones worn in Europe. There is no record as to whether gaiters were worn or discarded, but if they were worn they would probably have been of brown linen, rather than the white ones worn on parades. Headgear may have been the regulation black tricorne hat but on active service soldiers tended to slouch them and it would be very strange if they did not do so in India. Grenadiers were normally distinguished by mitre caps, which in the case of the 39th would have had a green front bearing the GR cypher in white, but Eyre Coote's grenadier company was an unofficial one and probably wore ordinary slouched hats. Once again, on active service King's officers will have worn lightweight red frock coats rather than their formal braided regimental ones. At this period it was common for officers to wear plain red frocks which did not display the facing colour.

Appendix 2

The Bengali Forces

It would probably be fair to say that the nature of the Indian armies which fought against the East India Company at this period has been misunderstood and their capabilities largely underestimated, but Robert Orme's contemporary account of Siraj-ud-Daula's army at Plassey bears repeating:

> The greatest part of the foot were armed with matchlocks, the rest with various arms, pikes, swords, arrows, rockets. The cavalry, both men and horses, drawn from the northern regions, were much stouter than any which serve in the armies of Coromandel. The cannon were mostly of the largest calibres, 24 and 32 pounders.[1]

Vivid as this picture is, it is also impressionistic and to a certain degree inaccurate, for together with other, similar descriptions by Europeans it creates a false impression of a colourful but tumultuous and undisciplined mob. Indeed, quite contrarily, Orme then goes on to admit how 'The infantry and cavalry marched in many separate and compact bodies',[2] which very clearly demonstrates their being formed up in reasonably well-disciplined military units.

Indeed it is important to emphasise that the military hierarchy of *subedars, jemadars, havildars* and *naiques* or *naiks*, adopted by the East India Company's sepoy units was not a local adaptation of European structures but represented a continuation of existing Moghul ones. The overwhelming majority of the Nawab's men at Plassey were not poorly-equipped peasant levies but proper soldiers raised by noblemen and other leaders, under the old Moghul *mansab* or contract system. The *mansabdars* were ranked according to the number of men that they had raised and in European terms it was very much analogous to the armies of the Thirty Years' War in that the Nawab's generals contracted with him to raise a certain number of men, either for hard cash or more commonly *jagdirs* or land grants, and they in turn farmed the recruitment out to lesser contractors who would engage to raise regiments and companies. Once accepted by the Nawab, he in turn undertook to pay them and on at least a couple of occasions had to do so liberally in order to rally them. In effect it was an army of mercenaries.

Just as in Europe a century earlier, there were also of course companies of freebooters outside of this system entirely, who attached themselves to the army for loot rather than pay and were armed in a manner that might charitably be described as various, including bows and pikes. Indeed, when the Nawab's army moved on Calcutta in 1756, it was said to include a corps of professional plunderers, armed with no more than clubs – presumably the long *lathis* or staves traditionally wielded with some enthusiasm by Indian policemen. It must be emphasised, however, that these men were in a minority, hung around on the fringes and were never expected to stand in the battle-line.

Cavalry

As in most armies, the cavalry enjoyed the highest status; after all they rode on horseback rather than trudged into battle, and being mounted enjoyed far greater opportunities to range wide in search of plunder. Some, known as *bargis*, were light and rather irregular cavalry, but what were regarded as the best cavalry units (sometimes referred to as Moghul Horse) were recruited under the *silladar* system, which required individual *sowars* or troopers to provide their own horses, armour and weapons – swords, lances and sometimes firearms or bows. This encouraged a fair degree of uniformity in both as they would be expected to conform to a certain standard in order to gain acceptance into a unit. At the same time, this could also be a source of weakness as the potential loss of a cavalryman's greatest asset – his charger – quite naturally tended to have something of a dampening effect on what ought to have been their dash. This is unlikely to have been a significant factor in ordinary combat, especially if it were a matter of cavalry being pitted against other cavalry. Infantry and artillery were a different matter, especially when the guns were European ones with a higher rate of fire than Indian ones and the infantry were European or at least European-trained and equipped with firelock muskets and bayonets rather than matchlocks. Orme, once again, tells how at Plassey, 'the cavalry advanced several times threatening to charge sword in hand, but were always stopped and repulsed by the quick firing of the English field-pieces'.[3] Whilst he was describing the heavy fighting at the northern end of the battlefield, this understandable reluctance to attack artillery and formed infantry head on, rather than Mir Jafar's indecisiveness, may also in at least part account for the hesitancy displayed by the rest of the Bengali cavalry.

Infantry

Whilst the cavalry invariably made the greatest impression on observers, and undoubtedly regarded their role as lending a little tone to what would otherwise be a vulgar brawl, they were considerably outnumbered by the infantry. How far the old Moghul *mansab* system survived in its original form by 1756 is unclear, but if we require a good model for the battalions and companies of *berkanduz* or musketeers, led by *subedars* and *jemadars*, making up the greater part of the Bengali army we need look no further than the East India Company's sepoys. The absence of European officers in those early sepoy units strongly suggests that the vaunted adoption of European drill and discipline by the Company troops was in fact limited to the weapon-handling training needed for the latter's adoption of firelock muskets and bayonets in place of the traditional matchlocks and tulwars. Otherwise, in terms of organisation, officer structure and fighting qualities, *berkanduz* and sepoys were in reality one and the same.

Of itself, the simple fact that the Bengali *berkanduz* were overwhelmingly armed with matchlock muskets allows us to make certain assumptions about their fighting methods. In the first place, men primarily armed with muskets need to be capable of standing in a reasonably straight line in order to use them effectively. In practice they actually need to be standing in several ranks and employing some kind of system to ensure that all of the men have the opportunity to fire, whether that involves their firing by successive ranks while stationary, or one rank passing through another or any of the other techniques devised to balance the need to maintain a rapid rate of fire with the time needed to reload the musket after firing. In Europe, that saw the employment of formations six ranks deep, gradually reducing to five or even four ranks while soldiers still carried matchlock muskets. Given that these deep formations were imposed by their weapon technology there is no reason not to suppose that the Bengalis, using the same weapons, did the same.

Almost by any definition, therefore, these *berkanduz* and their officers were proper soldiers. That is not to say their standard of training was necessarily up to contemporary European standards and they might not, it is true, have been so capable of manoeuvring as their European counterparts, but there is no doubting their dogged courage during firefights. Plassey once again provides ample evidence of this, for Bahadur Ali Khan's *berkanduz* engaged there in a sustained firefight for upwards of two hours, and as Orme notes, 'matchlocks from the intrenchments, from ditches, hollows, and every hole or shelter, as also from the bushes on the hillock east of the redoubt, kept up a constant although irregular fire.'

The 'irregular fire' or *feu a billebaude* as the French called it should not deceive us, for after the initial volleys it was as inevitable in European firefights as in Indian ones no matter what Humphrey Bland might pretend, so no criticism may be made on that score. On the contrary, the very fact that the Bengalis were able to sustain the firefight for so long strongly argues that they were able to hold their ground and that as ammunition ran low they were able to carry out reliefs of units in the front line and resupply them.

The real weakness of the Bengali *berkanduz* was a simple technological one, in that European firelock muskets were a generation ahead and capable of being loaded and fired faster. European ammunition was also packaged as paper cartridges, easy to transport, distribute and use, while contemporary illustrations show that *berkanduz* still relied on loose powder carried in flasks. What was more, although all or most Bengali soldiers carried tulwars or curved swords as a secondary weapon, using them meant discarding their matchlocks. By contrast the opposing Company forces, both Europeans and sepoys, had bayonets fixed on the ends of their firelock muskets, which was a much more effective combination.

Artillery

It was a similar story with the Bengali artillery. Their guns were magnificent and a highly-visible symbol of the power of the state, but there were two significant flaws. The first was that the gunners, although unquestionably as brave as gunners traditionally are, may not have been as technically proficient as their European counterparts; hence Siraj-ud-Daula's request for the loan of a detachment of British ones in the brief period of supposed amity which preceded the Plassey campaign. In all likelihood this was probably a simple consequence of the artillery's other drawback; the excessive reliance on very heavy cannon; 24- and 32-pounders. At a very basic level, conducting intensive loading drills with a short 6-pounder is a good deal easier and more practical than with heavier pieces.

As a result, whilst the smashing effect of the Bengali heavy guns and the moral effect of actually firing them should not be underestimated,[4] their rate of fire was considerably lower than European ones. Moving the guns was also problematic, and not even the best European gunners attempted to do so with guns of that weight once they had been emplaced. Instead, they almost exclusively used them for siege work. The Bengalis were more ambitious and once again we may turn to the ubiquitous Orme:

> The cannon were mostly of the largest calibres, 24 and 32 pounders; and these were mounted on the middle of a large stage, raised six feet from the ground, carrying besides the cannon, all the ammunition belonging to it, and the gunners themselves who managed the cannon, on the stage itself. These machines were drawn by 40 or 50 yoke of white oxen, of the largest size, bred in the country of Purnea; and behind each cannon walked an elephant, trained to assist at difficult tugs, by shoving with his forehead against the hinder part of the carriage.[5]

The famous platforms seem to have been an ill-fated attempt to achieve a degree of tactical mobility and to a degree the experiment can actually be said to have been successful in itself. The guns could indeed be moved on the battlefield. The fatal flaw was not the concept or its execution but rather the vulnerability of the famous white oxen, which were quickly shot down by Clive's gunners as the Bengalis tried to pass them through a single opening in their entrenchments.

Conversely, some use was made of lighter, more mobile guns, or rather would have been made had Mir Jafar not been so reluctant to fight. Also interlaced with the infantry (and indeed spoken of as part of the infantry by Orme) were detachments of rocket men, providing close fire support. Their range does not appear to have been great, their accuracy erratic and their effectiveness uncertain, but they did score at least one dramatic success in the night action outside Calcutta when a rocket strike scored a direct hit on the Madras Grenadiers and inflicted significant casualties.

***

In overall terms it remains difficult to form an accurately informed judgement as to the relative capabilities of European and Bengali troops and the degree to which the latter may have been underestimated by historians. It is striking, however, that they were capable of rapid marches wholly at odds with popular perceptions of Asiatic inefficiency, most notably in Siraj-ud-Daula's marches on Calcutta and his rapid advance from Murshidabad to Plassey which caught Clive off-balance. The infantry at least were capable of fighting doggedly, especially when well-led by men such as Bahadur Ali Khan and all in all it can be asserted that the Battle of Plassey would have had a very different outcome had some of the other Bengali leaders fought with equal determination.

Appendix 3

Captain Alexander Grant's Accounts of the Fall of Calcutta

Alexander Grant (1725–68) was a younger son of James Grant of Sheuglie, Inverness-shire, and commanded the Glen Urquhart men in McDonnell of Glengarry's Regiment during the last Jacobite rising. The circumstances of his pardon are unknown but he was probably the same Alexander Grant who was brought to trial in London on 16 December 1746. The Attorney-General helpfully pointed out that he had surrendered under the Duke's proclamation, and he was accordingly acquitted. This would be consistent with his shortly afterwards obtaining a commission in Captain Jonathan Forbes' Independent Company, raised in 1747 for Boscawen's secret expedition against Pondicherry.[1] From there he entered the Company's service and was serving as a captain at Calcutta in 1756 when he was appointed Adjutant General. Two of his surviving narratives as printed below, not only succeeded in vindicating him but probably supply the clearest and most detailed account of the defence of Calcutta.

An Account of the capture of Calcutta by Captain Grant[2]
The following passage appears to be the first draft of the letter, somewhat longer and varying in some minor particulars from the final version dated 'Fulta on board the *Success* Galley 13 July, 1756'.[3] An abridged version of the latter 'made for John Debonnaire 22 February 1774' appeared in the *Indian Antiquary* for November 1899 and is included in Hill, Vol. 3.

> As the siege of Calcutta and Fort William and the causes of the loss of them, will undoubtedly be represented in various ways; I think my duty, as well as my having had once the honor of your acquaintance and countenance, require that I give you, at least, the

135

particulars of the military transactions; which, my having been appointed to act as Adjutant General during the troubles, enables me to do with more certainty than I could, had I been stationed at any particular post, as I issued out all orders from the Governor, and saw most of them put in execution.

I must refer you to a narrative of Mr. Drake's for what relates to the negotiations and correspondence with the Government preceeding the surrender of Cossimbuzar on the 4th June, by the Chief's being decoyed under many specious pretences to visit the Nabob in his camp before that place, and, on his being made prisoner, induced to deliver it up, you must be informed of ere now, we having dispatched pattamars as soon as we received the news on the 7th.

We may justly impute all our misfortunes to the loss of that place, as it not only supplied our enemys with artillery and ammunition of all kinds, but flushed them with hopes of making as easy a conquest of our chief Settlement not near so defensible in its then circumstances. Cossimbuzar is an irregular square with solid bastions, each mounting 10 guns mostly 9 and 6 pounders with a saluting battery on the curtain to the river side of 24 guns from 2 to 4 pounders, and their carriages, when I left the place in October last, in pretty good order, besides 8 cohorn mortars of 4 and 5 inches, with a store of shells and grenades. Their garrison consisted of 50 military under the command of Lieutenant Ellet, a Serjeant, corporal and 3 matrosses of the artillery and 20 good lascars. The ramparts are overseen by two houses which lay within 20 yards of the walls, but as each is commanded by 5 guns from the bastions, the enemy could hardly keep possession of them. When we received the news of Cossimbuzar's being in the Nabob's possession, and of his intentions to march towards us with the artillery and ammunition of that place and with an army of 20,000 horse and 30,000 gunmen, who had been encouraged with the promise of the immense plunder expected in Calcutta, it was full time to enquire into the state of defence of a garrison, which had been neglected for so many years, and the managers of it lulled in so infatuate a security, that every rupee expended on military services was esteemed so much lost to the Company.

By last year's shipping there was positive orders from the Company to execute a plan sent home by Colonel Scot for their approbation, but his death was thought too sufficient an excuse to postpone what they had so little inclination to have executed. By a later ship we were still further pressed by the Company to put our

Settlement in the best state of defence possible, as there was great appearance of a French war. Captain Jones of the artillery, in September last, thinking it more particularly his duty to represent the defenceless state the garrison was in, and the situation of the cannon and ammunition, gave in a representation to the Governor and Council of what was immediately necessary for the defence of the place in case of a French war; such as making outworks, mounting the cannon which lay then useless for want of carriages, and putting their stores and ammunition in the best condition possible. The stile and form of this paper, and the manner of delivering it in, it seems gave offence, and Captain Jones was reprimanded for his irregularity in not delivering such representations first to the Commanding Officer of the troops.

However, though it contained many truths proper to be considered, there was no further notice taken of its contents, nor no orders given for any military preparations; trusting in the same kind fortune that had for so many years defended them in peace and security, though even at this time, we were dayly insulted by constant encroachments and impositions by the Country Government, and though it had been strongly recommended by the Directors, to keep our garrison at Cossimbuzar in a proper state of defence as troubles were likely to ensue on the death of the Nabob who was then very old and could not live long, so negligent were we as to disregard the precaution, and even after his death, when competitors were contending for the Government, we thought ourselves so little concerned in the consequences, that no addition of officers, men nor ammunition was made to the usual garrison of Cossimbuzar nor any demand from thence for it.

I will now proceed to inform you as well as possible what our situation was to stand a seige. The plan of Fort William and a part of Calcutta, which I here inclose you, and which since my comming on board I have sketched out from memory to give a clear idea of the manner we were attacked, will represent to you the situation of our small Fort in respect to the houses that surrounded it and the number of guns mounted upon it. Our military to defend it, exclusive of those at the subordinate Factory, amounted only to 180 infantry, of which number there were not 40 Europeans, and 36 men of the Artillery Company, sergeants and corporals included; hardly a gun on the ramports with a carriage fit for service. We had about three years ago 50 pieces of cannon, 18 and 24 pounders, with two mortars, 10 and 13 inches, with a good quantity of shells and balls for each; but they [had] been allowed to lay on the grass, where they were first landed ever since, with out carriages or beds. Only the 10 inche mortars we made shift to get ready by the time we were attacked, but neither shells filled nor fusees prepared for mortars or cohorns, made as well as the rest of little use. Our grape were eat up by the worms, and in short all our amunition of all sorts, such as we had, in the worst order; not a gun with a carriage fit be carried out of the Fort for any use, except the two feild pieces, which was sent us from your Settlement. What powder we had ready, for want of care the greatest part was damp and the season of the year improper to dry it.

It is true on the receipt of the letters by the Delawar a few weeks preceding our troubles, there was orders given to repair the old Line before the fort to the river side, and prepare carriages for 50 pieces of cannon 24 and 18 pounders (which had lyen unregarded at the wharff for three years past) in order to have them mounted on this Line, against an attack by water. The carriages on the bastions were at the same time ordered to be repaired, but so dilatory was the execution of these orders and so little was it thought necessary to have them forwarded with any expedition, that when we received the news of the loss of Cossimbuzar the 7th instant that it could be only said they were begun, and but very few of the carriages patched for the guns on the ramparts; and besides the two field pieces we had from Madarass, not another piece of ordinance, fit to be drawn out of the fort.

On receiving the unexpected news of the loss of a place, we thought capable to stand out against any numbers of a country enemy while they had provisions, and with such artillery and stores as they generally use. It was thought proper to join the military captains and Engineer to the Council in order to form a Council of war; they were afterwards desired to retire to consider of the properest methods for the defence of the inhabitants and Town of Calcutta in case of an irruption of the Moors. Accordingly we gave it as our oppinions, that batterys should be erected in all the roads leading to the fort at such distances as could be anywise defensible with the small number of troops we had; that the inhabitants should be immediately formed into a body of militia; all the carpenters and smiths in the place taken into the Fort to prepare carriages; the ammunition and stores put in the best order, and lascars and cooleys taken into pay for the use of the cannon and other works to be done, and likewise what sepoys and peons could be got to be formed into a body under the command of some European. It may be justly asked why we did not propose, the only method that as I thought then, and now do, could give us the least chance of defending the place, in case of a vigorous attack, the demolition of all the houses adjacent to the fort and surrounding it with a ditch and glacee; but so little credit was then given, and even to the very last day, that the Nabob would venture to attack us, or offer to force our lines, that it occasioned a generall grumbling and discontent to leave any of the European houses without them. Nay, the generallity wanted even to include every brick house in the place, Portuguese and Armenian, and thought it hard that any inhabitant should be deprived of protection against such an enemy. And should it be proposed by any person to demolish so many houses as would be necessary to make the fort defensible, his opinion would have been thought pusilanimous and ridiculous, had there been sufficient time to execute such a work as there was not, nor would it be possible to destroy half the number in triple the time, especially as we had not powder sufficient to blow them up.

From the 7th to the 16th (when the Nabob's advanced guard attacked our redoubt at Perrin's Gardens) all precautions were taken to forward every work that was thought necessary to be done. The militia was formed without loss of time, Mr. Manningham appointed Collonel, Frankland, Lieutenant-Collonel, and Messrs. Holwell, Macket and Mapletoft captains; and subalterns for 3 companys. Our batterys were finished and our troops disposed of as you see them in the plan which since my coming on board I have endeavoured to sketch out from memory, to give you a better idea of our situation. The Militia were constantly disciplined morning and evening and the utmost spirit and resolution shewn by every person concerned to prepare everything for the reception of an enemy from whom they expected no quarter. Our stores and ammunition were in the utmost bad order when we begun our preparations, no cartridges of any kind ready: the small quantity of grape in store had lyen by so long, that it was destroyed by the worms; no shells filled nor fuses prepared for small or great. The few that were thrown at the siege burst half way. There was 2 iron mortars, one of 13, and the (other) of 10 inches sent out about 3 years ago. The 10 inch mortar, we had just finished the bed for it, but the 13 inch one lay by useless for want of one; though there was upwards of 300 shells sent out for both, all that could be prepared was not above 20 and such as was thrown of them burst, some after quitting the mortar and others half way. We had but a small quantity of powder, and the greatest part of that damp. But you will be surprised to hear, that there was nothing known of this bad state of our stores and ammunition till the night before the Governor's retreat. There happened unfortunately, a misunderstanding to subsist between the Commandant and Captain Witherington who commanded the Train, which prevented Captain Minchin's having the Returns he ought of the stores and ammunition; at least the latter did not exert himself properly in his command, which I imagine was owing to the Governor's giving too ready an ear to Witherington's complaints of Minchin, he happening at the same time to be but upon indifferent terms with the Governor. These animositys amongst the persons who had the whole command and charge of the garrison in their hands did not contribute a little to our misfortunes.

Upon my being appointed Adjutant General I wrote down dayly what orders I thought might be necessary, and shewed them to the Governor for his approbation; They were afterwards issued out to the Adjutants of the military and militia, and by them carried to the commanding officer of each corps. Colonel Manningham, Lieutenant Colonel Frankland and Commandant Minchin for the more regular detail of duty were appointed Field Officers, to mount at the outworks dayly by rotation. I think amongst the first orders given on the news of the Nabob's approach. Captain Witherington was ordered to give in immediately a particular Return of the guns, ammunition and stores fit for service, as likewise of his company, volunteers entered, such as sea captains and Portuguese helmsmen and lascars, and everything else relating to the artillery. But the whole was never complyed with and only a return of the guns and ammunition given the night before the Governor retreated, being the 18th. I pressed dayly to the Governor the necessity there was of having his orders obeyed, and was sorry to receive no other answer, than that Witherington was a strange unaccountable man, and that he did not know what to do with him. Captain Minchin pressed likewise to have his orders complyed with in this respect, but in vain. From what motive or partiality to the man I cannot guess, without that his making a bustle and constant noise, recommended him as a very active man, who could not be supplyed was he suspended. I often repeated to the Governor the bad consequence that would ensue from trusting the safety of the garrison (as it chiefly depended on the state of our ammunition and stores) to the will and management of such a man, without giving any account or Return of his proceedings.

Our intelligence of the Nabob's motions, and numbers was always very uncertain, and we could never be thorowly perswaded that he would advance against our batterys. The most we imagined was that he would form a blockade and cut off our provision untill we came to an accommodation and comply with his requests; though I believe those demands were only pretences, and the generall oppinion that prevails is, that he was resolved for some time past to rout the English out of the country, having on some account been irreconcilably irritated with us. What greatly contributed to harrass us was our lascars and cooleys deserting us on the Nabob's approach, till at last we had not a cooley to cary a bale or sandbag on the ramparts, nor a lascar to draw or work a gun, but totally reduced for the working of our cannon to about 36 men of the artillery for the bastions, out batterys and Labratory, and those very badly disciplined. The volunteers were chiefly employed about the stores and some of them on the bastions.

In this situation we received advice from Ensign Paccard the 16th in the afternoon, that the enemy were then bringing up heavy cannon to play upon the redoubt and sloop that lay before it for the defence of the ditch. He was immediately reinforced with an 18 pounder the 2 brass fieldpieces and 40 men under the command of Lieutenant Blagg, being resolved to give them a warm reception on their approach. They had got six pieces of cannon playing on the redoubt and sloop when the reinforcement arrived, but on our fieldpieces beginning to play they withdrew their cannon, and abandoned that post, inclining to the southward, where they had on the opposite side of the ditch got possession of a tope of wood from whence they killed one of our gentlemen volunteers and 4 of the military. They killed 4 Europeans on board the sloop.

Before dark the whole body inclined to the southward, and crossed the ditch that surrounds the Black Town, the extent of it being so great, and passable in all parts, that it was impossible to do anything to interrupt them. Lieutenant Blagg about 8 at night demanded a further reinforcement to cover his retreat, as he was apprehensive of the enemys advancing through some of the lanes to cut off his communication. Captain Clayton was ordered with a party to that purpose, who returned safe with Lieutenant Blagg about 10 at night, and left Ensign Paccard in possession of the redoubt with his former detachment.

Next morning being the 17th, Monsieur le Beaume (who was a French officer, and left Chandnagor on a point of honor) desired to be permitted to take possession of the Gaol about 200 yards advanced before the battery, and where three roads terminates into the place. He was accordingly ordered with 2 small cannon, 12 military and militia, and 40 buxeries or gunners; he broke embrasures through the Gaol House for the cannon, and made loopholes all round for the musquetry. All this day the enemy did not advance in sight of any of our batterys, but the plunderers annoyed the black inhabitants greatly which we could not possibly help without risquing our men to be shot at from behind houses and walls. Our peons brought in severall of their people, but their reports were so different that we could not depend on it.

They informed us that they had all the Cossimbuzar cannon with some brought from Muxadavat of heavier mettall, about 25 Europeans and 80 Chittygong fringys under the command of one who stiled himself Le Marquis de St. Jacque, a French renegaid, for the management of their artillery, about 15,000 horse and 10,000 foot, but we found afterwards this to be short of their numbers. From the three grand batterys as many men as could be spared were detached to the breastworks thrown up in the small lanes, and such houses as most commanded our batterys taken possession with Serjeants and corporals' guards. This night all our peons deserted us, and in short every black fellow, who could make his escape, abandoned us. Upwards of 1,000 bearers left us in one night, on being ordered to carry the powder from the Magazeen into the Fort. And on the plunderers advancing into the town, all the Portuguese familys crowded within our lines for protection to the number of some thousands.

The 18th in the morning the enemy began to make their appearance in all quarters of the town, but did not seem as if they would advance openly against our batterys. And by their method of advance we could foresee that they intended to force their way within our lines by taking possession of the different houses one after another. This caused us to reinforce such houses as we could most annoy them from as much as possible. About II o'clock they brought up two pieces of cannon against the Gaol, one of them an 18 pounder by the size of the ball. We advanced an officer with 20 men and 2 field pieces to reinforce Monsieur le Beaume, but the walls of the Gaolhouse were so weak that they were hardly any defence against their cannon. However they kept possession of it till about 2 when Le Beaume and Ensign Carstairs (who commanded the party) being both wounded, and numbers of their men killed, had liberty to retire within Captain Clayton's battery. The enemy instantly took possession of that post, and all the adjacent houses, losing no opportunity to take advantage of our retreat. They did not long keep possession of the houses on which our cannon from the batterys could bear, though our metal was not sufficiently heavy to demolish strong pucka houses, as we afterwards found. They poured in numbers into the Gaol, Allsop's, Dumbleton's, and the houses behind that and Lady Russell's; and though our men from the tops and windows of the houses kept a constant fire on them as they advanced and our cannon from the fort and our batterys played, on every house they could see them in possession of, and endeavoured, though with little success, to fling shells amongst them (which had they been properly fitted for service would have been of much more use than our cannon) yet the superiority of their numbers under cover of the houses (which method and bush-fighting, these fellows are too near on a par with Europeans) soon enabled them to force one house after another, and oblige our people to abandon the houses they were in possession of. The first place where they broke in upon our line was at Mr. Nixon's, by breaking down the walls of the Compound behind, exposed to the fire of a sergeant's guard that had possession of that house and the adjacent breastwork, and pouring in through that into the Square at the corner of the Tank, the sergeant seeing them advance in such numbers made the best of his way to Captain Buchanan's battery where he was detached from, and left 8 or 10 of our gentlemen volunteers who had possession of Captain Minchin's house to force their way through the enemy where two of them were left behind and destroyed. [redacted in original] at all quarters made it impossible for our people to withstand such showers of small shott, as they fired into the houses we had possession of. They first broke into our lines through Mr. Nixon's house and fixed their collours (as is their custom every inch of ground they gain) at the corner of the Tank. We were now obliged to abandon the breastwork close to Mr. Putham's and all the houses of that Square, the enemy in multitudes taking possession of each of them. They brought some heavy pieces of cannon through the lane twixt Minchin's and Putham's houses and planted them at the corner of the Tank and door of Mr. Nixon's to play upon us as we passed and repassed to and from the batterys. Having thus lodged themselves in all the houses of the Square on which only two guns from the flank of the north-east bastion could bear, and that at too great a distance to annoy them much, they had a secure footing within our lines; and those houses (being most of them pucka) with the multitudes that occupied them were too strong lodgements for us to pretend to dispossess them of; being at the same time attacked in some manner at each of the other posts.

This situation of the enemy exposed the battery to have its communication cut off from the fort, as the enemy might surround them in the rear by advancing through the lane that passes by Captain Grant's and between Captains Buchanan's and Witherington's house; it was therefore thought necessary to order Captain Buchanan to retire with his cannon to the battery where 2 embrasures had been opened in expectation of such a retreat. I think it was about 4 afternoon when I delivered this order and I then proceeded to Captain Clayton's battery at where they had the warmest part of the attack since our retreat from the Gaol at 2, by the enemy's keeping possession of all the houses round it, and though we sent an 18 pounder (which by that time we had got mounted on a truck carriage, and were obliged to have drawen to the battery by the militia in the fort, all our lascars and cooleys having abandoned us) in order to play upon the houses which the enemy possessed, they still not only maintained their ground but advanced apace through one house to another; this occasioned Captain Holwell to go in person to the Governor. Whether by a representation of the state they were in or at his own request he obtained an order to abandon that battery; which having been of the utmost consequence, ought not to have been done but by a determination of a council of war: especially as there was not such numbers killed, but it might have been easily maintained, at least till dark. On my arrivall at the battery I found all the guns spiked, except the two field pieces, with which they were then ready to retreat. I was not a little surprised to find things in this situation, and by the Governor's orders, as they informed me. I therefore requested their stay for a few minutes till I galloped to the fort for further orders. The Governor made me answer that the post was represented to him as no longer tenible, and had accordingly ordered its being withdrawen. Now the guns were spiked, there was nothing further to be done than to get them likewise withdrawen, as leaving them behind must have greatly encouraged the enemy, and convinced them of the pannick that seized us, which only could occasion such a precipitate retreat. As I was going back to the battery I found Captain Clayton and his command with the 2 fieldpieces half way towards the fort. I prevailed upon him to return with me, that, if possible we might not undergo the ignominy of leaving our guns behind us in such a precipitate manner. But when I ordered half the men to lay down their arms in order to draw first the 18 pounder while the other half stood with their arms for defence of the battery, not a man would stir or pull a rope. As nothing could be done I left Captain Clayton to make his retreat as regular as he could. I found by this time Captain Buchanan had likewise received orders to retire from the battery, upon what account I know not. Captain Smith's battery was also ordered to be abandoned as maintaining that alone could answer no end, which was very regular done, and their guns brought to the fort gate. The next thing considered of, was a disposition for the defence of the fort, which was all that was left us now to maintain: for few expected that the batterys would have been so suddenly quitted, and most people foresaw that the fall of them would be attended with fatall consequences, as the enemy's getting possession of the houses contiguous to the fort, such as Cruttenden's, Eyre's, the Church and the Company's, all of them the strongest pucka, would in such a manner command the bastions and ramparts that it would be impossible to stand at the guns, exposed to the small arms of such a multitude as would occupy those and other houses, especially as the parapets of the bastions were very low, and the embrasures so wide that they hardly afforded any shelter. We had cotton bales and sandbaggs, which might in some measure supply this defect, but were so abandoned by all sorts of labourers that we could not get them carried upon the ramparts, and our military and militia so harrassed for want of rest and refreshments, that it was impossible to get them to do anything. This consideration determined us to take possession of the above houses and Church with the troops retired from the out batterys. We had laid in sufficient stores of provisions, but the irregularity in not appointing proper persons for this, as well as other particular duties (a fatall neglect to us from the beginning) and the generall desertion of the black fellows amongst whom were the cooks, left us to starve in the midst of plenty. All the men at the outposts had no refreshment for 24 hours, which occasioned constant complaints and murmurings all this night as well from them as those in the fort. Such was the irregularity and distress amongst them, that some had broke open godowns where liquors stood and where numbers made so free with it, that they were rendered incapable of any duty. The detachment in the Company's House finding the enemy had got possession of Captain Ranney's, thought that their post on the approach of day would not be tenible, and that their communication might be cut off by their being surrounded in the lane that leads to the waterside along the new godowns, where there was no guns to flank, so applied to the Governor and obtained leave to abandon it, in which situation it was left all night. This and our situation in generall left us but a bad prospect for next morning. Half of our men in liquor in the fort, no supply of provisions or water sent to those in the houses without, the drum beat to arms three different times on allarm of the enemy's being under the walls, but hardly a man could be got on the ramparts: the enemy's taking possession of the Company's House, as was expected, would have made it impossible to stand [on] the southerly bastions and new godowns nor any boats to stay at the gaut. At a council of war held at 8 at night, Collonels Manningham and Frankland were permitted to see the European ladies on board the ships, then before the fort, and afterwards to return, but such crowds of Portugees women and children filled all parts of the fort as occasioned the greatest noise and confusion. It was thought hard to refuse them protection, as their husbands carryed arms for the defence of the place, but undoubtedly it was wrong to risque the safety of the whole on such a consideration.

About one in the morning a second council of war was called, to consider of our then situation, and what in all probability we might expect it to be on the approach of day; as likewise, from every circumstance considered, for what time we might reasonably expect to maintain the fort. The Captain of the Artillery was first asked what quantity of amunition we had then in store (you must observe the Governor never procured a return of it) and for what time he thought it would last according to the expences of the day past. His answer was, that at the same rate, it would not be sufficient for above three days, and even a part of that, he was affraid was damp. This of itself, but added to the other circumstances still more, made it the unanimous oppinion that a retreat on board the ships must be determined on in that time, should no circumstances intervene to make it sooner necessary; as nothing but the utmost barbarity was expected from our enemy in case of surrender, as by fatall experience we have found to be the case, with such as fell into his hands. The majority were of opinion that as such a retreat was already fixed on, the delay of it even untill next morning could be attended with no sort of advantage, but might on the contrary produce such consequences as would either make it impracticable, or attended with the greatest risque and precipitation. For instance, did the enemy get possession of the houses we then occupied and the Company's, there was but little to prevent their forcing oppen the two barriers that lead to the fort from the Company's House and Cruttenden's; and from those two houses they might keep such a fire on the gaut and wharff, as would make it impossible for a boat to lye there; either of which would have effectually prevented our retreat.

By making our retreat that night, though late, having a sufficient number of boats then at the gaut, we might, at least, have carryed off all the Company's treasure, and secured every European safe on board before daylight. This opinion Mr. Holwell in particular maintained very strenuously, and several other gentlemen. It was proposed by others to send Omychaund to treat with the Nabob, but he absolutely refused to go, and it was then proposed to write to him, but our Persian writer with every black fellow deserting us made that impossible. In this state of irresolution attended with great confusion did we remain, without fixing on any settled scheme, till near daylight, then adjourning to wait what the morning might produce, in hopes of making our retreat the next night. For no person after the report of our ammunition and hearing the situation we were in stated, had any further thoughts of defending the place, longer than untill with any regularity and safety we could accomplish our retreat on board the ships. By break of day, finding the enemy had neglected in the night to take possession of the Company's House and Ensign Paccard (who had been ordered from Perrin's) having offered to maintain it with 20 military, his proposall was readily agreed to. The other out- post had been but little disturbed in the night, the enemy having satisfied themselves with setting some houses on fire, and taking possession of those from which they thought they could annoy us in the day, such as Captain Rannie's, Messrs. Watts's, Tooks's and Omichaund's to the east of Eyres's and all the houses from Mr. Eyres's to Mr. Griffith's, likewise the hospitall, Captain Clayton's and Captain Wedderburn's to the southward, and had brought some cannon to the gate of Mr. Bellamy's Compound, as well as behind the battery which we abandoned, and in the Compound of the Playhouse. From all these different places they kept a constant fire on the houses we occupied, as well as upon the ramparts. About 8 o'clock, Lieutenant Bishop who commanded in Mr. Eyre's House desired leave to retire, being no longer able to support himself against the fire of some thousands from the houses to the eastward and northward of him. He was ordered if possible to maintain his post till evening, but the fire thickening, and numbers of his men killed and wounded he was permitted to make his retreat. About the same time Ensign Paccard was brought in wounded, and the enemy had filled the Compound of the Company's House. Captain Clayton found himself very warmly attacked in the Church from the cannon planted behind our battery and in the Playhouse Compound, and the small arms from the houses. He had severall of his men killed with the cannon shott

147

which came through the Church. The outposts were then all ordered to be withdrawen. Messrs. Manningham and Frankland were not returned from on board the ships though the Governor alledges that he sent for them. The ship Dodly where they were on board dropt down below the fort, which the other ships and sloops seeing, they followed. This with the confusion in the fort occasioned numbers of the gentlemen to seize on such boats as they could get hold of, to provide for their own safety, and by this time more than half of the officers of the militia were on board the ships.

We fired on the enemy wherever they appeared from all the guns on the fort, and must have done terrible execution amongst them, but did not much contribute to slacken their fire. Betwixt 10 and 11 we were allarmed on the ramparts by a report that the enemy were forcing their way at the barrier that leads from the Company's House to the wharff. But when I came down I found it to be false, they were not then advanced so far. On my return to the back gate, I observed the Governor standing on the stairhead of the gaut. I came up to him to know if he had any commands, but found him only beckoning to his servant who stood in a ponsay a litle above the gaut. I saw numbers of boats setting off from different places with Europeans in them. The Governor just took time to mention the bad consequences of the ships droping down, that it discouraged everybody, and seeing the boats sett off, and not another then at the gaut except a budgerow where Mr. Macket and Captain Minchin were going aboard of, called to me, that he found every one were providing for their own security; and without giving me time to make answer run up along shore to the ponsay where his servant was aboard. I first thought he only wanted to speak to him to secure the boat, but seeing him step in in somewhat of a hurry, I followed, and before I came into the boat desired to know what he was about. On his making answer that he was going aboard the ships, I earnestly entreated he would first acquaint the garison of his design. He represented the impossibility of making a regular retreat on many accounts. That and the ships dropping down discouraged everybody, all the boats being carried off, the enemy being in possession of the Company's and Mr. Cruttenden's houses which would prevent any's coming to the gaut and the crowds of Portugeese women that crowded at the gaut to force themselves into any boats they could lay hold of, and said, that he supposed when they saw him retreat such as could possibly find boats would follow. Looking behind, I perceived Mr. Macket and Captain Minchin setting off in their hudgerow, and the stairs full of Europeans pressing to do the same. I concluded the retreat to be generall, and that everyone who could lay hold of a conveyance would choose to escape falling into the hands of a merciless ennemy, and so with Mr. O'Hara thought it justifyable to follow the Governor in a state of such apparent confusion and disorder, though greatly grieved to see how many of my friends and country-men were likely to fall a sacrifice for want of boats, as I believe there was not annother left at the gaut when the Governor came away. We got on board the Dodly, where Messrs. Manningham and Frankland with most of the women were. I then represented to the Governor the cruelty of abandoning so many gentlemen to the mercy of such an enemy, and requested he would order the ships and sloops to move up before the fort, by which means we should be able to send the boats under their cover, to bring off our distressed friends; but the captain of the ship representing the danger it would be attended with, and the impossibility of getting the ships back, in case they went up again before the fort, the Governor thought proper not to insist upon it; and the ships belonging to private owners, I doubt whether such an order would be complyed with, as everybody then pursued his own safety independent of command. We are informed, that as soon as the Governor retreated those that found it impossible to follow, shutt the fort gates, chose Mr. Holwell as Governor and resolved to dye upon the ramparts, in case they could get no conveyance that night to make their escape, rather than surrender to the mercy of the enemy. They endeavoured in the evening to get boats for that purpose, but in vain. Except a few budgerows that were then with the ships, every other boat was carried away by the blackfellows.

The ships fell down just within sight of the town. We could hear all the afternoon a constant [firing] of cannon and small arms; and at night saw numbers of the houses in fire. The place was taken next day the 20th afternoon, about 30 hours after the Governor left it, during which time upwards of 50 Europeans were killed on the bastions by the enemy's small arms from Mr. Cruttenden's, Eyres's, the Church and the Company's House. The firing was so hot from the top of the Church that they at last were obliged to abandon the easterly curtain and bastions. About 3 [in the] afternoon they made a signal for a truce; on which our people desisted firing. But they treacherously made use of it to crowd in multitudes under the walls, and with some ladders and bamboos scaled the easterly curtain and bastions which was abandoned under cover of their fire from the Church and other houses. Numbers were cut to pieces on the walls; all who wore red coats, without mercy. And such as were so unhappy as to be taken prisoners were at night put into the Black Hole, a place about 16 foot square, to the number of near 200 Europeans, Portugeese and Armenians, of which many were wounded. They were so crowded one upon another in this narrow confinement that by the heat and suffocation not above ten of the number survived untill morning. Some of those who give us the account, say that they fired upon them all night with small arms through the doors and windows, but this is contradicted by others. Mr. Holwell is one of the number who survived, and is now prisoner with the Nabob. 30 Company's servants and 15 officers we know to be dead and the Cossimbuzar and Dacca factorys prisoners.

Captain Minchin, and myself are all the officers here. Lieutenant Cudmore is at [Dacca], Ensign Walcot prisoner with Mr. Holwell. These are all the officers alive, the rest were either killed on the ramparts or died in the Black Hole. Lieutenant Ellet who commanded at Cossimbuzar, shott himself after the place was delivered up. The Dutch and French have made up matters with the Nabob, the former for 4 and the latter for 5 lacks of rupees, and he is now returned victorious to his capital of Muxidabad. There is about 3 or 4,000 troops in Calcutta, they keep possession of the fort but have destroyed the Factory House.

An Account of the manner of my retreat from Calcutta when besieged by the Moors, and of the causes which induced me to accompany the Governor on board the ships, by Captain Grant.[4]

On receipt of the advices of the capture of Cossimbuzar, and the Nabob's intention to march against Calcutta, amongst other regulations for the defence of the place, I was appointed to act as Adjutant General of our troops; in which station I afterwards issued out the daily orders from the Governor, and made such dispositions as had at different times been agreed on in councils of war. How far I have done my duty in that capacity and exerted myself in every other respect for the defence of the Settlement, I will submit it to the Governor and Council's answer to my letter given in to the Board of the 20th August last,[5] or the surviving inhabitants of Calcutta who were eye witnesses of my conduct. But as my retreat from thence is, I presume, the chief cause of the censure I have undergone (for want of a proper opportunity of acquitting myself) since that time; I will proceed to that particular: only in order to give a clearer idea of it, must first beg leave to represent the situation the garrison was in, and the resolutions taken the night preceding, being that of the 18th June.

Having withdrawn the batteries which defended the three principal avenues leading to the fort, the evening of the above day; the Company's House, Messrs. Cruttenden's and Eyre's, and the Church (all close to our walls) were taken possession of by the troops who retired from those batteries; and only the militia with 30 of the military continued for the defence of the fort. Till about eight at night I was employed in settling those outposts; in which time several resolutions had been taken in a council of war, of which I remained for some time ignorant; such as permitting Messrs. Manningham and Frankland, our two Field Officers, to escort the ladies on board the ships &c. The guard settled in the Company's House was soon after, on application made by some of the young gentlemen to the Governor ordered to be with-drawn, and that advantageous post left to be taken possession of by the enemy; whereby they would not only have a total command of the two southerly bastions and curtain, but likewise of the wharf and gaut where all our boats lay, and consequently have it in their power to obstruct our communication with the river. Continual duty and want of refreshment so harrassed both military and militia that before 12 at night, not a man could be brought on the ramparts, till dragged from the different corners of the fort where they had retired to rest; and by the help of liquor, which several of them met with, numbers were rendered incapable of any duty. This with constant calls from the out-posts for provisions and water, and none ready dressed to supply them, occasioned a disorder and confusion in all quarters, not easy to be described. In this situation a council of war was called about one in the morning, to consider of the methods necessary to be pursued in such an exigency. We concluded that before daylight the enemy would take possession of all the houses which our men did not occupy and with the superiority of numbers keep such a fire with their musquetry on our outposts, as would oblige them e'er long to retire into the fort; and consequently by the enemy's getting possession of those houses also, which lay so close to our walls, we saw ourselves liable in such a case, to be commanded from all quarters. The Captain of the Artillery reported at the same time that, at the rate of the consumption of amunition the preceding day, there was not remaining sufficient for two more.

This latter circumstance occasioned a general consternation, as no one had suspected any want or scarcity of this kind. Why those, whose duty it was to know the state of the amunition, should be so ignorant in an affair of such consequence, they best can answer. I only know that from the first day I was appointed to act as Adjutant General, there were daily orders to have such returns given in, but were never obeyed, though I represented to the Governor in the most earnest terms the bad consequences of not having those, as well as all other orders which he issued out, most strictly complied with. But such was the levity of the times, that severe measures were not esteemed necessary. This unexpected report, added to the situation we otherwise were in, easily determined every member of the council of war to vote for a general retreat on board the ships before the expiration of the above time, as the only means of saving the Company's treasure and effects, and the lives and properties of the inhabitants. It was then proposed that, as a retreat was already unanimously determined upon, and no hopes left of maintaining the fort, or accommodating matters with the Nabob; the sooner it was set about it would be the better, as consequences might attend the delay of it, which afterwards might make it impracticable. In this opinion I was one who seconded Mr. Holwell, who strongly pressed immediately to begin a general retreat, and clear the factory of the crowds of Portugueze women, as they were likely to cause great confusion in what afterwards might be necessary to be done. Other members of the council of war (who I imagine must have had something more in view than the publick interest) strenuously opposed this proposal, and would have a retreat deferred in hopes of some favorable change either by treaty or otherwise. These disputes lasted till near day light, and then each person repaired to his particular post without determining anything certain of the time or manner of a retreat. The enemy having neglected to take possession of the Company's House in the night, an officer and 20 men were placed in it about this time.

Such was the situation of things the 18th in the morning, when the want of rest for two nights before, and constant fatigue obliged me to retire for a little sleep, in order to fit me for the duties of the day, this being the time when the enemy gave us the least disturbance. As soon as I awoke, I came upon the ramparts and found that the enemy kept a pretty smart fire upon us, though not so as to annoy us much, as we still kept possession of the houses close to the fort. About 8 o'clock the outposts were very warmly attacked. The officer who commanded in the Company's House was brought in wounded, and those in the Church and Mr. Eyre's House had sent to acquaint the Governor, that the enemy poured in such vollies of musquetry upon them from the adjacent houses, as would oblige them to abandon their posts, if not soon relieved.

Having thus represented in as few words as possibly I could, the state of things in the fort and outposts to the time of my leaving it, there only now remains to lay before you the manner of it, and the motives which induced me to do it.

About 10 o'clock I received an alarm, when on the south east bastion, that the enemy had got possession of the Compound of the Company's House, and were forcing their way through the barrier that leads from thence to the fort; but when I came there, I found the report to be false. On my return towards the back gate, I saw the Governor standing on the stair head of the gaut beckoning to his servant, who was in a boat about 50 yards above.

I came up expecting he might have some commands for me, for I had not seen him before, since we broke up the council of war. When I addressed him, he pointed to me where the Doddaley and other vessells had fallen down below the Town, and numbers of boats full of Europeans were then proceeding on their way on board of them; saying that Messrs Manningham and Frankland, though sent for in the night, had still remained on board the Doddaley with the ladies; by which means they had so discouraged numbers of the gentlemen, as to induce them to provide for their own safety, in the same manner, and by their example. He then (without giving me time to make any answer) went down the stairs, up the waterside under the Line, and into the boat where his servant stood. I was somewhat amazed at his sudden departure being entirely ignorant of his intentions, and only supposed he had gone to give some particular orders to his servant: but finding he did not return soon, I thought it my duty to follow him, as I still remained unacquainted with his designs. When I came to the boat, and desired to know what he intended, he replied that he was resolved to provide for his own safety, as he found others were doing. I entreated him that if that was his resolution, he would wait till it was first intimated to Mr. Holwell and the rest of the garrison, and make as good a retreat as the situation of things would bear. He said it would be impracticable to make a regular retreat in the confusion things were then in; especially for want of boats, most of them being carried off by those who went before. That he therefore thought it would be in vain to wait any longer; and supposed when the rest of the garrison saw him come off, such of them as could find conveyance would follow.

I had but little time for recollection in such a juncture, and was therefore the more readily determined by the circumstances which immediately ensued. Looking behind me at the stairs of the gaut I saw it crowded with people pressing to get away; and amongst the rest Commandant Minchin and Mr. Mackett going into a budjerow. This I concluded to be in consequence of their seeing the Governor first make his escape; and according to what he told me before had not then the least doubts remaining, but every other person who observed him and could find conveyance would think the example of their Governor and Commander- in-chief a sufficient sanction for them to abandon a place, already declared not tenible above two days, and then in the greatest confusion. I likewise foresaw that those who should be obliged to remain behind for want of boats, would be exposed to the mercy of a cruel enemy, unless relieved by having conveyances sent them from the ships. My station of Adjutant General had fixed me to no particular post in the fort, but more properly was to attend the Governor for his orders, and act in a manner as his aidecamp. In the situation things appeared to me in this critical moment, my return to the shore when I saw every body was pressing to leave it, (and amongst them my Commander-in-chief; and other commanding officers being either already gone or setting off) could be attended with no advantage. To embark the Company's treasure, and other effects, public and private, on board the ships, and make a safe and regular retreat with the troops and inhabitants, is all that any person can pretend to say, was aimed at, or ever thought of, since the last council of war. As all this was oversett by the Governor's departure, and the boats being carried off before and after him, there only remained, of what was possible to be done for the public welfare, either to bring up the ships before the fort, or send boats to bring off those who were necessitated to stay behind for want of them. My accompanying the Governor to the ships was undoubtedly more likely to contribute to either of those purposes, than returning to the fort, as I should be more in the way of receiving his orders, and giving my assistance, by returning with what conveyances or succours he might think proper to send. I could make no doubt, that as soon as he got on board, he would immediately think of sending such relief to those who were left behind, as their situation required; and to that purpose soon after our arrival I spoke to him in presence of Captain Young, the Commander, to move up with the Doddaley, and other ships as the only probable method that then remained, (all the boats, excepting one or two, having abandoned us, and crossed to the other side of the water). But most unfortunately Captain Young representing to him the danger such an attempt would be attended with, the

Governor declined giving any orders in regard to it. I proposed the same thing at different times that day, but with as little effect.

Thus I have related the manner and motives of my retreat from Calcutta as minutely as my memory enables me; and in justice to myself I would long e'er now have submitted it to a proper enquiry, had not the scarcity of officers, and my long indisposition deprived me of the opportunity, and which in my above mentioned letter to the Governor and Council I declared to be my intention as soon as the troops then expected from Madras would arrive.

I shall only further add that if the reasons I have given appear not sufficient to justify my conduct in accompanying the Governor at such a time and with the circumstances above related, I desire any person to point out to me, what other method I could possibly have taken, that would have been attended with greater advantages; or whether, in the station I acted in, it was not the most consistent with my duty to attend the Governor, in order to rectify by the only means I could think of the disorders which then prevailed; and to give my assistance in executing what directions he might give for that purpose.

Having successfully vindicated himself, Grant then resumed command as the senior surviving Bengal officer and took his men to Plassey, where he voted in favour of fighting. Subsequently, he took part in the pursuit of the French commander Jean Law, but resigned in 1758, seemingly in a dispute over seniority.[6] Returning home with an illegitimate Eurasian son, William, he came out to India again in 1765 and was engaged for a time in the business of contracting for supplies and transport bullocks for the army, but died in Calcutta in October 1768, supposedly when on the point of coming home for good.

Appendix 4

The Black Hole of Calcutta

The story of the Black Hole of Calcutta is still very much an imperial legend and a controversial one. Notwithstanding the doubts of revisionist historians, there is a wealth of evidence, not least in the accounts left by the survivors, attesting to the events of that terrible night. Yet unlike the aftermath of the massacre at Cawnpore a century later, both survivors and bystanders took a pragmatic view and refrained from engaging in indiscriminate retaliation. No matter how it was presented in later schoolbooks, contemporaries recognised that it was due to negligence rather than a deliberate war crime. Moreover, whilst the traditional story holds that 146 unfortunates went into the Black Hole and only twenty-three emerged alive next morning, there is in fact a great deal of uncertainty as to the actual numbers involved.

In the end, all that can be stated with any confidence is that fifty-eight named individuals can be identified as certainly or at least probably having died either in the Black Hole or within hours of being liberated from it and that a further twenty-two named individuals, including a woman named Mary Carey, came out alive and lived beyond the morning afterwards, all for a verifiable total of eighty prisoners.

Whether there were more than those eighty individuals crammed into the Black Hole is at this remove quite impossible to determine. Holwell stoutly asserted that in addition to those he had named, there were also a further 'sixty-nine, consisting of Dutch and English serjeants, corporals, soldiers, topazes, militia, Whites and Portugueze (whose names I am unacquainted with) who died that night'.[1] However, of those supposedly anonymous victims, ten are in fact included within the fifty-eight named below. As to the rest, while there were no doubt a number of unidentified victims, lacking any real corroboration as we do it might be unwise to assert that the true number of dead was double that which can be verified, especially as the balance corresponds to the number of those who deserted on the last night.

Name	Fate	Notes
Abraham, Bernard	Died in Black Hole	Sergeant major, militia
Aillery, Richard	Survived Black Hole	Not in Holwell's list, but named by Mills (Hill, Vol. 1, pp. 43–4)
Alsop	Died in Black Hole	Seafaring man Not listed by Holwell or Mills (Hill, Vol. 3, pp. 72, 105)
Angell, John	Survived Black Hole	Corporal Not in Holwell's list, but named by Mills (Hill, Vol. 1, p. 44)
Arndt, John	Survived Black Hole	Not in Holwell's list, but named by Mills Probably a Dutchman (Hill, Vol. 1, p. 44)
Atkinson	Died in Black Hole	Not otherwise identified. Soldier?
Baillie, William	Died in Black Hole	Aged 34 Council Member One of his sons, also named William Baillie was reported as having been shot in the head during the fighting: anonymous letter published in various newspapers (Hill, Vol. 3, p. 71)
Bellamy, Rev. Gervase	Died in Black Hole	Aged 65 Chaplain

Bellamy, John	Died in Black Hole	Son of Rev. Gervase Bellamy Lieutenant in militia
Ballard, George	Died in Black Hole	Aged 18 Assistant in the Treasury
Bendal, Joseph	Died in Black Hole	Sea officer
Bishop, Richard	'died of his wounds before the place was taken' (Hill, Vol. 3, p. 72)	Lieutenant, Bengal military
Blagg, Thomas	This officer's fate is doubtful. Holwell places him in the Black Hole but other accounts state he was 'cut to pieces' on a bastion when the fort was stormed (Hill, Vol. 3, p. 72)	Lieutenant, Bengal military
Bleau, Jacob	Died in Black Hole	Carpenter and sergeant in militia
Boirs, John	Survived Black Hole	Sergeant Not in Holwell's list, but named by Mills. Probably Dutch (Hill, Vol. 1, p. 44)
Buchannan, John	Died in Black Hole	Captain Bengal military Of Craigievern, Stirlingshire, originally regular officer serving in 1st (Royal) Regiment, but entered Company's service in 1752.
Burdett, John	Survived Black Hole	Aged 18 Assistant in the Accountant's Office

Burgaft, John	Survived Black Hole	Not in Holwell's list, but named by Mills. (Hill, Vol. 1, p. 44)
Burton	Died in Black Hole	Seafarer Not listed by Holwell or Mills (Hill, Vol. 3, pp. 72, 105)
Byng, Robert	Died in Black Hole	Aged 19
Carey, Mary	Survived Black Hole	Eurasian, aged 15 or 16. Only woman known to have been in the Black Hole. Holwell hints and Law states that she was afterwards taken off to the Nawab's harem (Hill, Vol. 3, p. 171)
Carey, Peter	Died in Black Hole	Usually referred to as a seaman but identified by Holwell and others as an officer. Law rather more specifically refers to him as one of the Ganges pilots. Husband of Mary Carey (Hill, Vol. 3, p. 171)
Carse, John	Holwell places him in the Black Hole but another account states he was 'cut to pieces, having rashly fired a pistol after the place was taken' (Hill, Vol. 3, p. 72)	Aged 24
Cartwright	Died in Black Hole	Seafarer Sergeant and Quartermaster in militia

Caulker, William	Died in Black Hole	
Clayton, David	Died in Black Hole	Captain, Bengal military
Clelling, Barnard	Survived Black Hole	Not in Holwell's list, but named by Mills (Hill, Vol. 1, p. 44)
Coker	Died in Black Hole	Seafaring man Not listed by Holwell or Mills; probably a mistake for Caulker (Hill, Vol. 3, pp. 72, 105)
Coles, Thomas	'Had a shot in the breast and died in the Black Hole' (Hill, Vol. 3, p. 71)	Ensign in militia
Cooke, John	Survived Black Hole	Aged 31 Secretary
Cosall, Philip	Survived Black Hole	Not in Holwell's list, but named by Mills (Hill, Vol. 1, p. 44)
Court, Richard	Survived Black Hole	Aged 33 Sub-Accountant
Dalrymple, Stair	Died in Black Hole	Aged 22 Assistant in the Secretary's Office
Dickson, Alexander	Survived Black Hole	Sea Captain
Dodd, John	Died in Black Hole	Aged 18 Assistant in the Export Warehouse
Drake, Nathan	Died in Black Hole	Aged 23 Sub Export Warehouse Keeper

Stringer Lawrence (1797-1775) was effectively the founder of the East India Company's armies, turning the Madras one at least from a ruffianly collection of security guards into an effective military unit. Originally intended to command the Bengal expedition, he remained in Madras on health grounds.

Left: Mirza Mohammed, Nawab of Bengal (1733-1757), better known by his honorific Siraj-ud-Daula.

Middle left: John Zephaniah Holwell (1711-1798). Widely broadcast, not least by himself, as the hero of the hour when Calcutta fell, most of his contemporaries regarded him as a sanctimonious troublemaker.

Below left: Vice Admiral Charles Watson (1714-1757), a capable but sometimes pompous naval officer who contributed much to the success of the Plassey campaign but died little over a month after its conclusion.

Below right: Eyre Coote (1727-1783). One of the most outstanding British officers to serve in 18th Century India, Coote was also well known for his fiery temper and frequent exclamations of "Damme!"

Above: The East India House, Leadenhall Street, London, headquarters of the greatest multinational trading company in the world.

Left: Robert Clive (1725-1774). The legendary victor of the Battle of Plassey depicted in later life. In 1757 he was somewhat leaner but no less ruthless.

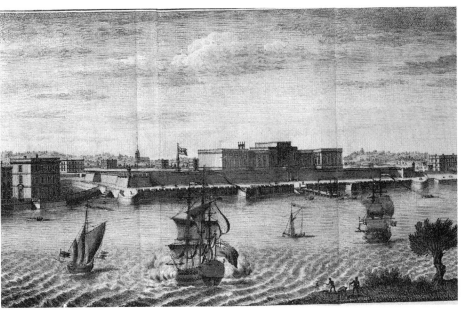

Above: Fort William, Calcutta. While published in 1760 this engraving provides a good view of the fort as it was in 1756 and the degree to which its walls were overlooked by neighbouring buildings.

Above left: Seventy miles from the sea, the Royal Navy's battleships played a substantial role in battering the French fortress of Chandernagore into submission. Above right: There is no evidence that Siraj-ud-Daula conducted the Battle of Plassey on board an elephant, as depicted by Richard Caton-Woodville, nevertheless it was still customary for Indian generals to do so at this period.

Below: Caton-Woodville was on surer ground with his depiction of the Bengali artillery mounted on mobile platforms at Plassey.

Above: A traditional view of the Battle of Plassey, improbably depicting the East India Company soldiers in European uniforms.

Right: The British Artillery at Plassey as depicted in traditional fashion by Caton-Woodville. In fact Clive's guns were manned by East India Company gunners, not British regulars.

Above left: Contemporary illustration of berkanduz or mercenary Buxarries armed with matchlock muskets and tulwars.

Above right: This Mughal infantryman was typical of the berkanduz or musketeers making up the greater part of the Bengali forces at Plassey.

Left: While unmistakeably strolling outside St. James's Palace in London, this engraving provides an excellent picture of the style of uniform worn by many East India Company officers such as Captain Alexander Grant.

Above left: HM 39th Foot. Ordinarily the green cuffs and lapels would be trimmed with worsted lace, but this was customarily stripped off on active service. Swords were not generally worn by the 1750s, but an inspection report after the regiment's return from India noted that the grenadier company sported tulwars.

Above right: Presenting a rather less martial appearance were the militia who helped defend Calcutta in 1756.

Right: The earliest known illustration of East India Company sepoys is this 1773 print depicting the 3rd Battalion at Bombay, but it is unlikely their appearance had much changed since the 1750s

Above: Little is known of the uniforms and equipment of the East India Company's European troops but this illustration from a contemporary British drill book probably gives a good idea. The coat is single breasted rather than lapelled and no gaiters are worn over his linen breeches. Conical hats like later solar topees were worn in Madras, but hats may have been worn in Bengal. Belly boxes may also have replaced the cartridge box on the hip.

Right: 18th century naval personnel were traditionally identified by short blue jackets and very loose trousers. The cap is untypical and identifies this seamen as a member of the crew of an admiral's or captain's barge.

Dumbleton, William	Wounded and died in Black Hole (Hill, Vol. 3, p. 72)	Ensign in Militia Notary Public and Registrar of Mayoral Court
Eyre, Edward	Died in Black Hole	Aged 28 Seemingly a very corpulent man, a French account says he lived until morning but Holwell positively identifies him as dying next to him during the night (Hill, Vol. 1, p. 50)
Frere	Died in Black Hole	Seafaring man Not recorded by Holwell and Mills (Hill, Vol. 3, pp. 72, 105)
Gatliff, John	Survived Black Hole	Not in Holwell's list, but named by Mills (Hill, Vol. 1, p. 44)
Gostlin, Francis	Died in Black Hole	Aged 20 Assistant in the Export Warehouse
Grubb, William	Died in Black Hole	Aged 19 Assistant in the Export Warehouse
Guy, James	Died in Black Hole	
Harrod, Aylmer	Died in Black Hole	Aged 19 Assistant in the Export Warehouse
Hastings, Henry	Died in Black Hole	Ensign
Hayes, Francis	Died in Black Hole	Lieutenant
Hillier	Died in Black Hole	Seafaring man Not listed by Holwell or Mills (Hill, Vol. 3, pp. 72, 105)

Holwell, John Zephaniah	Survived Black Hole	Aged 45 Zemindar Left a number of accounts and lists of those incarcerated in the Black Hole
Hunt	Died in Black Hole	Sea officer
Jebb, John	Died in Black Hole	Aged 23 Factor
Jenks, John	Died in Black Hole	Aged 28 Company Servant
Jennings	Died in Black Hole	Sea officer Not in Holwell's list (Hill, Vol. 3, p. 72)
Johnstone, Patrick	Died in Black Hole	Aged 19 Son of Sir James Johnstone of Westerhall Assistant in the Accountant's Office
Jones, John	Survived Black Hole	Not in Holwell's list, but named by Mills (Hill, Vol. 1, p. 44)
Knapton, William	Died in Black Hole	Aged 18 Zemindar's assistant
Law, John	Died in Black Hole	Aged 25 Factor
Leech, Thomas	Died in Black Hole	
Lushington, Henry	Survived Black Hole	Aged 18 Assistant in the Export Warehouse

Lyon	Died in Black Hole	Seafaring man Not recorded by Holwell or Mills (Hill, Vol. 3, pp. 72, 105)
Meadows, Thomas	Survived Black Hole	Holwell lists: 'John Meadows, and twelve military and militia Blacks and Whites, some of whom recovered when the door was opened.' Mills, however (Hill, Vol. 1, p. 44), identifies him as *Thomas* Meadows, a writer in the Company's Marine Yard – an employment which may explain a report of a seafaring man named Meadows dying in the Black Hole.
Mills, John	Survived Black Hole	Captain of the *Diligence* See Hill, Vol. 1, pp. 40–5 for important notebook
Moran, Patrick	Survived Black Hole	Hill states he was afterwards in the army but gives no source
Orr, William	Listed by Holwell as dead in the Black Hole but otherwise named as one of those who escaped on the ships. (Hill, Vol. 1,172)	Aged 19 Assistant in the Accountant's Office
Osborne, Michael	Died in Black Hole	Not in Holwell's list, but already wounded when confined in Black Hole

Paccard, John Francis	Fate uncertain. Holwell places him in the Black Hole but some accounts state he 'died of his wounds before the place was taken' (Hill, Vol. 3, p. 72)	Ensign, Bengal military
Page, Edward	Died in Black Hole	Aged 19 Assistant in the Accountant's Office
Page, Stephen	Died in Black Hole	Aged 20 Assistant in the Secretary's Office
Parker, William	Reported as having been killed in the attack but Holwell positively identifies him as having been pressed to death in the Black Hole (Hill, Vol. 3, p. 139)	Sea captain
Porter, Joseph	Died in Black Hole	Seafaring man Not listed by Holwell or Mills (Hill, Vol. 3, pp. 72, 105)
Purnell, Thomas	Holwell states he survived the night in the Black Hole but died next day. However he was another of those reported in newspapers to have been killed in the attack (Hill, Vol. 3, p. 72)	Sea officer

Reid	Died in Black Hole	Seafaring man Not recorded by Holwell or Mills (Hill, Vol. 3, pp. 72, 105)
Reveley, Roger	Died in Black Hole	Aged 29 Company Servant
Roop, John	Survived Black Hole	Probably a soldier (Hill, Vol. 3, pp. 72, 105)
Scott, William	Died in Black Hole	Ensign, Bengal military Nephew of Colonel Frederick Scott
Simpson, Colin	Died in Black Hole	Lieutenant, Bengal military
Stephenson or Stevenson, Francis	Another individual reported as killed in the attack (Hill, Vol. 3, p. 72) but positively identified by Holwell as dying in the Black Hole	Sea Captain
Street, John	Died in Black Hole	Aged 19 Assistant in the Secretary's Office
Talbot, Robert	Brought out alive from the Black Hole but died next morning	Lieutenant, Bengal military, served as Adjutant during siege
Thomas, Peter	Survived Black Hole	Not in Holwell's list, but named by Mills. (Hill, Vol. 1, pp. 43–4)
Tilley	Died in Black Hole	Seafaring man Not listed by Holwell or Mills (Hill, Vol. 3, 72, 105

Toriano, Richard	Died in Black Hole	Aged 18 Assistant in the Accountant's Office
Valicourt, James	Died in Black Hole	Aged 28 Assistant in the Accountant's Office
Walcott, Edward	Survived Black Hole	Ensign, Bengal military, but subsequently died at Fulta
Wedderburn, Charles	Died in Black Hole	Ensign, Bengal military Not to be confused with a sea officer, Henry Wedderburn, who was a lieutenant in the militia but fled aboard the ships with Frankland and Manningham
Wilson, George	Died in Black Hole	Seafaring man Not listed by Holwell or Mills (Hill, Vol. 3, pp. 72, 105)
Witherington, Lawrence	Died in Black Hole	Captain of the Train

Appendix 5

Clive's Headquarters Journal of the Expedition to Bengal

The official journal was written up daily by members of Colonel Clive's staff and copies periodically submitted to Fort St. George. In all three separate documents are transcribed here. The first, (a), was evidently written up by Clive's brother-in-law, Captain Neville Maskelyne, covering the period from the embarkation in October 1756 until 18 February 1757.

Document (b) commences on 2 March and ends on 25 March just after the fall of Chandernagore. The third document, (c), is a transcript covering the Plassey campaign, commencing on 12 June 1757 and ending with the army's taking up quarters in Cossimbazar on 27 June.

Whilst a great deal of factual information not to be found elsewhere is contained in these documents, the degree to which the narratives have been sanitised is quite remarkable and there are no references to the various rows between Clive and the British commanders which punctuated the campaigns.

(a) Journal of the expedition to Bengal from 13 October, 1756 to 18 February, 1757, kept by one of Colonel Clive's family.[1]

Oct. 13th. – This day all the forces consisting of 276 of the King's troops, 616 of the Company's, 1,048 *seapoys* and 260 *lascars* destined for the expedition, embarked on board the respective ships in the following manner, *viz.*:

	King's Troops	Company's Troops	Sepoys and Lascars
King's ships:			
Kent	65	77	59
Cumberland	97	150	67
Tyger	56	146	70

Salisbury	58	147	57
Bridgewater	–	96	–
Company's ships			
Walpole	–	–	413
Marlborough	–	–	360
Protector	–	–	132
Lapwing snow	–	–	90
Bonetta ketch	–	–	60
	276	616	1,308

Oct. 16th. – This day the fleet under the command of Vice Admiral Watson consisting of the above King's ships, the *Blaze* fire-ship, and the two Indiamen being victualled and watered for six weeks sailed from Madrass.

Nov. 6th. – Since sailing from the above port have been drove by the current into the latitude of 6° 36' N. occasioned by the baffling winds and calms usual at this season of the year.

Nov. 10th. – The appearance of a tedious passage obliged the squadron to be put to two-thirds allowance.

Nov. 13th – This night the *Salisbury* sprung a leak which kept all her pumps going to free her, and after making the signal of distress, the carpenter of the *Kent* and other ships were sent on board who found out the leak and in some measure stopped it, so that she was able to proceed on the voyage under an easy sail upon her foremast, as the leak was discovered to be in the wooden ends forwards.

Nov. 14th. – A Council of War being held on board the *Kent* concerning the *Salisbury*'s proceeding, it was agreed that the military, as well King's as Company's, should be transported on board of the *Kent, Cumberland* and *Tyger,* and they to replace the number out of the seapoys and lascars they had on board, the *Salisbury* to proceed with the fleet as far as the safety of the ship would permit and in case of necessity to bear away for Point de Gaul.

Nov. 15th. – The *Salisbury* made but little water, so that the hand-pumps kept her free, which induced the Admiral to defer the removal of the troops as it was thought she might proceed on her voyage with the fleet; this day the seamen and military were put to half allowance of provisions and two-third allowance of water. The scurvy began to appear in the fleet particularly amongst the seamen.

Nov. 16th. – The *Marlborough* Indiaman sailing very heavy and the passage already very long, the fleet proceeded without shortening sail for her, she having orders to join the squadron with all expedition at the place of rendezvous which was Ballasore Road, and lost sight of her in the evening. The squadron began to be very sickly. The *Blaze* fireship being leaky was ordered to bear away for Point de Gaul and from thence proceed to Bombay.

Dec. 1th. – This day struck ground off Point Palmiras being only six ships in company, having seen nothing of the *Marlborough* since the 16th November. About 8 p.m. the 2nd, *Cumberland* struck upon the reef off Point Palmiras, but was soon got off without any damage, the ship came to an anchor and lay till daylight; after making the signal of distress the fleet came to an anchor in seven, some in five and others in four fathoms water upon the edge of this dangerous shoal.

Dec. 3rd. – The *Kent* being the weathermost ship weighed and rounded the shoal, the point then bearing south by west, the *Tyger* and *Walpole* also weighed south, rounded the shoal in four fathom; the other ships endeavoured to weigh but parted their cables and stood off.

Dec. 4th. – Saw a pilot sloop standing towards us who put on board Mr. Grant the pilot; the *Tyger* and *Walpole* only in sight. The squadron was in great distress for water and provisions, having only eight days water on board and numbers down with the scurvy.

Dec. 8th. – Received some rice from the pilot sloop which was put aboard the *Walpole*, she being in greatest want of provisions. This day Messrs. Watts and Becher came on board as deputies from the Governor and Council to wait on the Admiral and Colonel Clive; they informed them of the sickly state of the remaining gentlemen of Calcutta and the party under Major Kilpatrick, of which only thirty men fit for duty.

Dec. 9th. – This day passed the Braces and anchored in company with the *Tyger* and *Walpole* in the kiln; and had no account of the remainder of the squadron, notwithstanding a sloop was despatched some days since to the point in order to look for them.

Dec. 12th. – Arrived at Ingerlee.

Dec. 13th. – Anchored in Culpee in company with the *Tyger* and *Walpole*, when Mr. Drake the Governor and Mr. Holwell waited upon the Admiral and Colonel Clive and confirmed the account of the sickness at Fulta.

Dec. 15th. – Anchored at Fulta in company with the *Tyger* and *Walpole*, where we found riding at anchor the *Kingfisher* sloop, the *Delawar* Indiaman and about twelve sail of country ships; the Governor, Council and the remainder of the inhabitants of Calcutta lived on board the country ships and the military under Major Kilpatrick were cantoned in huts ashore.

Dec. 16th. – The Company's troops and *seapoys* on the *Kent, Tyger* and *Walpole* landed at Fulta, where they joined the detachment under Major James Kilpatrick; the military encamped in a plain to the eastward of the town, and the seapoys were posted at the avenues leading to it.

Dec. 22nd. – The Grenadier and Artillery companies from the *Salisbury* and *Bridgewater* joined the battalion in camp where the whole continued till the 27th.

Dec. 27th. – When the Artillery [*sic*][2] reimbarked in the same order pursuant to the resolution of a Council of War held on board the *Kent*; but the *seapoys* marched over land keeping the ships in view and Captain Barker following in boats with 80 of the Train and two field pieces properly completed.

Dec. 28th – About three in the afternoon the troops and two field pieces were disembarked at Moyapore, where they joined the *seapoys* and at 5 in the evening marched northward in order to throw themselves into the road leading from the Fort of Bougee Bougee to Aligur and Calcutta and by that means cut off the enemy's retreat to those places, agreeable to the plan concerted at the Council of War. This was effected with infinite labour and fatigue by a continued march all night, which was made more difficult by the deep creeks and morasses the troops and cannon were obliged to pass.

Dec. 29th. – At 8 in the morning the troops passed through a place called Pike Parrah, where the enemy had been overnight, and about an hour after halted in the great road leading to Calcutta, having the ships at anchor in view, though not the Fort which was obscured by clusters of trees. Kessersing, commander of the seapoys, was detached from hence with 200 *seapoys* to reconnoitre, and was followed by Captain Pye at the head of the Grenadier company and the rest of the *seapoys*; Captain Guappe was likewise advanced with his company and the volunteers in the Calcutta Road to give timely notice of the approach of any of the enemy that might come that way. Captain Pye had orders to take possession of the suburbs and send an immediate report when he had effected it, but not to attempt anything further without order. Captain Pye finding the *pettah* or suburbs abandoned marched directly down to the river side, where Kesser Sing's party were lying under the bank, and put himself under the orders of Captain Coote who was landed with the King's troops; they had just struck a flag on one of the advanced batteries and were reconnoitring from behind it, when Kesser Sing was ordered back with the *seapoys*; Captain Weller landing soon after from the *Salisbury* and, hearing that the Colonel was attacked by the enemy, ordered the whole to march to his assistance; whilst these detachments were on their march to join the Colonel the main body of the enemy under the command of Rajah Monichund from the houses and thickets attacked the battalion consisting of 260 rank and file which was pushing for the plain; but they were soon dislodged by a few platoons that were ordered to advance.

The skirmish lasted about half an hour, in which time we had Ensign Kerr with nine private men killed and eight wounded. The enemy's loss must have been somewhat considerable as their number of horse and foot appeared to be about 2,000 and several of them exposed themselves pretty freely at first; but were much alarmed at the briskness of our fire and startled at the first appearance of the cannon which they thought impossible for us to transport over the ground we had marched the preceding night; 'tis said that 200 of inferior note were killed and wounded, four *jemidars*, an elephant and the Commander shot through his turban, besides about forty who perished in their confusion on passing a creek.

At noon the cannon of the fort being quite silenced, our forces marched down to the advanced battery near the river which the enemy had abandoned in the morning, and drew up in front of the fort under cover of a high bank.

At sunset two nine pounders were landed from the *Kent*, and were mounted on the enemy's advanced battery; some of the King's troops were wounded in forming the embrazures by exposing themselves too freely.

At 7 orders were issued out for storming the gateway at daybreak, under cover of the two guns, which was to be carried on by the King's troops, the Grenadier company, 200 *seapoys* and 100 seamen.

At 8 a drunken sailor straggling from his command, pushed into the fort, and giving three cheers was followed by the whole party without any order or regularity. As the enemy had been moving off ever since dusk not a man was lost on this occasion except Captain Dugald Campbell, who unfortunately fell as he was posting sentries over a magazine, it is thought designed by some of the military.

We found here twenty-two pieces of cannon of different calibre and thirty-three barrels of powder.

Dec. 30th. – After disabling the guns, carrying off the powder, demolishing the ramparts of the fort and batteries and burning the houses, the troops reimbarked in the evening; the *seapoys* taking their route along the bank of the river with the fleet in view, the artillery following again in boats.

Dec. 31st. – The fleet proceeded up the river and the next day.

1757. Jan. 1st. – At 10 a.m. came in sight of Tanna Fort from whence the enemy fired several guns out of random shot and at 2 p.m. came abreast of Tanna and Aligur which is a new mud fort erected by the enemy opposite to the former, and where twenty-four pieces of heavy cannon were mounted; upon our approach the enemy abandoned the forts without firing a shot and the boats crews of the squadron took possession of them; we found here fifty-six pieces of cannon, chiefly large, some shot and a small quantity of powder.

Jan. 2nd. – At 5 in the morning the Company's troops landed at Aligur where they joined the *seapoys* and at 8 marched with two field pieces towards Surman's gardens: the enemy abandoning their batteries near the river on approach of the fleet and land force, at 10 a.m. the ships coming abreast of Fort William (by the Moors called Alinagor) were fired upon pretty warmly as they lay becalmed, sheering round in the eddies of the tide; but soon, after coming to an anchor close in with the western line of guns on the river side, they drove the enemy from their batteries, who fled through the eastern gate before the military or *seapoys* could come up with them; in this action three of the King's soldiers and six sailors were killed. At 11 the boats landed a party of the King's troops from the squadron who took possession of Fort William in the King's name.

Jan. 3rd. – The Admiral came on shore and after being saluted, delivered up the Fort with all the stores and goods to the Company's representatives. There were found here many guns of different sizes, round and grape shots, shells, granadoes, a small quantity of powder (and some military stores) but no small arms; in the godowns were several bales of the Company's broad cloth and about 650 bales of goods for the Europe market; and in town about 1,400 bates of cotton, a small quantity of toothenague [zinx oxide] and some China ware.

Jan. 4th. – Arranged the garrison stores and mounted cannon on the ramparts; at 8 p.m. a detachment of 130 of King's troops, the Grenadier company, and 200 *seapoys* under command of Major Kilpatrick, embarked upon the *Bridgewater, Kingfisher, Thunder* bomb and other small vessells in order to proceed up to Hughly, Captain King having a party of 200 seamen in the boats of the squadron; the *Bridgewater* unfortunately grounded on the sand off Perrin's gardens, and notwithstanding her guns and stores were taken out the next day she was not got off till at 4 in the afternoon when she proceeded as far as Barnagore. Weighed with the morning flood, and at high water anchored abreast of the Danish factory.

Jan. 8th. – Got up as far as the French Gardens

Jan. 9th. – At noon the ships came to an anchor off Hughly and began firing to dislodge the enemy from the banks and houses where they might annoy us in landing. At 4 in the afternoon the troops landed about 700 yards below the Fort under cover of the ships which immediately moved farther up the river and anchored close to the fort and began to batter in breach. The troops on landing took possession of the houses and avenues leading to the Fort, got their scaling ladders on shore, burnt the houses and lay in Coja Wazeed's garden till the breach was practicable.

Jan. 10th. – About 2 o'clock this morning the troops marched up to the Fort and applying their ladders scaled the walls, making themselves masters of the place in less than an hour with little or no loss; having placed sufficient guards and posted sentries round the walls to prevent surprize, they lay on their arms till daylight.

Jan. 11th. About 8 p.m. two detachments were sent out each consisting of one Captain, three subalterns, fifty Europeans and seventy *seapoys* to search the houses and secure what effects might be found.

(During this time the commanding officer pitched upon a convenient spot of ground at the distance of five miles from the town of Calcutta to encamp upon, having secured it with batteries and entrenchments against the Nabob's army daily expected.)

Jan. 12th. – Captain Coote was sent out with a detachment to reconnoitre Bandell and protect the men of war's boats in bringing off any of the enemy they might find in the creeks.

Jan. 13th. – At six this evening upon information that several effects belonging to the Moors and bales of English goods had been lodged by our enemies in some empty storehouses at Chinchura (a Settlement belonging to the Dutch) and the Dutch Fiscal signifying his approbation to Captain Smith of our taking them by force, an officer was sent with thirty men to place sentries on such store houses there as the informer should point out, which was accordingly done, but to our surprize the Dutch Director denied his knowing anything of such effects and refused delivering them.

Jan. 14th. – This morning the detachment at Chinchura was ordered back on an alarm that the enemy had surrounded Hughly Fort.

Jan. 15th. – Having disabled the enemy's guns (carrying on board such as were serviceable) demolished the walls, bastions and gateways, and burnt the houses within and without we embarked in order to proceed higher up the river; we landed and burnt the *gunges* or granaries above the Portugueze church.

Jan. 17th. – Sent out parties to burn on the other side of the river.

Jan. 19th. – the King's and Company troops disembarked from His Majesty's ships and went on board the sloops in order to return to Calcutta where we landed (leaving the *seapoys* behind with Captain Smith) the next day.[3]

Jan. 25th. – The Grenadier Company joined the battalion in camp.

Jan. 28th. – The King's troops commanded by Captain Weller joined them. From this day to the 2nd February we remained in camp expecting the Nabob's army when we received intelligence that the van was advanced within four miles of us to the northward, and could discover their burning and destroying the villages as they marched along.

Feb. 3rd. – Early in the morning part of his army appeared on their march along the road leading from Dum Duma House to the Bridge, at the distance of two miles, which they crossed and proceeded to the southward of our camp towards Calcutta, and several of their horse came within about 400 yards of our advanced battery. About noon hearing that small parties of the enemy were got into the skirts of the town, Captain De La Beaume was detached with 80 Europeans, 150 *seapoys*, and two pieces of cannon, to the redoubt at Bogbuzar, from thence to defend that part of the town, and prevent the enemy's plunderers from annoying the inhabitants, which he effected having killed a good number and taken between thirty and forty prisoners. At 5 in the afternoon the major part of the battalion and *seapoys* with four field pieces advanced towards the enemy in order to harass them on their march and discover whether they were not making some lodgement in a wood within reach of our camp; and as soon as we came abreast of this place, they began a brisk fire upon us from nine pieces of cannon, some of them thirty-two pounders, which they had placed to cover their march; on this we immediately formed and returned the cannonadement which continued but a short time, it being near sunset when we began; we soon discovered the enemy draw off their cannon and proceeding on their march to their encampment; at the same time the forces returned to camp. The loss was inconsiderable on both sides; one *matross* and three *seapoys* killed and Captain Weller and Fraser slightly wounded, eight of the enemy's horse were killed and as many men.

Feb. 4th. This morning the main body of their army appeared in sight, in which we were informed the Nabob himself was. He having the preceding day signified his inclination to accommodate matters, and desired Commissaries might be sent for that purpose, Messrs. Walsh and Scrafton were accordingly dispatched with his messenger: they came to the place the Nabob had appointed, but contrary to his promise he had proceeded on his march and they did not get up with him till passing through his army in camp (which extended near five miles from the lake fronting our camp at the distance of two miles to the bounds of Calcutta) they came to Omichund's Garden: the Nabob and his ministers' behaviour to these gentlemen seeming to require some decisive blow to bring matters to a conclusion, it was determined on their return to attack the Nabob's camp the next morning before daylight, for which purpose Mr. Watson's assistance was requested, and he sent Captain Warwick with between five and six hundred seamen who joined our troops about 3 o'clock in the morning; half an hour after we marched with our battalion consisting of 500 Europeans rank and file, 800 *seapoys*, six field pieces and a howitzer with 70 of the Train, and the above mentioned seamen, one half of which were employed in drawing the guns and carrying ammunition, and the other carried arms; at break of day we arrived close to the Nabob's camp before we were challenged, when we received a brisk fire from several quarters, which was returned by our advanced *seapoys*; the enemy on this retreated and we entered their camp without further resistance and pursued our march for some time undisturbed; but upon our approaching nearer to the centre of the camp and the Nabob's quarters our battalion was briskly charged by a body of 300 horse almost within reach of bayonet; they were received with so much coolness and such a regular fire that few of them escaped: after this the whole army began to encompass us in great bodies; so that we were obliged to keep up a constant fire of artillery and musketry to keep the enemy at a distance; we marched through the whole camp which took us up full two hours; and several charges were made upon our rear by the horse, but not with equal courage to the first; about 11 we arrived at the Fort and in the evening set out for the camp which we reached by 7 in the evening.

An unlucky fog prevented our attack upon the Nabob's Head Quarters, which if successful would have made the action more decisive; however as it was, the enemy suffered very considerably; the sailors and *seapoys* in the rear destroyed everything which the van had passed. The Nabob's army consisted of 20,000 horse and 30,000 foot with 25 pieces of cannon, and by the best accounts 1,300 were killed and wounded including twenty-two officers, some of which were of great distinction; upwards of 500 horse were counted upon the spot with four elephants and a number of camels, cattle etc. The loss on our side amounted to twenty-seven killed in the battalion and seventy wounded, twelve seamen killed and as many wounded, eighteen *seapoys* killed and fifty-five wounded.

The apprehension of another attack was so great that the enemy kept up a constant fire of great guns and small arms, all the night and the next day decamped, the Nabob sending a messenger at the same time with offers to treat.

Whilst this treaty continued the enemy's army was encamped on the other side of Dum Dumma Bridge having a river between the two camps.[4]

Feb. 8th. – Everything was concluded and the Nabob decamped with his whole army and began his march to Muxadavad.

Feb. 14th. – We encamped about 400 yards nearer to the water side.

Feb. 18th. – We crossed the water and encamped camped opposite to Barnagul.[5]

(b) Colonel Clive's Military Journal, 2 to 25 March 1757

March 2nd, 1757. – The grenadiers and Captain Guapp's company were ordered to embark for the Coast.[6]

March 4th. – The orders for the embarkation of these two companies were countermanded, and this evening they returned to camp.

March 5th. – Lieutenant Molitur with 8 sergeants, 8 corporals, 2 drums and 53 privates besides 43 *topasses*, in all 114, arrived at camp from Bombay.

March 8th. – The army marched six miles to the northward and continued to march except a halt on the 11th at the French Gardens.

March 12th. – Captain Buchannan with 11 sergeants, 11 corporals, 3 drums, and 61 privates, besides 28 *topasses*, from Bombay, joined the troops at camp.

The army marched and encamped about two miles to the west of Chandernagore; same day the sailors belonging to the *Marlborough* and doing duty in our Train of artillery were ordered to return on board.

March 13th. – At night the Company's grenadiers were sent to join the picquet with orders to take possession of the French Bounds, and to annoy and alarm the enemy at their out batteries, which accordingly they did, and took possession of a battery to the north-west of Chandernagore Fort, which was abandoned by the French.

March 14th. – Captain-Lieutenant Edgerton with 4 sergeants, 4 corporals, 1 drum, 9 privates and 24 *topasses* from Bombay arrived at camp.

At 6 o'clock this morning the Declaration of War with France was read in camp. Immediately after Major Killpatrick with half the troops was ordered to advance to the post which the grenadiers had taken possession of the night before. In sight of this battery and within a hundred yards of the north-west bastion of the Fort was another, from which the enemy played down an avenue with two field pieces and musketry, but did little execution on account of the too great distance. Soon after some *seapoys* were ordered to advance under cover on each side the avenue with an intention of flanking the enemy's battery. The King's and Company's grenadiers followed to sustain them. On perceiving our people approach they began a smart fire; notwithstanding we gained ground, and took possession of some houses within fifty yards. A continual fire was kept up on both sides for a considerable time, in which the enemy lost several men; 1 sergeant and 4 Europeans we found dead and buried them. Captain Lin was ordered with two hundred Europeans and some companies of *seapoys* to reconnoitre the batteries to the westward and southward of the town, (though we had no particular information of the enemy's situation that could be depended on, we had been told that they had fortified all the avenues of the town that led to the Fort), and if possible to take possession of them, but on a nearer approach they were found too well maintained to be directly stormed, so, by the direction of a guide sent him, he marched to the southward, having one volunteer wounded, and about 6 o'clock in the evening lodged himself in the Prussian Gardens close to the river side, where when the enemy perceived him, they began a cannonadement from a half-moon battery 900 yards southward of the Fort, which continued (without doing any execution) till dark.

The attack on the north-west battery continued likewise till dark, during which time the enemy's voluntiers and other Europeans sallied out on an advanced party of the King's grenadiers, who soon repulsed them with considerable loss. On our side was only two grenadiers wounded, and Mr Tooke, a volunteer, received a shot through his body, of which he soon after died. We had besides several *seapoys* killed and wounded in this skirmish.

At night a detachment of the troops were left to maintain the post we got possession of, and the rest returned to camp.

March 16th. – This evening the 13 inch mortar began to play upon the Fort, and several small parties by way of alerts advanced under the walls to keep the enemy constantly awake. From this time to the 20th we were employed, whilst the ships were moving up, in erecting one five gun battery of 24 pounders, and one of three of the same calibre, bombarding the Fort at the same time, and keeping up a constant fire of musketry all round the place from the tops of the houses.

March 20th. – The ships came to an anchor off the Prussian Gardens a mile and a half distant from the Fort, while they sent up boats to sound the passage, where the enemy had sunk some vessels to prevent their approach. This day 200 *seapoys* arrived here from Madras.

We had now completed our two batteries, one of which was within a hundred and the other a hundred and eighty yards of the south-east bastion; the three gun battery was designed to play on a mud one of theirs close under the walls of the Fort and the southern flank of the north-east bastion, which could chiefly annoy the ships whilst coming up to the attack. Our three gun battery had been one of theirs which we had reversed.

The enemy having discovered where we were erecting our five gun battery, and seeing guns mounted on the other, kept a warm fire on both, by which they knocked down many adjacent houses, and by the fall of a verandah two artillery officers and two *matrosses* were wounded, and some *lascars* and *coolies* buried in the ruins.

Upon finding that the enemy attempted to dismount the guns of our nearest battery, we immediately threw a number of sand bags into the embrazures, and kept such a fire of musketry from behind them that the guns of the south-east bastion could no longer play on our battery. At night we completed our batteries, and ready to open them, on the ships moving up. At 6 in the evening the King's troops embarked on board the squadron.

March 23rd. – Before daylight all the troops were ordered to the batteries, and took possession of all houses that overlooked the bastions of the Fort.

At 6 o'clock we perceived the ships under way, and as soon as they came within reach of the enemy's guns we opened both our batteries and began an incessant fire of musketry from all quarters, as well as from a field piece and howitzer. This made it very difficult for them to stand to their guns, especially at the mud battery on the water side, from which the ships expected the greatest mischief.

About a quarter before seven the *Tyger* who led came to her station opposite to the eastern face of the north-east bastion, and the *Kent* soon after, opposite to the eastern face of the south-east bastion. The *Salisbury* followed. From this time till a quarter before 9 o'clock the attack continued with the greatest vigour on all sides, when the enemy's defences being almost ruined, as well by the fire from the ships as the batteries on shore, particularly the salient angle of the south-east bastion, which was in a manner entirely destroyed by our five gun battery, and an appearance of a breach in the eastern faces of both the northern and southern bastions, the French hung out a flag of truce, surrendered the Fort and themselves prisoners of war, which the King's troops landed and took possession of.

March 24th. – Lieutenant Corneille with the detachment of the King's troops from the *Cumberland* arrived at Chandernagore.

March 25th. – We removed our camp a mile to the northward of Chandernagore.

Lieutenant Corneille with his party joined us.[7]

(c) Journal of Military Proceedings on the Expedition to Muxadavad

June 12th. – Orders were given out that the troops at Chandernagore should hold themselves in readiness to march at a moment's warning, and this evening the military from Calcutta with Major Kilpatrick joined us.

June 13th. – The whole army, consisting of 190 artillery, between 8 and 900 military, and 2,200 sepoys with eight pieces of cannon and a howitzer, march from Chandernagore early in the morning. The Europeans embarked in boats, the *sepoys* marched by land, and this evening both reached Niasarray.

June 14th. – We left Niasarray, and about 8 at night arrived at Culna. This morning Mr. Watts and the gentlemen who had escaped from Cassimbuzar met us.

June 15th. – At 5 o'clock we landed and marched about five miles to Mirzapore. Notwithstanding the shortness of this march sixteen men fell sick on the road by the evening's being extremely sultry.

June 16th. – We proceeded to Tantesaul.

June 17th. – We were at Pattlee; we halted here to rest the army and sent Captain Coote with 200 Europeans, 500 *sepoys* and two field pieces, to possess himself of Cutwan town and fort about fourteen miles distant, and a post that might have proved extremely advantageous to us, not only from its situation, it lying just by the high road to Muxadavad, and a quantity of grain which we were informed was there, but also the assistance which the Fort would have afforded to our boats and the troops in case either of a retreat or their continuance there.

June 19th. – We proceeded to Cutwan and had an account from Captain Coote, while on our march, that he was in possession of both town and fort. We halted here two days, and on the

June 22nd. – At 5 in the evening crossed the river leaving a

179

subaltern's party and 500 *seapoys* in the Fort and about 12 at night we arrived at Placis after a very long and fatiguing march.

June 23rd. – At daybreak we discovered the Nabob's army at the distance of three miles in full march towards us, upon which the whole were ordered under arms, being in two battalions; the Europeans were told off in four grand divisions, the artillery distributed between them, and the *seapoys* on the right and left of the whole.

Our situation was very advantageous, being in a Grove surrounded with high mud banks; our right and front were entirely covered by the above mud banks; our left by Placis House and the river, our rear by the Grove and a village. The enemy approached apace, covered a fine extensive plain in front of us as far as the eye could discern from right to left, and consisted as we since learned of 15,000 horse and 35,000 foot with more than forty pieces of cannon from 32 to 9 pounders. They began to cannonade from their heavy artillery, which though well pointed could do little execution, our people being lodged under the banks. We could not hope to succeed in an immediate attempt upon their cannon as they were planted almost round and at a considerable distance both from us and each other, we therefore remained quiet in our post in hopes of a successful attack on their camp at night.

About 300 yards from the bank under which we were posted was a pool of water with high banks all round it, and was apparently a post of strength. This the enemy presently took possession of, and would have galled us much from thence but for our advantageous situation with some cannon managed by 50 Frenchmen. Their heavy metal continued to play very briskly on the Grove.

As their army (exclusive of a few advanced parties) were drawn up at too great a distance for our short sixes to reach them, one field piece with a howitzer was advanced two hundred yards in front, and we could see they played with great success among those that were of the first rank, by which the whole army was dispirited and thrown into confusion.

A large body of horse stretching out on our right, and as by that movement we supposed they intended an attempt on the advanced field piece and howitzer, they were both ordered back.

About 11 o'clock a very heavy shower of rain came on and we imagined the horse would now if ever have charged in hopes of breaking us, as they might have thought we could not then make use of our firelocks, but their ignorance of the brisk fire of our artillery prevented them from attempting it. At 12 a report being made that a party of horse had attacked and taken the boats the picquetts of the night before were ordered out, but the account proving false they were countermanded. The enemy's fire now began to slacken and soon after entirely ceased. In this situation we remained till 2 o'clock, when perceiving that most of the enemy were returned to their camp, we thought it a proper opportunity to seize one of the eminences from which the enemy had much annoyed us in the morning; accordingly the grenadiers of the first battalion with two field pieces and a body of sepoys supported by four platoons and two field pieces from the second battalion were encouraged to take possession of it, which accordingly they did. This encouraged us to take possession of another advanced post within three hundred yards of the entrance to the enemy's camp; all these motions brought the enemy out of their camp a second time; but in attempting to bring out their cannon they were so galled by our artillery that they could not effect it, notwithstanding they made several attempts. Their horse and foot however advanced much nearer than in the morning, and by their motions made as if they intended to charge us, two or three large bodies being within one hundred and fifty yards. In this situation they stood a very brisk and severe cannonadement, which killed them upwards of 400 men, among which were four or five principal officers. This loss put the enemy into great confusion and encouraged us to attack the entrance into their camp, and an adjacent eminence at the same time, which we effected with little or no loss, although the former was defended by 50 French and a very large body of infantry, and the latter by a body of foot and horse intermixt together. During the heat of the action the remainder of our forces were two or three times ordered to join us, and that order as often countermanded on account of the movement of a large body of horse towards the Grove, whom we had often fired upon to keep at a proper distance; these afterwards proved to be our friends commanded by Meer Jaffier.

The entrance to the camp being gained a general rout ensued and the whole army continued the pursuit for upwards of six miles which for want of horse answered no other purpose than that of taking all their artillery consisting of 40 pieces of cannon, and all their baggage.

This night we lay at a small village called Daudpore.

June 24th. – At 5 in the evening we marched to Binna (or Burrua)

June 25th. – We reached Maudipore and remained there till the

June 27th. – When we marched one battalion to the English and the other to the French Factory at Cassimbuzar.

Letter from Colonel Clive to Select Committee, Fort Saint George, dated Muxadavad, 2 July 1757

Gentlemen, Sometime since I acquainted the President by a letter, despatched under a Dutch cover, of the necessity there was to overset Surajah Dowla. I have now the happiness to inform you that great event is completely brought about. He still delayed under different pretences to fulfil the grand points of the treaty, such as delivering us the villages, making good the Calcutta ballance and admitting the currency of our siccas. At the same time we found him designing our ruin by a conjunction with the French; pressing invitations were sent to Monsieur Bussey to come into the province and Monsieur Law's party (then in his pay at 10,000 rupees per month) was ordered to return from Patna, of all which we had certain knowledge by authentic copies of his own letters. At this juncture some principal officers of his army made overtures to us, at the head of whom was Jaffir Ally Khan who had long been *Buxey*, and was a man as generally esteemed as the other was detested. We soon entered into a private treaty to make him Nabob, and, having prepared everything with the utmost secrecy, the army consisting of 1,000 Europeans and 2,000 sepoys with eight pieces of cannon marched from Chandernagore the 13th in the morning and arrived the 18th at Cutwa Fort which was taken without opposition. The 22nd in the evening we crossed the river and landing on the island marched straight for Plassey, where we arrived by 1 in the morning. At daybreak we discovered the Nabob's army, consisting of about 15,000 horse and 35,000 foot with upwards of 40 pieces of cannon, moving towards us. They approached apace and by 6 began the attack with a number of heavy cannon supported by the whole army, and continued to play upon us very briskly for several hours, during which our very advantageous situation saved us greatly, being possessed of a large *tope* surrounded with a good mud bank. To succeed in an attempt on their cannon was next to impossible, as they were planted in a manner round us and a considerable distance from each other; we therefore remained quiet in our post in expectation of a successful attack upon their camp at night. The enemy retiring to their camp about noon with their artillery we sent a detachment and two field pieces to take possession of a Tank with high banks from whence they had considerably annoyed us with some cannon which were managed by Frenchmen. This brought them out a second time, but as we found they made no great effort to dislodge us we proceeded to take possession of one or two more eminences lying very near one angle of their camp, round which run a ditch and breastwork, from whence and an adjacent eminence, still in their possession, they kept a smart fire of musquetry upon us. They made several attempts to bring out their cannon, but our field pieces played so warmly and well upon them that they were always drove back. The Horse exposed themselves a good deal on this occasion; many of them was killed and among the rest four or five officers of the first distinction, which, dispiriting the enemy and throwing them into some confusion, we were encouraged to storm the eminence and angle of their camp. Both which were attempted at the same time and carried with little or no loss, though the latter was defended, exclusive of blacks, by forty French and two pieces of cannon, and the former by a large body of Foot and Horse. On this a general rout ensued, and we pursued the enemy six miles taking upwards of forty pieces of cannon which they had abandoned. The roads were strewed with hacarys and filled with baggage of all kinds. Their loss is computed at about five hundred men. On our side there were twenty-two killed and fifty wounded and those chiefly blacks. Surajah Dowla saved himself on a camel and reached the City early next morning; dispatched away what jewels and treasure he conveniently could, and followed himself at midnight attended only by four or five persons.

During the warmest part of the action we observed a large body of troops hovering on our right, who proved to be our friends, but, as they made no signal by which we could discover them, we frequently fired on them to make them keep their distance. After the action they sent their compliments and encamped that night in our neighbourhood. The next morning Jaffir Ally Cawn [Khan] paid me a visit and expressed much gratitude for the great services we had done him, assuring us in the most solemn manner that he would faithfully fulfil the treaty he had made with us. He then proceeded to the City which he reached some hours before Surajah Dowla left it. As on his flight Jaffir Ally Cawn was in quiet possession of the palace and City, I encamped without to prevent ravage and disorder, first at Mandipoor and afterwards at the French Factory at Sydabad. The 29th I entered the city with only a party of 200 Europeans and 300 sepoys and took up my quarters in a spacious house and garden near the palace. The same day I waited on Jaffir Ally Cawn who refused seating himself on the *musnud* till placed on it by me, which done he received the homage and congratulations of all the courtiers as Nabob. The next morning he returned the visit and on my recommending to him to consult Jaggat Seat on all occasions, who as the man of the greatest property in the Kingdom, would give him the best advice for its tranquility and security, we agreed to pay him a visit immediately together, at which a firm union was entered into by us three, and Jaggatseat engaged to use his influence at Delhi (which is very great) both to get the Nabob confirmed and procure for us such *phirmaunds* as we should have occasion for.

The principal Articles of our treaty with the present Nabob are a confirmation of all grants both in the Mogul's *phirmaund* and the treaty with Surajah Dowla; an alliance offensive and defensive against all enemies, Europeans or country; the delivery of the French and their property into our hands and a perpetual exclusion of them from these provinces; a tract of land extending between the lake and river from Calcutta to Culpee to be given to the Company, also one *crore*[8] of rupees 50 lack to the European sufferers at the loss of Calcutta, twenty lack to the blacks, seven to the Armenians, and fifty to the army and navy. All the Articles to be fulfilled within one month from his accession to the *Subahship*.

As the sum in the Treasury did not appear enough to satisfy our demand, much less leave a sufficiency for the Nabob to pay his troops, which was indispensably necessary, it was left to Jaggat Seat as a mutual friend to settle what we should receive, whose determination was that we should immediately be paid one half, two thirds in money and one third in jewels, plate and goods, and that the other half should be discharged within three years at three equal and annual payments.

I have just had advice of Surajah Dowla's being taken near Rajahmaul in a distressed condition with hardly cloaths to his back, such is the misery he has been reduced to by his injuries to the English and by a general course of folly and wickedness throughout the short time he has reigned. Our victory is very complete, and the present Nabob seems happily settled in his government and with universal approbation. My presence therefore in this quarter I imagine will not be required much longer. When you have thoroughly considered the critical situation the Company's affairs were in on this Establishment after the taking of Chandernagore and the nice and important game that was to be played with the late Nabob, I flatter myself you will alter the sentiments you are pleased to express in your late letters with regard to my having kept the troops here. I cannot at this time reply to those letters, nor even acquaint you what are received, as all my papers are left at Chandernagore.

I am now using my utmost endeavours to secure Monsieur Laws

and his party who are still at Patna. The French I spoke of in the action were some fugitives, who had assembled at Sydabad under Monsieur Sinfray, late secretary of Chandernagore, and who advised, and I understand had the principal hand in, burning and destroying Cassimbuzar Factory.

I must acquaint you that some days before I left Chandernagore letters arrived from the Nanna desiring our friendship, for that he would engage to enter the Province with 150,000 Marattas and make good to us double of all the losses we had sustained; that as we were powerful in ships we might keep out the French by sea, and he would take care to do it by land. In answer I have just wrote him of our success, and that Jaffir Ally Cawn is in peaceful possession of the kingdom, and will duly pay him the *chout*.[9]

The late Nabob's spies have hitherto prevented any *cossids* passing through Cuttack, but now I hope they will meet no further impediment. Jaggat Seat has promised me to forward this safely

to your hands. In a few days I expect to have an opportunity of addressing the Court of Directors by a twenty-gun ship dispatched from hence.

I have, &c. &c., Robert Clive.

P.S. – Surajah Dowla arrived in the city the 2nd at night and was immediately dispatched having created some commotions in the army by the letters he wrote on the road to the several jemidars. Monsieur Laws and his party came as far as Rajamaul to his assistance, and were within three hours' march of him when he was taken. A party of the Nabob's horse and foot, followed by some of our military and seapoys are gone after the French, and I hope will give a good account of them. Gouzeoden Cawn and the Mogul's son are come down to Halabass and the Nabob of Owde with a numerous army is within seven coss of them. It's expected every hour to hear of a battle or compromise.

Robert Clive.

Appendix 6

Captain Eyre Coote's Journal

Eyre Coote (1726–83) was one of the most remarkable officers to serve in India at this time, Clive not excepted. His debut was inauspicious in quarrelling furiously with Clive at the retaking of Calcutta in January 1757, but notwithstanding this he went on to become one of Clive's most trusted subordinates and on the strength of his record in India returned home to be given his own regiment. Coming out to India again he decisively defeated the French at the Battle of Wandewash in 1760 and continued to have a distinguished career before dying as Lieutenant General Sir Eyre Coote at Madras in 1783.

This extract from his journal covers the period 17 October 1756 to 30 June 1757.[1]

> *Saturday, 17th October, 1756* – Sailed from Madrass on the expedition on board Admiral Watson's ship the *Kent*, in company with His Majesty's ships *Cumberland, Tyger, Salisbury, Bridgewater,* and two Indiamen *viz. Marlborough* and *Walpole.*
>
> *Tuesday, 30th Nov.* – Came to anchor in Balasore Road, the *Cumberland* and *Salisbury* struck and fired some guns.[2]
>
> *December 1st.* – Stood more into the Road and lost company from the *Cumberland, Salisbury* and *Bridgewater.*
>
> *Dec. 8th.* – Sailed for the river Ganges.
>
> *Dec. 15th.* – Arrived at Fultah with the *Tyger* and *Walpole* Indiaman.
>
> *Dec. 16th.* – Colonel Clive landed with the Company's troops.
>
> *Dec. 22nd.* – Landed the Company's troops from the *Salisbury* and *Bridgewater.*
>
> *Dec. 27th.* – Colonel Clive re-embarked the Company's troops, the *seapoys* to the number of 600 marched by land.
>
> *Dec. 28th.* – Colonel Clive disembarked the Company's troops at Moyapore.

Dec. 29th. – The Admiral's ship with the *Tyger* who took the van, and *Salisbury* the rear, arrived before Bougeebougee about 7 o'clock in the morning, the *Tyger* began to cannonade the Fort, and a quarter of an hour after the *Kent*, the *Salisbury* did not come up till near 12; about 11 o'clock the Admiral made the signal for the King's troops to land, and to join some of the Company's troops we saw marching under the bank of the river; upon my landing I found they were a detachment from Colonel Clive's army composed of the Grenadier company and sepoys; Captain Pye, who commanded them, told me he had orders from Colonel Clive to take possession of the bank under the fire of the ships; but that as he was under my command, he was ready to obey what orders I pleased to give; upon which I formed the King's troops into platoons,[3] (who were by this time all arrived from the *Kent* and *Tyger*) the Company's Grenadiers in the rear of me, and divided the *seapoys* into the advanced and rear guards. I immediately advanced and took possession of two out forts the enemy had evacuated without taking away their colours. From one of the forts I could plainly see that there was a narrow road into the interior fort and that the gate was made of wooden bars, so that I thought we might enter without much difficulty, especially as the men-of-war had silenced all of their batteries; I therefore ordered a march to be beat and was advancing to storm the Fort, when word was brought to me that Captain Weller (who was my senior) was landed with the troops from the *Salisbury*, and desired I would halt till he came up, which I did, and while I was representing the situation of affairs, word was brought that a very large body of horse and foot had attacked Colonel Clive, therefore Captain Weller thought it necessary to desist from my project, and to go to the Colonel, whom we knew to be very weak, and after three miles march, we joined him; he was the drawn up in a plain, and had a smart skirmish with the enemy before he could disengage himself from some enclosures and houses that the enemy had possessed themselves of; after remaining for about an hour, we marched back to the place I had been before in possession of, and the Colonel went on board to consult with the Admiral; on his return I found we were to have a body of seamen to join us, and that we were to storm the place when night came on; all this time the enemy fired nothing but small arms at us, by which they killed and wounded some of our men. When night came on, 400 sailors came on shore under the command of Captain King; the Colonel and Major Kilpatrick were retired to rest as they had a very fatiguing march all the night before, and Captain Weller was gone sick on board; so that

I then had the command, and as my opinion was all day for storming the place, I was in hopes to have the honour of doing it, but the Colonel sent me word he'd have nothing done till the morning; upon which I went to him to represent how things stood, and that the sailors were all landed, and that our men would suffer from lying out all night; he sent me then on board the Admiral to know if he would have the sailors sent on board till morning; while I was on board a sailor that was drunk stole away to the fort gate, and fired his pistol and cried out the place was his, upon which the King's, who were next the gate, entered the fort without any opposition; thus the place was taken without the least honour to anyone; we found the fort very strong, with a wet ditch all around it, and I had the honour to command it that night.

Dec. 30th. – Re-embarked the troops, the *seapoys* marched by land.

Dec. 31st. – The Fleet proceeded up the river.

1757, Jan. 1st. – Came in sight of Tannah Fort, which the enemy had evacuated.

Jan. 2nd. – Colonel Clive landed with the Company's troops and the *Kent* and *Tyger* proceeded to Calcutta. About 9 o'clock the Fort fired smartly on the *Tyger;* she was half an hour before she could get a gun to bear; as soon as we could get our guns to bear from the *Kent* and *Tyger,* we ply'd so warmly that they left before 12 o'clock. The Admiral ordered me on shore to hoist the English colours and take the command of the Fort for His Majesty and sent me the following orders.

By Charles Watson Esq., Vice Admiral of the Blue Squadron of His Majesty's Fleet and Commander in Chief of all His Majesty's ships and vessels, employed in the East Indies, and of the marine force of the United Company of Merchants trading to and in these parts.

You are hereby required and directed to garrison the Fort of Calcutta with His Majesty's troops you have now on shore, and take care to post your sentinels and guards so as not to be surprised by the enemy. In the evening I shall be on shore, and you are not to quit your post, or deliver up your command till further orders from me. During your continuance on shore you are to take care no disorders are committed by His Majesty's troops or any other people, but to treat the natives with humanity and take particular care there is no plundering, as such offenders may depend on the severest punishment.

Given under my hand on board His Majesty's ship *Kent* off Calcutta 2nd January 1757.

CHARLES WATSON

By Charles Watson Esq., Vice Admiral of the Blue Squadron of His Majesty's Fleet and Commander in Chief of all His Majesty's ships and vessels, employed in the East Indies, and of the marine force of the United Company of Merchants trading to and in these parts.

In honour of His Majesty's colours on our success in reducing this place, you are hereby required and directed to fire a salute of twenty-one guns, for which this shall be your order.

Given under my hand on board His Majesty's ship *Kent* off Calcutta 2nd January 1757.

CHARLES WATSON

Jan. 2nd. – Sometime after, Colonel Clive came with the Company's troops.

Jan. 3rd. – The Admiral came on shore and delivered up the place to the Company. I then marched out with the King's troops and quartered in the town.

Jan. 4th. – I received orders to embark with the King's troops on board the twenty gun ship and sloop of war, and the rest of our detachment that was on board the *Salisbury* all joined except Captain Waller who was left sick on board; Major Kilpatrick with the Company's grenadiers and 170 *seapoys* were also embarked; we were in all about 200 Europeans and 170 *seapoys*.

Jan. 9th. – The ships came to an anchor off Hughly.

Jan. 10th. – The troops landed and took possession of the town, the twenty gun ship [*Bridgewater*] and sloop went abreast of the Fort and began to cannonade it, which they continued doing till about 12 o'clock at night; the Major sent me to examine the breach that the ships had made which I found practicable to enter, on which we formed two attacks, one of 50 men went to the main gate and kept a great noise with continual firing, whilst we entered privately at the breach; the sailors under Captain King, that were on shore with us, put up our scaling ladders and assisted us in getting in, which we did without any loss, for the enemy (as we had imagined) went all to the place where our false attack was made, and run away through one of the gates; we found the Fort much stronger than we first imagined and the garrison consisted of 2,000 men; we had some of our men killed and wounded before we stormed.

Jan. 11th. – I was sent into the town with 50 soldiers and 100 *seapoys* and Captain Pye with the like number to examine the houses.

Jan. 12th. – I was detached with 50 soldiers and 100 *seapoys* to burn a village about three miles from the Fort, and was to be joined by some sailors on my march. I took possession of a Portuguese convent, where I was informed that between 3 and 4,000 of the enemy were encamped behind the village that I was going to burn; however as it was a very great granary I knew it must be of very great service could I succeed: I therefore marched into the village about a mile and a half, and then ordered the *seapoys* and sailors to set fire in the rear of me as I marched back again, which I did but before I had got halfway back some of my advanced guard came running in, and told me the enemy, consisting both of horse and foot, were marching up the street, and had taken possession of several houses, and also the men-of-war's boats. As my rear was well secured by the houses being all on fire, I made no doubt but I should give a good account of them that attacked me in the front; as I could see they were all horse my 50 men were formed into three platoons, but the street was so narrow I was obliged to march by files, I therefore made every platoon into two firings and advanced by street firing very briskly upon them, but found them not so eager as they seemed to be at first.[4] Upon our first fire we killed their chief officer and four or five of their men, upon which all their horse went away, but I found they fired up the lanes upon my right flank as I marched by, I therefore ordered some of the men to fire down as we passed; as soon as I had got out of the village, I drew up the men and halted, and formed an advance and rear guard of *seapoys*, whom I found had not continued burning in my rear as I ordered them. I found the men-of-war boats all safe. In this skirmish we killed ten of the enemy and had but one sergeant wounded. Major Kilpatrick upon hearing our firing but had marched out of the garrison to support me, but the affair was over before he joined us.

Jan. 16th. – Demolished the Fort at Hughly and re-embarked.

Jan. 17th. – Sailed for Calcutta, but left the twenty gun ship and sloop behind.

Jan. 19th. – Disembarked at Calcutta, where Captain Weller took the command of the King's troops.

Jan. 23rd. – Marched out and joined Colonel Clive who was in an entrenched encampment about three miles to the northward of Calcutta.

Feb. 2nd. – Intelligence was brought that the Nabob with his army consisting of 40,000 horse and 60,000 foot, 50 elephants and 30 pieces of cannon was within a few miles of us. Our body, for I cannot call it our army, consisted of 711 men in battalion, about 100 artillery with 14 field pieces 6 pounders besides the cannon on our batteries and 1,300 *seapoys*.

Feb. 3rd. – we could see the Nabob's army marching along the road to Calcutta, and had begun to set fire to the suburbs of the town. About 4 o'clock in the afternoon we marched about two miles out of our camp with six pieces of cannon and drew up opposite to their line of march, upon which both sides began to cannonade and continued it till night; they fired from ten pieces of cannon, some of them thirty-two pounders; we had a few men killed and Captain Weller was wounded in the thigh. The enemy continued their line of march, and encamped on a plain to the eastward of the town, about four miles from us; the Colonel sent Messrs. Walsh and Scrafton to treat with the Nabob on pacific terms, who returned in the evening, having obtained nothing more than evasive answers, but were desired by the Nabob to come again the next day and matters should be settled amicably.

Feb. 5th. – About one in the morning we were joined by 600 sailors from the squadron, under the command of Captain Warwick and soon after marched to attack the Nabob's camp, our force being 500 rank and file in battalion, 800 sepoys, 600 sailors, six field pieces, one cohorn and 60 artillery men; the sepoys were divided in front and rear, the artillery were all in the rear with the sailors to guard them; about daybreak we arrived unperceived at an encampment of their horse, but the alarm was soon given, and some popping shots fired at us, upon which our *seapoys* in the front began firing but with some confusion. As I had a company of grenadiers formed out of the King's troops, and my post being next to them, I was not without some apprehension of being broke by them; I therefore endeavoured to make them advance as fast as I could and sent for a piece of cannon to come in my front; while this was doing a shower of arrows came among us with some fire rockets, one of which unfortunately fell on one of the Company's grenadiers (who were in my rear) and blew up almost the whole platoon; immediately after this a body of their choice horse came riding down upon us sword in hand; as there was a very great fog we could not perceive them until they were within ten yards of us, upon which our battalion faced to the right and gave them a full fire, which destroyed almost the whole of them; after this we kept marching through their encampment without any of their horse or elephants offering to come near us; their foot kept firing as us from several places, being dispersed up and down behind banks; about 9 o'clock the fog began to disperse, and we found ourselves nearly opposite the Nabob's quarters, which was behind an entrenchment made many years ago by the English for the defence of the town against the Morattoes. Here we could perceive their greatest force lay, and they began to cannonade us briskly; they sent some bodies of horse to surround us, but they never attempted to come near for us to fire our musketry at them; finding we could not force this part of the intrenchment we marched about a mile further in order to get over at another place; while we were marching the carriage of one of our cannon in the rear broke and we were obliged to leave it behind; soon after being pressed in the rear, and the people that drew the cannon being very much fatigued, another shared the same fate. Ensign York with a platoon of the King's was ordered from the front to the rear, in order to recover the cannon; when he arrived he found the rear in some confusion, and another piece of cannon in great danger of being taken, as there was a body of horse and foot pressing upon it; it being at some distance from the battalion; he then marched beyond the gun and drew up his platoon in the rear of it, and by keeping a constant fire secured the gun till it was drawn to the front; in this affair he had one man killed and three wounded; after we had passed the entrenchment at the place intended, we began to cannonade on both sides very briskly, and continued it for half an hour, after which we marched for Fort William, which was about a mile distant; about 5 in the evening marched out of our camp.

The Nabob sent an Embassador to treat. He began his march back to his capital Muxadavad.

[Coote at this point inserted a transcript of the peace treaty then agreed, before resuming his narrative on 14 February.]

Feb. 14th. – Broke up our camp, marched and encamped upon the bank of the river.

Feb. 18th. – Crossed the river and encamped opposite Barnagore.

March 4th. – The first division of the Bombay troop consisting of 150 men, joined us, under the command of Captain Andrew Buchannan.

March 8th. – Broke up our camp, and marched about eight miles towards Chandernagore.

March 9th. – Marched and encamped near Serampore, a Factory belonging to the Danes.

March 10th. – Marched and encamped about two miles from the French Gardens.

March 11th. – Halted; 2nd division of the Bombay troops consisting of 150 men, joined us, under the command of Captain Andrew Armstrong.

March 12th. – Marched and encamped about two miles to the westward of Chandernagore.

March 14th. – Read His Majesty's Declaration of War against the French King; the 3rd division of the Bombay troops consisting of 100 men, joined us; Colonel Clive ordered the picquets with the Company's grenadiers to march into the French Bounds, which is encompassed with an old ditch, the entrance into it a gateway with embrasures on top, but no cannon, which the French evacuated on our people's advancing; as soon as Captain Lynn (who commanded the party) had taken possession, he acquainted the Colonel, who ordered Major Kilpatrick and me, with my company of grenadiers to join Captain Lynn, and send him word after we had reconnoitred the place; on our arrival there we found a party of French was in possession of a road leading to a redoubt that they had thrown up close up under their Fort, where they had a battery of cannon, and upon our advancing down the road, they fired some shot at us; we detached some parties through a wood and drove them from the road into their batteries with the loss of some men; we then sent for the Colonel, who as soon as he joined us, sent to the camp for more troops; we continued firing at each other; in an irregular manner till about noon, at which time the Colonel ordered me to continue with my grenadier company and about 200 *seapoys* at the advance post, and that he would go with the rest of our troops to the entrance which was about a mile back. About 2 o'clock word was brought to me that the French were making a sortie; soon after I perceived the *seapoys* retiring from their post, upon which I sent to the Colonel to let him know the French were coming out. I was then obliged to divide my company which consisted of about fifty men into two or three parties (very much against my inclination) to take possession of the ground the *sepoys* had quitted; we fired pretty warmly for a quarter of an hour from the different parties at each other, when the French retreated again into their battery; on this occasion I had a gentleman (Mr. Tooke)[5] who was a volunteer, killed, and two of my men wounded; the enemy lost five or six Europeans and some blacks; by their retiring I got close under their battery and was tolerably well sheltered by an old house, where I continued firing until about 7 o'clock, at which time I was relieved and marched back to camp; this night the Colonel sent a party to take possession of the southward of the town.

March 15th. – The army marched to the southward except the party that relieved me yesterday to the northward; the commanding officer of which party sent word to the Colonel, while on the march, that the French had evacuated the battery we attacked the preceeding night, and had spiked their guns, and that he was in possession of it; we were likewise informed during our march that the French had evacuated all their batteries to the southward and had retired to the Fort; the chief of which was a half-moon battery newly erected in order to defend a narrow part of the river where they had sunk some ships in order to hinder the passage of our men-of-war. The others (three in number) were thrown up at the end of the three principal streets of the town, all which batteries we took possession of before 12 o'clock at noon, which made us masters of the town, and brought us within half a musket shot of the Fort. Colonel Clive ordered me to take the command of that advanced post with 200 Europeans and 300 *seapoys*; the enemy fired some cannon and musketry, but being covered by a number of houses they did very little execution.

March 16th. – Relieved all the posts and marched back to camp, which was in the suburbs of the town.

March 17th. – Got some cohorns and one 13 inch mortar which we played upon the Fort.

March 18th. – Continued throwing shells into the Fort and firing musketry from the tops of the houses.

March 19th. – Began to erect a battery of five 24 pounders behind the wall of a house that was close to the glacis and opposite to the south face of the south-east bastion, and mounted three 24 pounders. Admiral Watson with the *Kent, Tyger* and *Salisbury* arrived this morning from Calcutta, which they left the 14th instant, and anchored just out of gunshot from the Fort.

March 20th. – The enemy began to play upon our three gun battery, which we returned, but they soon silenced it and almost demolished the work.

March 21st. – Continued making the five gun battery and almost finished the three; when the enemy began firing warmly again at it and knocked down a veranda close by the battery, the rubbish of which choked up one of our guns, very much bruised two artillery officers, and buried several men in the ruins. Admiral Pocock and Captain Grant (of our regiment)[6] arrived from Culpee, where they had left the *Cumberland*.

March 22nd. – Finished our 5 gun battery, but got no more than 4 guns in it; the enemy in the evening found out where we were making our battery and fired very warmly on it; the detachment of the King's troops were ordered on board His Majesty's ships *Kent, Tyger* and *Salisbury*. At night Admiral Pocock hoisted his flag on board the *Tyger*.

March 23rd. – At 6 o'clock in the morning signal was made for weighing; soon after the Colonel marched with the Company's troops from camp into the town, opened the four gun battery and began to fire from the three gun battery which was tolerably well repaired; the Colonel had likewise placed musketry on several houses, who kept a continual fire on the south east bastion; at half past six the *Tyger* was under sail and stood up the river for the Fort, the *Kent* following her, and the *Salisbury* bringing up the rear; the enemy had a mud battery of six guns close to the water's edge, from which they kept a continual fire on the *Kent* and *Tyger*, as well as from the south-east and north-east bastions, which did the *Tyger* some damage, but on her coming abreast of the mud battery, the enemy spiked up their guns and retired into the Fort; at 7 o'clock the *Tyger* came to an anchor opposite the south-east, both of which bastions consisted of five guns in face and three in flank; they fired very warmly and with a good deal of success; the *Kent* very unfortunately dragging her anchor exposed her quarter to the fire of the flank of the south-west bastion; the *Salisbury* brought up in the rear. After a very warm engagement of two hours, the French having bravely defended their Fort hung out a flag of truce. Admiral Watson then ordered me on shore to know what they wanted; when I got into the Fort everything seemed in very great confusion; in about a quarter of an hour I returned to the Admiral with the Governor's son, and a letter concerning the delivery of the place.

I was ordered on shore to take possession of the Fort with a company of artillery, my own company of grenadiers, and the Company's grenadiers. During the engagement the *Kent* had three of her 32 pounders dismounted, 19 men killed and 74 wounded; among the former was Mr Perreau First Lieutenant, and among the latter Captain Speke, Mr Hay Third Lieutenant, Captain Speke's son and four or five petty officers; my detachment consisting of 30 rank and file, had nine men killed and five wounded; the larboard side (which was the side we engaged with) was hulled in 138 places, besides three or four shot through our main mast, and as many through the mizzen; the *Tyger* had 14 men killed and 56 wounded, the master being the only person of rank among the former; among the latter Admiral Pocock slightly hurt; of the King's detachment under Captain [Archibald] Grant one man killed and two wounded; the *Salisbury* had none killed or wounded, and the enemy were so much employed against the ships that the army ashore under Colonel Clive had but one man killed and ten wounded; the number of the enemy in the garrison were 500 Europeans and about 500 blacks. The Fort of Chandernagore is a regular square about three-quarters of a mile in circumference with four bastions, each of which mounts sixteen guns, besides guns on the curtain and a battery of four pieces of cannon on the top of a church, a dry fosse [ditch] round the three sides to the land, with a glacis of about forty yards; out of the northward port a small ravelin mounting five guns, and opposite the port, towards the waterside, a mud battery of six guns which flanked down the river.

March 27th. – Marched and encamped a little to the northward of Chinsura.

March 29th. – The detachment of the King's troops from the *Cumberland* consisting of about ninety men joined the camp, where the whole army continued till the 1st of May.

May 2nd. – Broke up our camp, the Bombay and Bengal troops marched to Calcutta, the King's and Madrass troops went into garrison at Chandernagore.

June 12th. – Major Kilpatrick marched from Calcutta with the military and sepoys under his command; at 5 in the afternoon embarked at Barnagore in boats and joined the Colonel at Chandernagore about 11 at night.

June 13th. – Delivered the Fort of Chandernagore to the care of Mr. Clerke (Admiral Watson's First Lieutenant who took the command of it with 100 sailors). Our army under the command of Colonel Clive consisting of 750 military (including 100 topasses) about 150 of the Train (including 50 sailors), with eight pieces of cannon 6 pounders and one hobit [howitzer] embarked in boats, the *seapoys* (being 2,100) marched to the north-ward through Hughly; about noon arrived at Niaserray; at 3 in the afternoon the *seapoys* joined us.

June 14th. – At daybreak the *seapoys* marched, and at 8 o'clock the artillery embarked; about 11 at night, the first of the boats arrived at Culnah, where we met the *seapoys*, who this day had a very fatiguing march; one *jemadar*, one *hauvildar*, and about twenty-nine of the Madrass *seapoys* deserted on the march. About 3 in the afternoon met Mr. Watts (Chief of Cossimbazar) some other gentlemen and about thirty soldiers who had made their escape from Cossimbazar.

June 15th. – The Colonel thought proper to appoint Captain Archibald Grant a Major. About 3 in the afternoon marched (the artillery only embarking) to a small creek about six miles northward of Culnah, where the guns and tumbrils were landed.

June 16th. – The whole artillery under the command of a subaltern and twenty men of the Train and the *seapoys* marched, the military embarked in the boats about 7 in the morning and landed at 4 in the afternoon; lay in a large grove by the river side; this day the Colonel appointed Captain Eyre Coote a Major.[7]

June 17th. – Embarked in the morning and landed at 4 in the afternoon; were joined here by the artillery and *seapoys*.

June 18th. – The army halted here. About 9 o'clock the Colonel ordered me with a detachment of 200 Europeans and 500 *seapoys*, one field piece 6 pounder and a hobit to march and reduce Cutwah, a fort belonging to the Nabob, distant from us about twelve miles; at noon embarked the military with the two pieces of artillery, the *seapoys* marching along the bank of the river; about 10 o'clock at night disembarked the military about three miles below Cutwah and gave orders to the officer of artillery to go with his boats in the front and proceed on to Cutwah where I should take care to secure his landing; marched on towards Cutwah where I arrived that night about 12 o'clock, took three prisoners who informed me that the enemy to the number of 2,000 had quitted the town and retired into the Fort which was at half a mile's distance, and that Rajah Monickchund (late Governor of Calcutta) was expected that night with 10,000 horse to reinforce the garrison. As soon as I had found a place proper for disembarking the artillery, I sent to the officer and ordered him to lead with all expedition, and went with a small party to reconnoitre the Fort; about this time one of the King's soldiers being suddenly taken ill grew delirious, and whilst in the agonies of death made so great a noise as to discover to the enemy where we were drawn up, on which they began firing at us pretty briskly; I then marched from thence and made a lodgement on a large bastion belonging to the town, exactly opposite the Fort, by which I secured myself from any parties of horse.

June 19th. – The officer of artillery sent me word that he could not bring the boats any higher up, most of them being aground, upon which I ordered him to land the artillery at the place where he was. At daybreak he himself came and informed me, he could not find the limber of the 6 pounder nor the wheels of the hobit carriage; at this time the enemy perceiving where we lay, began to fire on us very briskly. Finding I could have no dependence on the artillery and being apprehensive of Minickchund's arrival, I altered the plan I had before resolved on, and sent a *jemadar* (Mirza Shah Abbasbeg) with a flag of truce, to acquaint the Governor of the Fort, that, being invited by the principal men of the country, we came as friends to assist them against the tyranny of the Nabob, and notwithstanding his continual firing upon me, I had resolved not to return it (though in my power, my batteries being all ready) until I received his answer with regard to delivering up the place, which if he refused I would immediately storm and give no quarter; to which he sent me answer that as he had received the command of the Fort from the Nabob he could not deliver it up without his orders, and was resolved to defend it to the last; the *jemedar* likewise informed me that he had not been permitted to cross the river, which divides the town from the Fort, but that the Governor had come down to the waterside to him. I then formed the whole into two divisions, the Europeans making one, and the sepoys the other, and gave orders to Mootenbeg, who commanded the sepoys, to march on very briskly, cross the river, and lodge himself under the opposite bank which was about thirty yards from the Fort, and from thence to keep up a continual fire whilst the Europeans crost the river a little higher up. On our advancing the enemy fired some shot without effect, and I could perceive them running out of the Fort, which we immediately entered and found fourteen pieces of cannon of different calibers and a quantity of ammunition. The Fort of Cutwah is about half a mile in circumference, made of earth with eight round towers, situated on the bank of the Cossimbazar river, which covers the east face, with a large creek that covers the south face, which we were obliged to cross and found it very deep and rapid; this face with the other two are surrounded by a deep dry ditch having a narrow passage to walk over without a drawbridge. As soon as I had made myself master of the place, dispatched a letter to the Colonel acquainting him with it, and receiving a congratulatory letter in answer, about 2 in the afternoon he joined me. The army arrived here about 12 o'clock at night.

June 20th. – Halted here and pitched the tents, but the heavy rains prevented the men from lying in them.

June 21st. – A Council of War was held, composed of the following members – **viz.**:[8] –

Lieutenant-Colonel Robert Clive President, against an immediate action.

Majors:	*Service:*	
James Kilpatrick	Madras	against
Archibald Grant	HM 39th Foot	against
Eyre Coote	HM 39th Foot	For immediate action

Captains:		
George Frederick Gaupp	Madras	against
Alexander Grant	Bengal	for
John Cudmore	Bengal	for
Thomas Rumbold	Madras	against
Christian Fischer	Madras	against
Charles Palmer	Bombay	against

Andrew Armstrong	Bombay	for
George Grainger Muir	Bengal	for
Melchior Le Beaume	Bengal	against
Robert Campbell	Madras	for
Rudolph Waggoner[9]	Madras	against
John Corneille	HM 39th Foot	against

Richard Hater Lieutenant in the navy did not give his opinion because he thought he had not his proper seat in Council.[10]

Captain Lieutenants: Service

Peter Casters [Carstairs]	Bengal	for.
William Jennings	Artillery	against
John Francis Paschoud[11]	Madras	against
[J. W.] Molitore[12]	Bombay	against

The Colonel informed the Council that he found he could not depend on Meer Jaffier for anything more than his standing neuter in case we came to an action with the Nabob, that Monsieur Law with a body of French was then within three days march of joining the Nabob, whose army (by the best intelligence we could get) consisted of about 50,000 men, and that he called us together, to desire our opinions, whether in those circumstances it would be prudent to come to immediate action with the Nabob, or fortify ourselves where we were and remain till the *monsoon* was over, and the Morattoes could be brought into the country to join us. The question being put began with the President and eldest members, whose opinions are opposite their names; and I being the first that dissented, thought it necessary to give my reasons for doing so, which were, that as we had hitherto met with nothing but success which consequently had given great spirits to our men, I was of opinion that any delay might cast damp; secondly, that the arrival of Mr. Law would not only strengthen the Nabob's army and add vigour to their councils, but likewise weaken our force considerably, as the number of Frenchmen we had entered into our service, after the capture of Chandernagore, would undoubtedly desert to him upon every opportunity; thirdly, that our distance from Calcutta was so great, that all communication from thence would certainly be cut off, and therefore gave us no room to hope for supplies, and consequently that we must be soon reduced to the greatest distress; therefore gave it as my opinion that we should come to an immediate action, or if that was thought intirely impracticable, that we should return to Calcutta, the consequence of which must be our own disgrace and the inevitable destruction of the Company's affairs.

About an hour after we had broke up, the Colonel informed me, that, notwithstanding the resolution of the Council of War, he intended to march the next morning, and accordingly gave orders for the army to hold themselves in readiness, leaving a subaltern officer's command together with all our sick in the Fort at Cutwah.

June 22nd. – At 6 o'clock in the morning the army crossed the river and marched to a large tope about two miles' distance; at 4 o'clock in the afternoon marched and reached Plassey Grove about 12 at night; on advice that the Nabob's vanguard (consisting of 6,000 men) being within three miles of us, an advanced guard of 200 Europeans, 300 *seapoys*, and two pieces of cannon were posted at Plassey House, and several *seapoy* guards posted round the Grove.

June 23rd. – Soon after daybreak in the morning discovered the Nabob's army marching in two lines towards Plassey Grove (which we were in possession of) as if they intended to surround us; upon which we formed the line a few paces without the Grove, our army consisting of 750 men in battalion (including 100 *topasses*) which were told off into four divisions; the first division was commanded by Major Kilpatrick, the second by Major Grant, the third by Major Coote, and the fourth by Captain Guapp; we had besides 150 of the Train (including 50 sailors) eight pieces of cannon 6 pounders and one hobit, with 2,100 *seapoys,* who were formed on the right and left; the enemy took possession of the adjacent eminences with their cannon which appeared to be regularly supported by their horse and foot; and a large detachment of their army commanded by Meer Modun, (one of their chief generals), together with a body of about 40 French men, with four pieces of cannon lodged themselves within the banks of a tank, distant from us about 200 yards; from whence and the rest of their advance posts, they began to cannonade so briskly that it was adviseable we should retire into the Grove, where we formed behind the ditch that surrounded it, our left being covered by Plassey House which was close to the riverside; in this situation we cannonaded each other till 12 o'clock, when the Colonel came from Plassey House and called the Captains together in order to hold a Council of War, but changing his mind returned without holding one; the cannonading continued on both sides till about 2 o'clock when we could perceive the enemy retiring into their Lines; upon which Major Kilpatrick marched out with his division and took possession of the tank the enemy had quitted; here the Colonel joined him and sent to the grove for another detachment upon which I marched out and joined him with my division; the Colonel then sent for the King's grenadiers and a grenadier company of *seapoys* to lodge themselves behind a bank that was close upon the enemy's lines, from whence they kept a continual fire with their small arms, as we likewise did from four pieces of cannon from the tank; perceiving the enemy retire on all sides, I was ordered to march into their lines, which I entered without opposition; the remainder of the army were then ordered to march, while we pursued the enemy which we continued till it was dusk, and halted at Doudpore, about six miles from the field of battle, where the rest of the army under the command of Major Kilpatrick joined us. In this action we had six men of the artillery killed, two artillery officers and eight privates wounded, and of the King's one serjeant and one private man wounded. The Nabob's army consisted of 20,000 foot [*sic*] and 40,000 foot, had about 500 men killed, amongst whom was Meer Modun (whose death was the first occasion of their retreat); besides three elephants and a great many horses; they had 53 pieces of cannon 18 and 24 pounders all of which we got possession of. Whilst we were pursuing the enemy, a large body of horse was observed on our right, and upon our firing some shot at them, a messenger arrived with a letter to the Colonel from Meer Jaffier, acquainting him, that he (Meer Jaffier) commanded that body, and requested an interview with him that night, or the next morning.

June 24th. – Marched from Doudpore, and halted that night by a large tank; the Colonel had a meeting with Meer Jaffier, who confirmed the treaty he had before agreed to with Mr. Watts:

[A copy of the treaty then follows.]

June 25th. – Marched at daybreak and arrived at Moydepore about 11 o'clock. Meer Jaffier was proclaimed Nabob at Muxadavad.

June 26th. – Halted.

June 27th. – Halted. A subaltern officer with 30 military and 50 sepoys was sent to take possession of Cossimbazar Factory.

June 28th. – The army marched to Cossinbazar; the King's and Bengal troops quartered in the English Factory, the Madrass and Bombay troops quartered in the French Factory.

June 29th. – A detachment of 100 of the King's troops with 300 sepoys under the command of Major Grant ordered as a guard to the Commander-in-Chief to go with him to Muxadavad.

June 30th. – The detachment ordered yesterday, reinforced by the Company's Grenadiers, 200 sepoys and two field pieces, escorted Colonel Clive to Muxadauadad, the whole army ordered in readiness to march at a moment's warning.

Appendix 7

Various Contemporary Accounts of the Battle of Plassey

Robert Orme's History

Orme was not an actual eyewitness to the events described but his account is nevertheless an extremely important one since he was at the time actively engaged in writing his *History of the Military Transactions of The British Nation in Hindostan, From the Year MDCCXLV*, and so was constantly kept supplied with information by those involved; not least his friend Robert Clive. As a result, his narrative is both authoritative and includes many details which would otherwise be lost.[1]

The English army arrived and halted on the 16th at Patlee, a town on the western shore of the river of Cossimbuzar, about six miles above the junction of this with the Jelingeer river. Twelve miles above Patlee, on the same shore, is the fort of Cutwah; the walls of which were only of mud; but it commanded the passage of the river. The governor of this fort had promised to surrender after a little pretended resistance, and Major Coote was sent forward on the 17th with 200 Europeans, 500 Sepoys, one field-piece, and a small mortar, to summon the place. The town of Cutwah lies about 300 yards south of the fort, and is separated from it by the Agey, a river which takes rise in the high lands of Berbohin. The detachment landed at midnight, and found the town abandoned; but not being able to make use either of the field-piece or mortar because some of their appurtenances had been left behind, remained quiet until day-break, when Major Coote went to the bank of the river, and waved a white flag, which for some time was answered only by shot. However, the governor at length came down to the opposite bank, but instead of compliance, defied the attack. As soon as he was returned into the fort, the Sepoys crossed the river, and, under shelter of a ridge, fired

202

upon the ramparts, whilst the Europeans marched to the left, in order to ford at some distance from the fort. As soon as the garrison saw them entering the river, they set fire to a shed of matts, which had been raised to protect the walls from the sun and rain, and as soon as all parts were in a blaze, they made their escape to the northward. Within the fort, and in several granaries in the neighbourhood, was found as much rice as would sustain 10,000 men for a year. The main body of the army arrived at Cutwah in the evening, and encamped on the plain; but the next day the rainy season began with such violence, that they were obliged to strike their tents, and shelter themselves in the huts and houses of the town.

The Nabob's troops, seeing in the impending warfare no prospect of plunder, as in the sacking of Calcutta, and much more danger, clamorously refused to quit the city, until the arrears of their pay were discharged: this tumult lasted three days, nor was it appeased until they had obtained a large distribution of money. Colonel Clive had dispatched a letter every day since he left Chandernagore, informing Meer Jaffier of his progress and stations, but he had hitherto received only one letter from Jaffier, which arrived on the 17th, and was dated the day before. In this Jaffier acknowledged his seeming reconciliation with the Nabob, and his oath not to assist the English against him; but said, nevertheless, that the purport of his covenant with them must be carried into execution. This ambiguous communication, at so decisive a time, made Colonel Clive suspect that he might betray the English, by leaguing with the Nabob, and determined him not to cross the river into the island of Cossimbuzar until this doubt should be removed. The two next days passed in disappointed expectations of farther intelligence; but, on the 20th returned the messenger whom Mr. Watts had dispatched to Muxadavad on his arrival at Culnah. He reported, that he had been introduced to Meer Jaffier and his son Meirum, in a private court of their palace, into which, as soon as they began to question him, came some other persons, whom he supposed to belong to the Nabob; for as soon as they appeared, Meirum threatened to cut off his head as a spy, and the heads of all the English, if they should dare to cross the river into the island. From this report no consequences could be drawn; but in the evening arrived two letters from Meer Jaffier, dated on the 19th, one written to his agent Omarbeg, who was in the English camp, and the other to Colonel Clive. This only mentioned that he should begin his march that day from the city, and that his tent would be either on the left or the right of the army, from whence he promised to send more frequent and explicit intelligence; having hitherto been deterred by the fear of discovery, as guards were stationed on all the roads to intercept all messengers. His letter to Omarbeg contained several particulars of the reconciliation between himself and the Nabob, and gave some account of the state of the army. But neither letter explained his own designs in the field, or proposed any plan of operations for the English army. This communication, therefore, although it abated Colonel Olive's suspicions of Jaffier's treachery, did not confirm him in any reliance upon his resolution or assistance: and much confounded by this perplexity, as well as by the danger of coming to action without horse, of which the English had none, he wrote the same day to the Rajah of Burdawan, who was discontented with the Nabob, inviting him to join them with his cavalry, even were they only a thousand. But, recollecting that the princes of Indostan never join the standard which doubts of success, his anxieties increased by the dread of those imputations, to which he foresaw the present caution of his conduct would be exposed, if, after having engaged the public welfare in a project of such importance and risque, he should recede from the attempt in the very hour of event. He, therefore, determined to consult his officers, and assembled them the next day in council. They were 20, and he proposed to their consideration, 'Whether the army should immediately cross into the island of Cossimbuzar, and at all risques attack the Nabob? or whether, availing themselves of the great quantity of rice which they had taken at Cutwah, they should maintain themselves there during the rainy season, and in the mean time invite the Morattoes to enter the province and join them. Contrary to the forms usually practised in councils of war, of taking the voice of the youngest officer first, and ascending from this to the opinion of the president, Colonel Clive gave his own opinion first, which was, 'to remain at Cutwah; and then descended to the lowest according to the succession of rank. The Majors Kilpatrick and Grant were of the same opinion as himself, but Major Coote reasoned otherwise. He said, that the common soldiers were at present confident of success; that a stop so near the enemy would naturally quell this ardour, which it would be difficult to restore; that the arrival of the French troops with Mr. Law would add strength to the Nabob's force and vigour to his councils; that they would surround the English army, and cut off its communication with Calcutta, when distresses not yet foreseen might ruin it as effectually as the loss of a battle. He therefore advised, that they should either advance and decide the contest immediately, or immediately return to Calcutta.' It is very rare that a council of war decides for battle; for as the commander never consults his officers in this authentic form, but when great difficulties are to be surmounted, the general communication increases the sense of risque and danger which every one brings with him to the consultation. Thirteen officers were against, and only seven voted for immediate action. The sanction of this council in no wise alleviated the anxieties of Clive; for, as soon as it broke up, he retired alone into the adjoining grove, where he remained near an hour in deep meditation, which convinced him of the absurdity of stopping where he was; and acting now entirely from himself, he gave orders, on his return to his quarters, that the army should cross the river the next morning.

The sick were lodged in the fort of Cutwah, and at sun-rise, on the 22d, the army began to pass: all were landed on the opposite shore by four in the afternoon, at which time another messenger arrived with a letter from Jaffier, which had likewise been dispatched on the 19th, but had taken bye-roads, and was delayed by other precautions. The purport was, 'That the Nabob had halted at Muncara, a village six miles to the south of Cossimbuzar, and intended to entrench and wait the event at that place, where Jaffier proposed that the English shuld attack him by surprize, marching round by the inland part of the island.' Colonel Clive immediately sent back the messenger with this answer, 'That he should march to Plassy without delay, and would the next morning advance six miles farther to the village of Daudpoor; but if Meer Jaffier did not join him there, he would make peace with the Nabob.' Accordingly the troops proceeded before sun-set, conforming their march to the progress of the boats, which, as before, were towed against the stream; and having, by unceasing toil, advanced fifteen miles in eight hours, arrived at one in the morning at Plassy. The army immediately took possession of the adjoining grove, when, to their great surprize, the continual sound of drums, clarions, and cymbals, which always accompany the night watches of an Indian camp, convinced them that they were within a mile of the Nabob's army. His intention to remain at Muncarra, had arisen from a supposition that the English would advance immediately after they had taken Cutwah, and would arrive at Plassy before his own could get there; but as soon as he found that they were not so active, he continued his march, and arrived at the camp of Plassy twelve hours before them.

The guards and centinels being stationed, the rest of the troops were permitted to take rest. The soldiers slept; but few of the officers, and least of all the commander. On the other hand, the despondency of the Nabob increased as the hour of danger approached. Sitting in his tent in the evening of his arrival at the camp, it chanced that his attendants quitted him one after another in order to say their usual prayers at sun-set, until they left him quite alone; when a common fellow, either through ignorance, or with an intention to steal, entered the tent unperceived, until he was discovered by the Nabob; who starting from the gloomy reflections in which he was absorbed, hastily recalled his attendants with this emphatic exclamation, 'Sure they see me dead.'

The grove of Plassy extended north and south about 800 yards in length, and 300 in breadth, and was planted with mango-trees, in regular rows. It was inclosed by a slight bank and ditch, but the ditch was choaked with coarse weeds and brambles. The angle to the south-west was 200 yards from the river, but that to the north-west not more than 50. A little to the north of the grove, and on the bank of the river, stood a hunting-house of the Nabob's, encompassed by a garden-wall. The river, a mile before it reaches this house, curves to the south-west nearly in the shape of an horse-shoe, including a peninsula about three miles in circumference, of which the neck, from the stream to the stream again, is not more than a quarter of a mile across. About 300 yards to the south of the peninsula, began an entrenchment, which Roydoolub had thrown up to secure his camp: the southern face, fronting the grove of Plassy, extended nearly in a straight line, about 200 yards inland from the 1757 bank of the river; and then turning to the north-east by an obtuse angle, continued nearly in this direction about three miles. Within this entrenchment encamped the whole army, of which a part like-wise occupied the peninsula. In the angle was raised a redoubt, on which cannon were mounted. About 300 yards to the east of this redoubt, but without the camp, was a hillock covered with trees; and 800 yards to the south of this hillock and the redoubt, was a small tank or pond; and 100 yards farther to the south was another, but much larger tank: both, as all such public reservoirs of water in Bengal, were surrounded by a large mound of earth at the distance of some yards from the margin of the water.

At day-break, the enemy's army issuing from many different openings of the camp, began to advance towards the grove; 50,000 foot, 18,000 horse, and 50 pieces of cannon. The greatest part of the foot were armed with matchlocks, the rest with various arms, pikes, swords, arrows, rockets. The cavalry, both men and horses, drawn from the northern regions, were much stouter than any which serve in the armies of Coromandel. The cannon were mostly of the largest calibres, 24 and 32 pounders; and these were mounted on the middle of a large stage, raised six feet from the ground, carrying besides the cannon, all the ammunition belonging to it, and the gunners themselves who managed the cannon, on the stage itself. These machines were drawn by 40 or 50 yoke of white oxen, of the largest size, bred in the country of Purnea; and behind each cannon walked an elephant, trained to assist at difficult tugs, by shoving with his forehead against the hinder part of the carriage. The infantry and cavalry marched in many separate and compact bodies. Forty vagabond Frenchmen under the command of one Sinfray, appeared at the larger tank, that nearest the grove, with four pieces of light cannon. Two larger pieces advanced and halted on a line with this tank, close to the bank of the river. Behind these posts 5,000 horse and 7,000 foot took their station under the command of Meer Murdeen, and the son of Moonlol. The rest of the army in large columns of horse and foot extended in a curve from the left of the hillock near their camp, to the ground about 800 yards east of the southern angle of the grove of Plassy; and in this part were the troops of Meer Jaffier, Roydoolub, and Latty. In all the openings between the columns were interspersed the artillery, two, three, and four pieces together.

Colonel Clive, viewing the enemy's array from the top of the hunting-house, was surprized at their numbers, as well as the splendor and confidence of their array: but judging, that if his own troops remained in the grove, the enemy would impute the caution to fear, and grow bolder, he drew them up in a line with the hunting-house, and facing to the nearest tank. They were 900 Europeans, of whom 100 were artillery-men, and 50 were sailors; 100 Topasses, and 2,100 Sepoys; the artillery were eight field-pieces, all six-pounders, and two howitz: the Topasse were blended in the battalion with the Europeans, the sailors assisted the artillery-men. The battalion with three field-pieces on the right, and the same number on their left, were in the centre; on the right and left of which extended the Sepoys in two equal divisions. The other two field-pieces and the howitzers were advanced 200 yards in front of the left division of Sepoys, and posted behind two brick-kilns. This line extended 600 yards beyond the right of the grove; but the distance of the enemy in this quarter, prevented any danger of their falling upon the flank before whatsoever troops were ordered could fall back, and range along the east side of the grove. The first shot was fired by the enemy, at eight o'clock, from the tank; it killed one, and wounded another of the grenadier company, which was posted on the right of the battalion. This, as a signal, was followed by the continual fire of the rest of the Nabob's artillery on the plain. But most of their shot flew too high. The two advanced field-pieces answered the fire from the tank, and those with the battalion acted against the different divisions of heavy artillery on the plain; but firing out of the reach of point-blank shot, hit none of the enemy's guns; nevertheless, every shot took place, either in one or other of the bodies of infantry or cavalry. But ten for one killed, was no advantage in such a disparity of numbers, and in half an hour the English lost 10 Europeans and 20 Sepoys, on which Colonel Clive ordered the whole army to retire into the grove. The enemy elated by this retreat, advanced their heavy artillery nearer, and fired with greater vivacity than before; but their shot only struck the trees; for the troops were ordered to sit down, whilst the field-pieces alone answered the enemy's cannon from behind the bank. Explosions of powder were frequently observed amongst their artillery. At eleven o'clock Colonel Clive consulted his officers at the drum head; and it was resolved to maintain the cannonade during the day, but at midnight to attack the Nabob's camp. About noon a very heavy shower covered the plain, and very soon damaged the enemy's powder so much, that their fire slackened continually; but the English ammunition served on. The Nabob had remained in his tent out of the reach of danger, continually flattered by his attendants and officers, of whom one half were traitors, with assurances of victory; but about noon he was informed, that Meer Murdeen, the best and most faithful of his generals, was mortally wounded by a cannon-ball. The misfortune disturbed him to excess; he immediately sent for Meer Jaffier; and as soon as he entered the tent, flung his turban on the ground, saying, 'Jaffier, that turban you must defend.' The other bowed, and with his hands on his breast, promised his utmost services; and returning to his troops and associates, immediately dispatched a letter to Colonel Clive, informing him of what had passed, and advising him either to push forward in the instant, or at all events, to attack the Nabob's camp at three the next morning; but the messenger was afraid to proceed whilst the firing continued. In the mean time, the terrors of the Nabob increased continually: Roy-doolub taking advantage of them, counselled him to return to his capital: his advice prevailed, and the Nabob ordered the army to retreat into the intrenchments.

Accordingly, about two o'clock, the enemy ceased the cannonade, and were perceived yoking the trains of oxen to their artillery, and as soon as these were in motion, their whole army turned and proceeded slowly towards the camp. But Sinfray with his party and field-pieces still maintained his post at the tank. This was a good station to cannonade the enemy from, during their retreat; and Major Kilpatrick impatient to seize the opportunity, advanced from the grove with two companies of the battalion, and two field-pieces, marching fast towards the tank, and sent information of his intention, and the reason of it, to his commander, who chanced at this time to be lying down in the hunting-house. Some say he was asleep; which is not improbable, considering how little rest he had had for so many hours before; but this is no imputation either against his courage or conduct. Starting up, he ran immediately to the detachment, reprimanded Kilpatrick sharply for making such a motion without his orders, commanded him to return to the grove, and bring up the rest of the army; and then proceeded himself with the detachment to the tank, which Sinfray, seeing his party left without support, abandoned; and retreated to the redoubt of the intrenchment, where he planted his field-pieces ready to act again.

As the main body of the English troops were advancing to the tank, that part of the Nabob's army, which in the beginning of the action had formed opposite to the south-east angle of the grove of Plassy, lingered in the retreat behind the rest, and when they had passed the parallel of the grove, halted, faced, and advanced towards the north-east angle. These were the troops of Meer Jaffier; but their signals not being understood, it was supposed that they intended to fall upon the baggage and boats at the grove, whilst the English army were engaged at the tank. Three platoons of the line, whilst in march, and a field-piece, were detached to oppose them, under the command of Captain Grant and Lieutenant Rumbold; and Mr. John Johnstone, a volunteer, managed the field-piece, the fire of which soon stopped the approach of the supposed enemy.[2] Meanwhile the army being arrived at the tank, got all their field-pieces upon the mound, and from thence began to cannonade into the Nabob's camp; on which many of the troops came again out of the intrenchment, and several pieces of their artillery were likewise preparing to return; on this, Colonel Clive advanced nearer, and posted half his troops and artillery at the lesser tank, and the other half at a rising ground about 200 yards to the left of it. From these stations the cannonade was renewed with more efficacy than before, and killed many of the oxen which were drawing the artillery, which threw all the trains that were approaching into disorder. On the other hand, the Frenchmen with Sinfray plyed their field-pieces from the redoubt; and matchlocks from the intrenchments, from ditches, hollows, and every hole or shelter, as also from the bushes on the hillock east of the redoubt, kept up a constant although irregular fire, whilst the cavalry advanced several times threatening to charge sword in hand, but were always stopped and repulsed by the quick firing of the English field-pieces. Nevertheless, the English suffered as much in this, as they had during all the former operations of the day. At length the troops of Jaffier appeared moving away from the field of battle, without joining the rest of the Nabob's army; which convincing Colonel Clive who they were, he determined to make one vigorous effort for victory by attacking at once Sinfray's redoubt, and the eminence to the eastward of it, in the cover of which an ambuscade was suspected. Two divisions of the army were appointed to the two attacks, and the main body advanced in the centre ready to support both, and to act, as occasion should offer, of itself. The division on the right gained the eminence without firing or receiving a single shot. At the same time the left marched up to the redoubt, which Sinfray, finding himself again deserted by his allies, quitted without farther resistance, and without carrying off his field-pieces. Thus the whole of the English army entered the camp at five o'clock, without other obstacle than what they met from tents, artillery, baggage, and stores, dispersed around them, and abandoned by an army which out-numbered them ten to one, and were flying before them on all sides in the utmost confusion.

The cause of this sudden panic was the flight of the Nabob, who hearing that Meer Jaffier remained inactive on the plain, and that the English were advancing to storm his camp, mounted a camel, and fled at the utmost pace of the animal, accompanied by about 2,000 horsemen. The victory was decided, and was confirmed by the arrival of the messenger with the letter sent by Meer Jaffier at noon; soon after came another, whom Colonel Clive immediately returned with a note, requesting Meer Jaffier to meet him the next morning at Daudpore.

The English soldiers being told, that they should receive a donation of money, received the orders to march on to Daudpore with acclamations, nor shewed any desire to stop for the plunder which lay spread around them. They halted, however, until the commissaries had taken possession of as many oxen as sufficed for all the artillery and carriages of the army; their own being much inferior to the Nabob's. A detachment was sent forward, under Major Coote, to pursue, or rather to observe if the enemy rallied;

and the whole army arrived at eight o'clock, and rested at Daudpore. This important victory was gained with little loss. Only 16 Sepoys were killed, and 36 wounded, many of whom slightly: and of the Europeans about 20 were killed and wounded; of which number, six of the killed, and ten of the wounded, were of the artillery, as were likewise the only two officers who were wounded during the different operations of the day.

In the morning, Colonel Clive deputed Mr. Scrafton and Omarbeg to conduct Meer Jaffier to Daudpore, who received them with reserve, and an air of anxiety, as if he apprehended that the English refented his conduct, in not having joined them, conformably to his promises; he, however, immediately proceeded with them to Daudpore, accompanied by his son, Meirum, and his usual retinue. On entering the English camp, he alighted from his elephant, and the guard drew out, and rested their arms, to receive him with the usual honours. Not knowing the meaning of this compliment, he started back, as if he thought it a preparation to his destruction but Colonel Clive advancing hastily, embraced, and saluted him Nabob of Bengal, Behar, and Orixa, which removed his fears. They conferred about an hour, he making some apologies, and the Colonel no reproaches; but advised him to proceed immediately to the city, and not to suffer Surajah Dowlah to escape, nor his treasures to be plundered. Meer Jaffier returning to his troops, hastened with them to Muxadavad, and arrived there in the evening, that is, of the 24th. Colonel Clive then dispatched letters to Roydoolub, Latty, and Monickchund, and to Monickchund he promised that no enquiry should be made concerning the plunder of Calcutta. The army proceeded in the afternoon, and halted six miles beyond Daudpore.

'A Narrative of the Battle near Muxidavad,' dated 'Cossimbazar, 29 June, 1757'.
Authorship of this account is unknown, but it appears to have been written by one of Clive's staff.[3]

Messrs Boddam and Sykes must have carried to Calcutta the situation of the army at Catua on the 20th instant. The 22nd in the morning we crossed the river, and at 4 [in the] afternoon marched.

After a fatiguing march of twelve or fifteen miles the van arrived at Plassey Grove (twenty miles from Muxidevad) at 11; the rear hardly came up before 3 in the morning. We had advice that night, that the Nabob was advanced as far as Doudpoor, within four miles of us; but the accounts were afterwards contradicted, that it was only

211

Raydoolab with an advanced guard. In the morning of the 23rd, our advanced picquet perceived the enemy in possession of a camp, which Raydoolab had fortified with an entrenchment, within a mile of us, along the banks of the river, but as it may enable you and any other of your friends to conceive a better idea of it, I enclose you a sketch of the field of battle.[4] About 7 from the top of the brick house we perceived the enemy moving out of their camp, some few advanced along the bank of the river, but their main body as you see marked in the plan; at this time our two battalions lay upon their arms, as they did all night, their front towards the river and their right towards the brick house, without the Grove fronting the Nabob's camp; the sepoys most in the Grove, our picquet with two pieces of cannon to the northward of the Grove, fronting the Nabob's camp. We were likewise informed that the body of the enemy which was in sight, had no cannon with them. On thus seeing them in motion, we formed our whole line a few yards to the northward of the Grove, our left close to the brick house, and our right extending beyond the Grove. We were scarcely drawn up in this manner, when a 24 lb. shott from their camp, bounding along, and carrying off the arm of one of the King's granadiers, convinced us that their cannon was come up. Finding we were thus exposed to their heavy artillery, at a distance too great for ours to annoy them much, the battalions and sepoys were ordered to retire and lye upon their arms within the bank of the Grove, fronting the enemy as before and drawn up in the same order. Our houbitz was advanced about half way to the first Tank, and our eight guns properly divided in the intervals, betwixt the battalions and sepoys but advanced a little distance without the banks of the Grove. In this situation our men lay in pretty good security from the cannonadement, and as the enemy advanced out towards our right, which they now begun to do in vast multitudes, our artillery played upon them pretty briskly, though the distance was still too great. The enemy's cannon moved along, and in front of their main body, in such a manner that their whole front was almost covered with the bullocks that drew them. They filed off to their left till they covered the ground you see marked in the plan, and every now and then made a halt to turn their artillery upon us; then proceeded small bodies advanced to the two Tanks, and they brought some of their cannon down along the banks of the river, and from thence played very briskly. We perceived amongst them numbers of Europeans, and as we afterwards found about fifty French had possession of that part. In this situation we continued cannonading till 2 [in the] afternoon; the artillery being most exposed suffered considerably. About 12 a heavy shower of rain came on, we had some apprehension that the enemy would take advantage of this opportunity, and make a push with their horse, but our guns continued to play very briskly, prevented any such motion. The enemy's guns during the rain which lasted half an hour did not fire a shott. The enemy whether from the smartness of the fire from our guns, or some of their chiefs being killed, or what other motive, begun at this time to retire, and withdraw their cannon within their entrenchments. The opportunity of attacking them in such a situation was too great to be neglected. Accordingly Major Kilpatrick advanced to the first Tank with two pieces of cannon, covered with the King's granadiers, and three platoons from the right of the battalion. The few of the enemy who possessed it soon retired from this advantageous post; our two guns put them in some disorder, but notwithstanding they filed off again to their left, and brought such of their cannon out of their camp as they had retired. They extended their line still further to their left than they had done before, which gave us reason to apprehend they had intentions to enter the Grove to the southward, but our sepoys, moving to our right, put a stop to it. The enemy's cannonadement beginning afresh the Colonel moved up with two pieces of cannon more to the Tank. A little before this our whole line moved out some distance on the Plain, but finding they did not attempt any push on the Tank, they were again ordered to retire into the Grove, to save them from the enemy's cannon. Our four guns from the top of the Tank, being a rising ground, played upon the enemy, who covered the Plain with their numbers and at no very great distance, with vast success. They had got possession of the second Tank with horse and burgundasses or gunmen, (as many as it could hold or cover themselves from our cannon behind it), and from thence with their musquetry wounded several of our men: amongst them Lieutenant Cassells and Holts of the Train, but slightly. The body of the enemy stood in this manner exposed to our guns; they endeavoured to use theirs but as we perceived them turn them towards us, we took care to fire on those parts, which put their bullocks in such confusion that we received but few shott; their cannonadement slacked gradually and ours rather quickened. It seemed now time to possess ourselves of the second Tank, though the fire of musquetry from thence was very warm. The detachment at the first Tank with some sepoys in front (being ordered) accordingly rushed on, fired on the enemy when they got to the top, and drove them off with such precipitation that their whole army, (seeing the fury with which we advanced and they

213

not following) abandoned their guns, took to their heels, and left us masters of the field and their entrenchments. We pursued as close as order could permit, by which means the pannick so seized the Nabob and most of his army that before 12 that night he and them arrived at Muxidavad, leaving behind them scattered on the road most of their carriages and baggage. They left us forty-two pieces of cannon, mostly large and the bullocks in the draught. Thus we obtained a victory with about 1,000 military, a third hardly Europeans, and 2,000 sepoys, without the assistance of the expected junction of Jaffer Ally Khan, against 40,000 Gunmen and 20,000 Horse, as we are since informed by Monloll the Nabob's Prime Minister and dewan. We had killed and wounded Europeans and sepoys 80, and by Jaffer Ally Khan's own account the enemy had 500 killed, and as many wounded, amongst them several chief jemidars. The Nabob made his escape next morning from Muxidevad and Jaffer Ally Khan waited on Colonel Clive, and is now proclaimed Nabob.

Captain John Corneille's Account

Corneille (an Irishman) was a lieutenant in HM 39th Foot when he arrived in Bengal aboard HMS *Cumberland* and was immediately given a brevet promotion to captain in order to cover for the wounded Captain Weller.[5]

The city of Murchidabad is situated on a large island made by two branches of the Ganges. We had hitherto pursued our route on the opposite side but on 22 June, after the forementioned resolution, we crossed the river and advanced to the enemy with no impediment in the way to hinder our meeting. We made a forced march this day in order to reach a grove near which we were informed some of the nabob's army had encamped, but our intelligence was very vague and little to be depended on. It was twelve at night before the first division of the of the army arrived, having a rear of upwards of three miles in length, our men fatigued to the last degree. Altogether we were in such a situation as would have made us an easy prey to four hundred men of any spirit that dared to have attacked us. But the enemy we had to encounter were luckily not of that stamp.

On our arrival we had certain information that the nabob with his whole army was encamped within two miles of us. Piquets consisting of two captains and two hundred men were sent to take possession of a pleasure house belonging to him, called Plassey, situated about two hundred yards from the grove. This was done without meeting any opposition. Thus we remained all that night, the whole army lying on their arms.

The 23rd June about six o'clock in the morning, our spies brought us word that the nabob had drawn his army out of their camp and was moving towards us, on which the whole was ordered under arms. The Europeans from the time we had set out had been divided into two battalions and were now drawn up accordingly, the first on the right (in which was the detachment of our regiment) and the second on the left. Each battalion was subdivided into two grand divisions with an equal proportion of artillery, and the sepoys were distributed on the right and on the left. In this order we marched to that side of the grove which faced a fine extensive plain. Our left was covered by the house of Plassey, our rear by the grove. About four hundred yards in our front was a pond, well banked and apparently a post of strength, situated not very far from the first entrenchment of the nabob's camp.

Scarcely were we drawn up when we received the fire of the enemy's cannon, which killed two of the King's grenadiers. On that we were ordered to retire into the grove and cover ourselves behind a bank which surrounded it. The enemy soon took possession of the pond in our front, from whence they plied us with grape and kept a very warm and brisk fire on the grove with their heavy artillery, consisting of thirty-two, twenty-four and nine pounders, but as we were sheltered behind the bank it did little execution.

The plain seemed covered with their army, consisting of horse, foot, some Europeans whom we since learned numbered about fifty, elephants and camels – affording us a grand, though terrible, prospect. As they were drawn up, except for some few advanced parties, at too great a distance for our short sixes to do any execution, out hobit was advanced two hundred yards in the front and fired with success. But a party of horse made a movement as if they intended to seize it and the men were ordered back for fear of bringing on a general engagement – which at that time was not thought expedient. However, from the grove we returned their fire, which was very heavy and would have annoyed us much but for the shelter we had luckily found there. Their movements gave us a reason to imagine that they intended surrounding us in order to make a general attack, and this seemed all the more likely when there fell a heavy shower of rain that might have been expected to render our firearms useless. But this was a case of our own apprehensions forming schemes for the enemy that they themselves never thought of.

At twelve o'clock it was reported that a party had attacked our boats and were destroying them. This sounded true, as it would then have been the most effectual thing they could have done to distress us, and might easily have been accomplished since the guard left to secure them was but small and they were about a quarter of a mile from the grove. The picquets of the night before were ordered to reinforce them but the report proved false and the orders were countermanded.[6]

The enemy's fire now began to slacken and, shortly after, entirely ceased. In this situation we remained until two o'clock, when it was perceived that they were leaving the field, returning to their camp. Part were even in camp. The lucky moment was seized and the company of grenadiers belonging to the first battalion, with a couple of guns and some sepoys, were ordered to take possession of the pond which the enemy had held that morning. This was immediately executed without any loss, the enemy having quitted it some time before. Four platoons from the same battalion were ordered up to support them. Then the grenadiers with some sepoys were sent to take possession of a post about two hundred yards nearer the enemy's camp.

When we made these motions the enemy halted and immediately sent a strong party of horse towards our grove as if with intention to cut off the communication between our advanced parties and main body and took possession of a rising grund a little distance from the pond. There steps were the most prudent that they could have taken, we had just reason to expect a vigorous attack. We fired now with great success, they being within full reach of our cannon. At this period, orders were sent for the whole army to march out of the grove, but then it was considered that all our ammunition was there and that the enemy's party of horse seemed to be tending that way, so the orders were countermanded except for four platoons of the second battalion and two more guns. The enemy by this time had got some of their cannon to bear on us and plied us with small-arms fire from the first entrenchment of their camp as well as from their advanced party on the rising ground. But they had little effect, for our grenadiers' fire was so very warm as to prevent their returning it otherwise than in hurry and confusion, and their cannon was of little use, being large unwieldy pieces moved with great difficulty and most of them already lodged in their camp.

In this situation we remained about half an hour, when our cannon – which was very well served that day – seeming to have thrown them into some confusion and having, as we afterwards learned, killed their principal general and three or four of their elephants, the grenadiers with the platoons from the pond were ordered to drive the enemy from their advanced post on the rising ground. This was done with little danger, as they abandoned it as soon as it became clear we were making the attempt. From that moment they never more made head against us. We immediately pursued them into their camp and they as fast fled from it. Here we found most of their heavy cannon, some with upwards of a hundred oxen yoked to them, others dismounted, and all in the utmost confusion. That body of horse which had moved towards the grove in our first attempt, and on whom we still continued to fire, belonged we were now informed, to our friend – being commanded by Mir Jafar. We had orders immediately to desist.

Our whole army now marched out of the grove and continued to pursue until five o'clock in the evening. Not having horse, this answered no other purpose than to keep up the panic which had made them so easy a conquest to our arms. This was manifest in the great confusion in which they fled, leaving all their cannon behind amounting to upwards of fifty pieces. According to their own account, they had above one hundred thousand fighting men in the field that day of whom we killed and wounded about five hundred. Our loss was very inconsiderable, not above seventy. We continued the pursuit to a small village about six miles from the field of battle, where we lay that night. Thus ended the battle of Plassey, which left us without obstacle masters of fulfilling our intentions.

Letter from Mr. Vernet to the Dutch Director and Council, Hugli, 24 June 1757

George Lodowijk Vernet was the Dutch factor at Cossimbazar. Whilst not an eyewitness to the battle he provides some useful information on the aftermath.

The purport of this is only to inform you, that the English army having encamped the day before yesterday in the groves of Plassey, being attacked yesterday morning by the vanguard of the Nawab, consisting of 15,000 men, commanded by Mohonlaal, Meer Modum, Manik Chand, Coja Haddie, and Nauwe Singh Hazarie, the English offered such a vigorous resistance that the Moors were compelled to quit the field and retreat to Mangor Parra where the Nawab had pitched his tents. The English lost but few men and were, therefore, encouraged to resume the attack without leaving the foe much time for consideration, in which they succeeded so well, that the Nawab's entire army was completely routed. The Nawab arrived with his defeated hordes, after a hurried and disorderly flight, at Moorshedabad about midnight, but Jafar Ali Khan, Rajah Durlabh Ram and Khodadad Khan Latty have joined the English, so it is said, with the view of besieging the Nawab who holds Mansurganj (which he has had fortified) and to proclaim Jafar Ali Khan Nawab.

In the first attack there were sixty Frenchmen and several Portuguese, commanded by Monsieur St. Frais, late Secretary of that nation, and an officer at the head of the army, of whom until now but twenty common soldiers have come in. The others are supposed to have been killed, and taken prisoners. Of the Chiefs of the Nawab's army Mir Madan and Nouw Singh Hasarie have perished, Mohan Lal, Manikchand and Coja Haddie have been wounded.

We have the honour to be, with great respect, &c., &c.

Appendix 8

Orme's Account of the Pursuit of the French up the Ganges

This expedition, which saw Major Eyre Coote and Captain Alexander Grant lead a small detachment over 300 miles up the Ganges beyond Patna in what turned out to be an unsuccessful attempt to capture or destroy a French force under M. Jean Law, does not, strictly speaking, form a part of the Plassey campaign but it is not devoid of interest.[1]

The party of Frenchmen, with Mr. Law, advanced from Boglipore as soon as they received the last summons of Surajah Dowlah, but so late, that they had not passed Tacriagully, when they heard some confused reports of the battle of Plassy, on which Mr. Law halted, waiting for more certain information. Had he immediately proceeded 20 miles farther, he would the next day have met and saved Surajah Dowlah, and an order of events, very different from those which we have to relate, would in all probability have ensued. After waiting two days at Tacriagully, Mr. Law received intelligence that he was taken; on which he immediately marched back into Behar, intending to offer his service to Ramnarain, the vice-nabob of the province.

Of all the Gentoos whom Allaverdy had raised to high appointments, Ramnarain seems to have been the only one, whose gratitude had not been estranged by the despotic caprices of Surajah Dowlah. But they were connected by the same resentments: for, whilst Surajah Dowlah was harbouring grudge against Meer Jaffier at Muxadavad, Ramnarain was at variance with a brother, and a brother-in-law of Meer Jaffier, who held considerable employments at Patna.

The knowledge of this animosity had deterred Roydoolub, although connected with Ramnarain by religion as well as business,

219

from attempting to gain his concurrence to the confederacy; nor does it appear that Ramnarain knew any thing of it until it was brought to the point of decision. In the mean while, he regarded the party with Mr. Law as an important resource to Surajah Dowlah, in case hostilities should be renewed with the English, and had accordingly supplied them, although secretly, with the means of subsistence ever since they had retreated into his province. The new regency at Muxadavad had, therefore, no reason to expect his willing acquiescence to the revolution, or not to suspect that he would not entertain the party with Mr. Law, and even strengthen himself still more by alliances with the neighbouring powers to the westward. The best means of averting these consequences consisted in sending a detachment expedite and strong enough to destroy the French party before they reached Patna, or a force sufficient to deter Ramnarain from taking them into his pay when they should arrive there.

Meer Jaffier, notwithstanding the seeming acquiescence of the soldiery to his accession, was afraid to trust any considerable body of them at a distance, and especially in the precarious province of Behar; but was ashamed to acknowledge his mistrust, which Clive penetrated, and determined to undertake the expedition with the English troops alone. The detachment consisted of 230 Europeans, three companies each of 100 Sepoys, 50 Lascars, and two field-pieces, both six-pounders, and Major Coote was appointed to the command. The baggage, stores, carriages, ammunition, and provisions, were laden in 40 boats, all of which were very ill equipt, whether with rowers or tackle; and, nevertheless, were not ready before the 6th of July, when they left Muxadavad; by which time the French party had got half-way to Patna. [At this point Orme turns to events in Murshidabad before resuming]

… interval continual advices had been received from Major Coote of the progress of his detachment, which had met with even more interruptions than might have been expected from the insufficiencies of the outset. The boats, for want of rowers, could not be towed as fast as the troops marched on shore, which obliged him, before they arrived at the head of the island of Cossimbuzar, to take 87 men out of three large trading boats which were coming down the river. On the 10th of July, which was the 4th day after their departure from Muxadavad, the troops, and on the 11th the boats, arrived at Rajahmahal, 40 miles beyond Muxadavad, where a brother of Meer Jaffier commanded; he had sent 120 horse to meet the detachment on the road, and promised every other kind of assistance, but afforded none. However, after five days delay, the boats were repaired, but the horsemen refused to proceed without two months pay, which Major Coote had neither money or orders to furnish: he therefore continued his march without them on the 13th, and on the 18th arrived at Boglipore, which is 65 miles from Rajahmahal.

Here he received intelligence, that Mr. Law's party had four days before passed the city of Patna, which is 55 miles beyond Boglipore. Major Coote left this place on the 19th, and was followed the next day by 60 horsemen, sent by the governor under the command of his son. On the 21st, the horsemen, troops, and boats, arrived at Mongheir, which by the road is 35 miles farther. The garrison, on the appearance of the detachment, who expected to have been admitted into the fort, manned the ramparts, and shewed their lighted matches, which obliged the troops to march round the walls. On the 23d they arrived at Burhia, 30 miles farther on. By this time so many mischances had happened to the fleet of boats, several having been lost, others stranded, and some continually breaking from the towing lines, that Major Coote landed the field-pieces and ammunition at Burhia, and the same evening proceeded six miles farther to Darriapore. At two in the afternoon of the next day the troops arrived at Panarack, 11 miles farther. During this march all the European soldiers were holding mutinous language in complaints of their hardships and fatigues. Major Coote, impatient to reach Patna, resolved to reserve their chastisement until he arrived there, but, as an immediate disgrace, put them all into the boats, and the same evening marched himself at the head of the Sepoys 5 miles farther to the town of Bhar. Proceeding with them the next day, which was the 25th, whilst the Europeans were following at leisure, he arrived at night at Futwah, which is 26 miles from Bhar, and only seven from Patna. During this day's march he received two letters, and they were the first, from Ramnaraim, apologizing for the escape of the French party, and imputing it to the want of timely notice from Meer Janier. Soon after a deputation of his principal officers arrived at Futwah, under the pretence of compliment , but in reality to observe the force, and discover the intentions of Major Coote. They informed him that Ramnarain had returned only two days before from an expedition against two disobedient chiefs of Moy and Sader, whose districts lay about fifty miles south-east of Patna; that immediately on his return he had proclaimed Meer Jaffier Nabob of Bengal, Behar, and Orixa; that he had sent forward 2000 of his troops, horse and foot, in pursuit of Mr. Law, and that he had disbanded the greatest part of the rest. The next day, the 26th, at ten in the forenoon, the whole detachment, as well as the boats, arrived at the English factory, which is a spacious building situated on the bank of the river, just without the western wall of the city. Major Coote immediately prepared to visit Ramnarain, but was prevented by a message, desiring him to take some repose, and to defer his visit until the next day: in the afternoon three Europeans and some Sepoys, who were leading some cattle to the factory, were, without provocation, assaulted and wounded by a number of Peons belonging to the garrison. Complaint was immediately made to Ramnarain, who shewed no inclination to redress the outrage; and moreover desired Major Coote not to visit him, as was intended, the next day, lest the ceremonial should give occasion to quarrels betwixt their respective attendants. An English officer, likewise, walking in the town, overheard two men of condition, who did not suppose him to understand their language, talking of a design to massacre the English detachment. In the night many of the Europeans got drunk, and 30 of the most disorderly, who had likewise been foremost in the mutiny on the road, were selected, and confined for punishment.

The next day Major Coote conferred with Mahmud Amy, the brother, and Meer Cossum, the brother-in-law, of Meer Jaffier. They informed him that the French party might easily have been stopped, if Ramnarain had so willed; that, on hearing of the death of Surajah Dowlah, he had sent to Sujah Dowlah, the neighbouring and powerful subah of Oude, proposing to render himself independent of Bengal, if Sujah Dowlah would assist him with his forces, and requesting him to protect the French party on the frontiers, until it, might be necessary to recall them to Patna; that Sujah Dowlah encouraged his views, but was prevented by events, which more immediately concerned himself, from marching with his army into Bahar. They likewise asserted that Ramnarain had consulted his confidents on the means of destroying the English detachment. This information determined the Major to proceed with all expedition to the frontiers of Oude.

The next day the 30 mutineers were tried and flogged; this punishment was judged adequate to their offence, because of the great fatigues they had endured: for they had marched from Rajamahol to Patna in eleven days and a half, without the intermission of one day's halt, and the distance, measured by a perambulator, is 201 miles.

A day passed in making preparations for the outset; but all the attendants of the camp, and many of the boatmen, finding they were to go farther, took fright and ran away; and it was impossible to collect others without the assistance of the government, which Ramnarain promised, but did not supply half the requisite number. However in this and the succeeding day all the boats, as well as the troops, assembled at Bankipore, a garden belonging to the company about five miles from the city, and on the same side of the river. The next day the detachment moved six miles farther to Dinapore, and, the day after, which was the first of August, joined the troops which Ramnarain pretended to have sent forward in pursuit of Mr. Law, with whom they halted at Moneah, a considerable town fifteen miles from Dinapore, situated at the confluence of the river Soan with the Ganges, where Hybutjung, their commander, refused to proceed any farther. The troops of the detachment, with their ammunition, crossed the Ganges, and marched on the other side, whilst the bullocks, baggage, and attendants, crossed the Soan, and proceeded along the southern side of the Ganges until they came opposite to Chuprah, when it took three days to ferry them over; for the bed of the river is in this part three miles broad, and the officer of the district failed to furnish the boats and other assistances he had promised. At Chuprah the company have a house established to collect saltpetre, of which great quantities are made in this, and some of the neighbouring districts. Here intelligence was obtained, that the several Chiefs in this part of Behar had enlisted forces to assist Ramnararn; and spies reported that they had left Mr. Law's party at Benarez, which is by the road at least 140 miles beyond Chuprah, and that they were supplied there by Bulwansing, the Rajah of the district, who was dependant on Sujah Dowlah the subah of Oude. Farther pursuit was evidently vain, but certain of producing immediate hostilities with Sujah Dowlah, whose territory commenceth at the river Dewah, which disembogues into the Ganges 18 miles to the west of Chuprah. The Major, therefore, resolved to wait here for farther orders, and on the 12th received a letter from Colonel Clive, instructing him, as a scheme of Meer Jaffier's, to return to Patna, and endeavour, in concert with Mahmud Amy Cawn, to wrest the government from Ramnarain. The troops, leaving the baggage to follow, embarked early the next morning; and such is the strength of the stream at this season of the year, that they arrived at Patna by noon, although the distance along the course of the river is 44 miles. It appeared to the Major that the only means of executing his instructions would be to assault the citadel, in which Ramnarain always resided, and at this time only with 2000 men; but Mahmud Amy represented that their force was not sufficient to invest it so closely as to prevent Ramnarain from escaping by some of the secret passages, and proposed to defer the attempt until he himself should be joined by 1500 of Ramnarain's troops, whom he had engaged to desert.

But by this time Ramnarain had taken the alarm, probably by information from his friends at Muxadavad of the orders sent to Major Coote and Mahmud Amy, which, confirmed by the hasty return of the detachment from Chuprah, frightened him so much, that he now spared no attentions to the Major, and received his visit with much affectation of complacence. Two days after, the Major received a letter from Meer Jaffier, fraught with suspicions that Mahmud Amy had borne false witness against Ramnarain, as a pretext for levying forces, with the intention of seizing the government for himself. Enough has not been discovered of the secrets of Jaffier to account for this abrupt change and contradiction of an opinion, which had hitherto been the greatest anxiety in his mind. His letter, however, precluded all farther intentions of hostility; and on the 22d a conference was held by appointment in the citadel, to discuss and reconcile all differences. Major Coote and the two brothers, Mahmud Amy and Meer Cossim, came each with strong escorts, and Ramnarain was attended by all his principal officers. The two brothers, with the calmness peculiar to the manners of Indostan, accused him of a design to assassinate them, which indeed had been reported in the city; then of his intention to rebel against Meer Jaffier, in proof of which they urged his connivance at the passage of the French troops through Behar, the oaths he had taken from the officers of his army, his correspondence and proposals to Sujah Dowlah. Ramnarain solemnly denied all these accusations, and produced a letter he had just received from Sujah Dowlah, which indicated no such intentions as were imputed to their correspondence: he then said, it was true, that he had been attached to the late Nabob, because his fortunes had been raised by the princes of his family; but now that Surajah Dowlah was no more, and none of his family remaining worthy or capable of the government, on whom should he so naturally wish to depend as on Meer Jaffier, whom their common patron, Allaverdy, had raised so near his own person and dignity. He then called a bramin, and, in the presence of his officers, and a crowd of attendants, solemnly swore allegiance and fidelity to Meer Jaffier, and friendship and good-will to Meer Cossim and Mahmud Amy. The two brothers returned the compliment, by taking an oath on the koran that their heart was clear of all ill-will to Ramnarain, and should continue so.

They then embraced him, and all the three Major Coote, as the mediator of this reconciliation. Nevertheless, neither side believed the other, but each wished to gain time, and to wait events: for Ramnarain knew that the orders from Muxadavad would prevent Major Coote and the brothers of Meer Jaffier from acting against him at present; and they knew that he, disappointed of the assistance of Sujah Dowlah, would be submissive until he was better prepared to assert independence.

Before this conference Meer Jaffier had determined to recall the detachment; but Major Coote did not receive the orders to return until the beginning of September, and in the interval the troops remained, uninterrupted by any alarms, in the company's factory adjoining to the city. All proceeded in the boats, which left Patna on the 7th of September, and arrived in seven days at Muxadavad, although the distance is 300 miles.

Appendix 9

A General Return of all the Troops Under the Command of Lieutenant-Colonel Robert Clive

Bengal, 22nd February 1757

	King's	Coast Establishment	Bengal Establishment	Train	Total
Officers Doing Duty					
Lieutenant-Colonel	-	1	-	-	1
Major	-	-	1	-	1
Captains	1	3	4	1	9
Captain-Lieutenants	-	-	1	1	2
Lieutenants	3	4	2	3	12
Ensigns	3	6	13	-	22
Adjutants	-	1	1	1	3
Quartermasters	-	1	1	-	2
Voluntiers	-	5	8	-	13
Officers Sick					
Captains	1	3	1	-	5
Lieutenants	-	1	-	-	1
Ensigns	-	-	1	-	1
Voluntiers	-	2	-	-	2

Non-Commissioned Officers and Centinels Doing Duty

Serjeants	5	35	12	6	58
Corporals	6	23	12	7	48
Drummers	5	14	2	3	24
Centinels (Europeans)	123	242	36	-	401
Centinels (Topasses)	-	-	91	-	91
Bombardiers	-	-	-	21	21
Gunners	-	-	-	19	19
Mattrosses	-	-	-	43	43
Total	*139*	*314*	*153*	*99*	*705*

Non-Commissioned Officers and Centinels Sick

Serjeants	-	4	6	2	12
Corporals	-	6	2	-	8
Drummers	-	1	4	-	5
Centinels (Europeans)	14	58	16	-	88
Centinels (Topasses)	-	-	17	-	17
Bombardiers	-	-	-	3	3
Gunners	-	-	-	4	4
Mattrosses	-	-	-	7	7
Total	*14*	*69*	*45*	*16*	*144*

Total of the whole

	153	383	198	115	849

Casualties

Entertained	-	2	15	1	18
Deceased	11	43	4	9	67
Discharged	-	-	1	1	2
Deserted	2	6	-	-	8
Killed	6	26	4	4	40
Wounded	9	51	8	10	78
Missing	-	-	-	1	1

Killed

Captain Dugald Campbell
Do. Timothy Bridge
Do. William Pye

Ensign Charles Kerr
Volunteer Davidson
Mr William Belchies, Secretary to the Army

Wounded
Captain Nicholas Weller
Do. Geo. Fred. Gaupp
Do. John Fraser
Do. Thos. Rumbold
Capt. Lieut. Peter Carstairs
Ensign William Ryder
Do. William Ellis
Volunteer Dundas
Do. Stibber

Appendix 10

A General Return of the Sepoys Under the Command of Lieutenant-Colonel Robert Clive

Bengal, 22nd February 1757

	Coast Establishment	Bengal Establishment	Total
Doing Duty			
Subadars	9	4	13
Jemadars	29	13	42
Havildars	63	25	88
Naiks	64	32	96
Colourmen	21	12	33
Tom-Toms	16	-	16
Trumpeters	8	1	9
Seapoys	713	371	1,084
Total	*923*	*458*	*1,381*
Sick			
Subadars	-	-	-
Jemadars	2	-	2
Havildars	6	-	6
Naiks	4	-	4
Colourmen	-	-	-
Tom-Toms	-	-	-
Trumpeters	-	-	-
Seapoys	67	-	67
Total	*79*	*-*	*79*

Total of the			
whole	1,002	458	1,460
Casualties			
Deceased	14	-	14
Killed	12	6	18
Wounded	49	6	55

Appendix 11

A General Muster Of The Troops Under The Command Of Colonel Clive In Camp Near Chinsura

Chinsura, 7th April 1757

	Major	Captains	Captain-Lieutenant	Lieutenants	Ensigns	Adjutants	Quartermasters	Volunteers	Serjeants	Corporals	Drummers	Europeans	Topasses	Total
King's Troops														
Captain Grant's	-	1	-	1	2	-	-	-	3	3	2	72	-	80
Do. Weller's	-	1	-	1	2	1	-	-	3	3	2	71	-	79
Do. Cooote's	-	1	-	2	1	-	1	-	2	4	3	70	-	79
Madrass Troops														
Grenadiers –														
Captain Lin	-	1	-	3	-	-	1	2	6	5	2	65	-	78
Major Kilpatrick's	1	-	-	-	-	-	-	-	4	3	2	26	-	35
Captain Maskelyne's	-	-	-	1	1	1	-	3	3	5	3	60	-	71
Do. Callender's	-	-	-	-	1	-	-	-	3	3	-	32	-	38
Vacant Company	-	-	-	-	-	-	-	-	3	3	2	17	-	25
Captain Gaupp's	-	1	-	1	2	-	-	-	7	6	4	60	-	77
Supernumerary's	-	3	-	-	-	1	-	-	15	1	1	11	-	28

	Major	Captains	Captain-Lieutenant	Lieutenants	Ensigns	Adjutants	Quartermasters	Volunteers	Serjeants	Corporals	Drummers	Europeans	Topasses	Total
Bengal Troops														
Captain Grant's	-	1	-	1	2	-	-	3	3	2	1	9	29	44
Do. Muir's	-	1	1	-	2	-	-	3	3	5	2	25	25	60
Do. Cudmore's	-	1	-	-	3	-	-	3	3	1	1	20	43	68
Do. Fraser's	-	1	-	1	2	1	1	3	9	6	6	51	66	138
Bombay Troops														
Captain Buchanan's	-	1	-	1	1	-	1	2	12	10	3	66	56	147
Do. Armstrong's	-	1	-	1	1	-	-	-	9	9	3	64	61	146
Total	1	14	1	13	20	4	4	19	88	69	37	719	280	1,193

MEMORANDUM.

There are returned in the above Muster, 3 Captains, 1 Captain-Lieutenant, 1 Lieutenant, 1 Ensign and 132 Military (being 11 Serjeants, 11 Corporals, 2 Drummers, 79 Europeans, and 29 Topasses) who are sick in the Hospital. Pay Rolls exact with the above Muster, allowing casualties. There have been 1 Serjeant, 3 European Centinels, and 6 Topasses died since the 15th of March who are drawn pay for this month. There are missing and deserted, 6 European Centinels and one Topass (being 1 European from Captain Buchanan's Company, 4 Europeans from Captain Armstrong's, 1 European and 1 Topass from Captain Cudmore's, and 1 European from Captain Fraser's).

OFFICERS' NAMES TO THE COMPANYS AS THEY STAND IN ORDER

King's Troops	Captain Grant, Lieutenant Corneille, Ensigns Adnett and Blair
Do.	Captain Weller, Lieutenant Pierson as Lieutenant and Adjutant, Ensigns Yorke and Balfour
Do.	Captain Cote, Lieutenant Bush as Lieutenant and Quartermaster, Lieutenant Power, Ensign Fenton
Madrass Troops	Grenadiers Captain Lin, Lieutenant Campbell as Lieutenant and Quartermaster, Lieutenants Knox and Tuite
Do.	Major Kilpatrick to his Company
Do.	Captain Maskelyne's Company – Lieutenant Scotney as Lieutenant and Adjutant, Ensign Stenger

Do.	Captain Callender's Company – Ensign Tabby
Do.	Do. Gaupp's do. Captain Gaupp, Lieutenant Joecher, Ensigns Oswald and Wiecks
Do.	*Supernumerarys.* – Captains Rumbold, Wagner and Fischer, Captain Fraser as Adjutant
Bengal Troops	Captain Grant, Lieutenant Dyer, Ensigns DeLubers and Varelst
Do.	Captain Muir, Captain-Lieutenant Carstairs, Ensigns Maclean and Ellis
Do.	Captain Cudmore, Ensigns Demee David, Prichard and Champion
Do.	Captain Fraser, Lieutenant Keir, Ensigns Gibbons and Barnes
Bombay Troops	Captain Buchanan, Lieutenant Walsh, Ensign Robertson, Mr McLean, Quartermaster, Captain Armstrong, Lieutenant Palmer, Ensign Tottingham, Lieutenant Corneille of the King's Troops appointed to do duty as Captain

Appendix 12

A General Muster of the Troops in the Train Under the Command of Colonel Clive in Camp Near Chinsura

Chinsura, 7th April 1757

	Madrass Detachment	Bengal Detachment	Bombay Detachment	Total
Captain	1	-	-	1
Captain-Lieutenants	2	-	1	3
Lieutenants	3	2	3	8
Serjeants	4	2	2	8
Corporals	5	1	2	8
Drummers	2	1	1	4
Bombardiers	16	5	6	27
Gunners	18	9	10	37
Mattrosses	37	12	41	90
Totals	*82*	*30*	*62*	*174*

MEMORANDUM

There are sic 2 Captain-Lieutenants, 2 Lieutenants, and 22 of the Train (being 1 Serjeant, 5 Bombardiers, 8 Gunners, 8 Mattrosses) who are sick in the Hospital and returned in the above Muster. Pay rolls exact with the above Muster. There are on Command at Cossimbazar, 1 Lieutenant (Mr. Cassells) and 14 of the Train who are drawn pay for, but not returned above. Entertained in the Service this month, 1 Mattross of the Madras Detachment, and 2 Mattrosses of the Bengal Detachment.

OFFICERS'S NAME TO THE COMPANYS

Madras   Captain Barker, Captain-Lieutenants Paschoud and Jennings
         Lieutenants Bonjour, Ford and Charles de Torriano
Bengal   Lieutenants Lewis and Johnson
Bombay Captain-Lieutenant Egerton, Lieutenants Molitore, Turner and Kinch

SEPOYS

	Subadars	Jemadars	Havildars	Naiks	Colourmen	Seapoys	Tom-Toms and Trumpeters	Total
Madrass Sepoys								
Kaser Sing's	1	3	7	8	2	79	3	103
Vurdarauze's	1	4	8	9	2	76	3	103
Bawan Sing's	1	4	7	7	2	81	2	104
Comrapah's	1	4	8	8	3	75	2	101
Peer Mahomed's	1	3	8	9	2	79	3	105
Rasool Khan's	1	4	7	7	1	83	-	103
Mahomed Khan's	1	4	8	9	3	74	4	103
Raganaigne's	1	4	6	9	3	71	3	97
Hyder Saib's	-	3	7	7	3	77	3	100
Survian's	1	3	7	5	2	79	2	99
Shaikh Daoud's	1	4	10	9	2	83	1	110
Tim Naik's	1	4	8	8	2	71	3	97
Vengana's	1	4	9	9	2	69	3	97
Jaffer Mahomed's	1	4	9	8	2	55	1	80
Bengall Sepoys								
Shaik Emaum	1	4	8	9	3	79	-	104
Condojee's	1	3	7	7	3	96	1	118
Syed Hassan's	1	4	7	9	3	98	-	122
Moideen Saib's	1	4	5	7	3	95	3	118
New Seapoys entertained	-	2	1	-	-	99	-	102
Total	*17*	*69*	*137*	*144*	*43*	*1,519*	*37*	*1,966*

There have been killed of the Madrass seapoys at Charnagore – 1 Subadar, 3 Jemadars, 3 Havildars, 1 Naik, and 7 Seapoys. The four last companys of the Madrass arrived here from thence last month, the sick being 1 Jemadar, 3 Havildars, 2 Naiks, and 47 Seapoys returned in this Muster.

Notes

Introduction

1. S. C. Hill (ed.), *Bengal in 1756-1757*, London, John Murray, 1905, Vol. 2, p. 464 (Clive to Orme 1 August 1757).
2. John Corneille, *Journal of My Service in India*, London, Folio Society, 1960, p. 129.

Chapter 1

1. The curious might care to note that the site is now occupied by the Lloyd's building.
2. Presidencies were so called because they were administered by a council of merchants headed by a president. Initially elected by his fellow merchants, the office was quickly deemed too important to be dealt with locally and instead appoinments were made or confirmed by the directors in London.
3. Rumour had it that Francis Day, the Company's factor responsible, chose the spot for no better reason than that it was conveniently situated to his local girlfriend.
4. Fort St. David lay some 100 miles south of Madras and only 16 or 17 miles south of the French station at Pondicherry. It was originally built and then subsequently abandoned by the Dutch before being sold to the East India Company by the local Indian ruler in 1688.
5. Hill, Vol. 3, p. 408.
6. Marquis of Cornwallis to Henry Dundas, 16 November 1787, quoted in Raymond Callahan, *The East India Company and Army Reform 1783-1793*, Harvard, 1972, p. 76.
7. In the share-out after Plassey, Eurasians were actually awarded two-thirds of the bounty given to Europeans, which presumably reflects their pay scales. In noting that they cost only half as much as Europeans the directors were presumably factoring in the capital cost of shipping European soldiers out to India in the first place.
8. Madras Mayoral Court Range 328 Vol.61. Bannatyne's elder brother served as an officer in the regular 13th Foot and a stepbrother, Forbes MacBean, became a distinguished artillery officer, but he himself had to settle for India.
9. Contemporary pamphlet published by dissident officers of the Bengal army, 1797.

10. By this he presumably means the Cape of Good Hope at the southern tip of Africa, rather than India's Cape Comorin – an important distinction since using the Cape of Good Hope as the demarcation point would ensure the neutral status of Mauritius and other French possessions in the Indian Ocean.

11. Unsurprisingly, he was censured for this desertion by the East India Company and arrested and sent home by his successor Commodore Thomas Griffin – who ironically was himself court-martialled for negligence on his own return to England in 1749.

12. The apparent discrepancy between the 545 men listed in 1720 and the lower number present in 1746 is probably accounted for by the detachment of a garrison for Fort St. David and the probable inclusion of the gunroom crew in the earlier total.

13. The term 'peon' appears to derive from a Portuguese word signifying a poor, landless labourer. In this case it was applied to bands of mercenaries, serving on foot with matchlocks rather than on horseback.

14. Construction of Fort George had commenced in 1644 and now, a century later, it was badly in need of updating. Works had been planned but nothing substantial done.

15. James P. Lawford, *Britain's Army in India; From its Origins to the Conquest of Bengal*, London, Allen & Unwin, 1978, pp. 72–4.

16. Officially the *Compagnie des Indes* troops wore white wool coats turned up with blue, but in the 1740s they had adopted more practical blue gingham cotton coats with red serge cuffs. Like their British counterparts, about 40 per cent of those serving in the ranks at this time were actually Eurasians. The *cypayes* were also issued with blue jackets of some description turned up with red, but seemingly objected to the cost being deducted from their pay.

17. The National Archives (TNA) SP41/18/106, 26 August 1747.

18. TNA SP41/18/72 & 84, unlike Major Mompesson, both of them also commanded companies of their own.

    Frustratingly it is extremely difficult to track down the rest of the officers serving with these companies as not all of them are recorded in the commission registers. Sometimes these merely authorised the granting of commissions but as no names appear they were presumably in the gift of Major Mompesson.

    Nevertheless, the 2nd or Scotch Battalion's company commanders can largely be identified from a variety of sources:

    Captain William Muir [Major, commanding]
    Captain Jonathan Forbes
    Captain Alexander Campbell of Barcaldine
    Captain John Campbell of Dunoon
    Captain George Gordon
    Captain Archibald Grant

19. A Return in Boscawen's journal of 17 October 1748 numerates them on their arrival at Fort St. David as follows (TNA ADM1/160):

Marine Battalion	32 officers	818 men
1st Battalion Independent Companies	33 Officers	591 men
2nd Battalion Independent Companies	34 Officers	593 men

| Company's European Battalion | 28 Officers | 725 men |
| Royal Artillery | | 148 officers and men |

In addition there was later a 'Seamen's Battalion', adding another 1,097 men. The Artillery comprised two companies, one of them belonging to the Royal Artillery as mustered below, and a second, smaller company recruited by the East India Company (TNA WO10 34/38: January, 1748, to April, 1750).

Similarly, although the overall figure for the Company contingent is about right, Neill's history of the Madras Europeans breaks it down as follows:

European Battalion	400
Topasses [Eurasians]	300
Dutch [from Negapatam]	120
Artillerymen	70
Peons	2,000

20. Captain-lieutenant was a thankless appointment. In theory three of the ten companies in a battalion were commanded by each of the three field officers; that is, the colonel, lieutenant colonel and major. In practice it was recognised that the colonel was unable to devote any time to doing so and in any case was normally absent, either effectively in retirement or serving as a general officer. Day-to-day command of his company therefore devolved upon his lieutenant, who for his pains was designated captain-lieutenant, and addressed as captain merely by courtesy. His only consolation was that as the senior lieutenant he was first in line for any death vacancies and on appointment to a captaincy his regimental seniority was determined by the date of his earlier commission as captain-lieutenant.

21. Lawrence also procured proper uniforms for them. They had always worn red coats, but now they had the buff facings of his old 14th Foot. They did not, however, have the tight gaiters and cocked hats wished upon them by Victorian artists. Instead, Lawrence specified 'a hat or cap suitable to the climate', which appears to have been a forerunner of the solar topee, made of white fabric stretched over a rattan frame, and gingham rather than wool breeches. Equipment was probably limited to the lightweight belly-box and bayonet combination in black leather issued to colonial troops in North America, rather than the broad buff belts used in Europe – see Appendix 1.

22. Both the Independent Companies and the Marines were certain to be disbanded on their return home, so signing on with the East India Company offered some security.

23. Helpfully, Bussy, who also happened to be Dupleix's son-in-law, raised a very colourfully-dressed private army of his own, quite independent of the regular *Compagnie des Indes'* troops.

Chapter 2

1. While they were expected to take Chittagong with the aid of the neighbouring Arakanese, the Nawab, on discovering that they really were intent on leaving Calcutta in favour of that place, offered to charter space on the Company ships to transport some of his troops across the Bay to fight the Arakanese! Needless

to say the proposal was turned down and in the event the Arakanese flatly declined to take part in the farce.

2. A very good summary is provided in J. Keay, *The Honourable Company*, London, HarperCollins, 1991, pp. 148–168.

3. Quoted in Hill, Vol. 3, p. 384.

4. M. Edwardes, *The Battle of Plassey and the Conquest of Bengal*, London, Batsford, 1963, p. 24.

5. It is difficult to assess Siraj-ud-Daula's real character objectively since all those concerned were rather too eager to blacken it. He was certainly impulsive and had even rebelled briefly against his grandfather in 1750. He was also supposedly vicious in his habits and vindictive (especially when contrasted with his abstemious and universally-admired grandfather) but he was also under a great deal of pressure on all sides.

6. Hill, Vol. 3, p. 394. The original letter to the Nawab has apparently not survived, but in January 1762 John Cooke, a member of the Council at Calcutta in 1756 gave Robert Orme the gist of it to the best of his recollection. Cooke also asserted that Drake advised the Council of its contents only after it had been sent. Whether this really was the case is uncertain, but Drake was certainly on sufficiently bad terms with the other Council members for this to have been the case.

7. Hill, Vol. 1, p. 3 (Siraj-ud-Daula to Coja Wahid, 28 May 1756). Coja Wahid was an Armenian merchant who acted as a go-between through which correspondence passed between the Nawab and the Company. The reference to the time of the Nawab Jafar Khan was an allusion to the time before the Company enjoyed the power of issuing *dustucks*.

8. Ibid., pp. 73–4 (Alexander Grant). It is not entirely clear what Grant was doing at Cossimbazar. He may, obviously, have been commanding the military detachment there, but similar ones at Jagdea and Dacca were commanded by lieutenants as a matter of course. It does appear, however, from later events that he was more than ordinarily well informed about Murshidabad and the surrounding area and may have been employed in a tour of inspection or some other kind of exploration. That would certainly explain why in the following year he was chosen to serve as second-in-command under Coote on the expedition up the Ganges proper to Patna and beyond.

9. Ibid., p. 47 (Watts, Collet and Batson to the Council, Fort St. George, Madras, 2 July 1756).

10. Ibid., p. 2 (Watts, Collet and Batson to the Council, Fort William, 25 May 1756).

11. Ibid., p. 6 (George Lodowijk Vernet [the Dutch Factor] to his superior at Hugli, 3 June 1756).

12. In fairness to the Bengalis this act shocked them sufficiently that Mrs Watts and some of the other civilians were promptly allowed to take refuge in the French factory, where they were treated with considerable kindness.

13. Edwardes, pp. 27–8.

14. Hill, Vol. 1, p. 74. See Appendix 3.

15. The oddly-named Lieutenant Colonel Caroline Frederick Scott of the 29th Foot, a former ADC to the Duke of Cumberland, had been appointed Engineer-General of the Company's settlements in October 1752, and was also made major commandant of Fort William and commander-in-chief of the Bengal

presidency's troop, just as Stringer Lawrence had been in Madras. He accordingly surveyed and proposed improvements to Fort William, Calcutta, but as Grant observes, his death in May 1754 put a stop to the proceedings – and any reform of the military in Calcutta.

16. Hill, Vol. 1, p. 74. See Appendix 3.
17. Hill, Vol. 3, pp. 386–7 (Rennie).
18. Ironically the building of a quite innocent brick-walled summer house known as Kelsall's Octagon on the landward side of the ditch had been misinterpreted by the Nawab's spies as a new fortification and its demolition was one of the few demands which the Council *were* prepared to accede to.
19. Even at this early date saltpetre was an important export and the major reason why British gunpowder was reckoned the best in the world.
20. The reason for the name is now lost but at the end of the eighteenth century the bungalow appears to have been a genteel sort of tavern and the name may have derived from its offering refreshments.
21. Hill, Vol. 3, pp. 75–6 (Rennie) and p. 408.
    According to a return dated 29 February 1756, the military forces in Bengal were then disposed as follows:

At Calcutta

Officers and soldiers,	Europeans	260
	Eurasians	225
		485

At Cossimbazar

Officers and soldiers,	Europeans	24
	Eurasians	16
		40

At Dacca

Officers and soldiers,	Europeans	31
	Eurasians	15
		46

At Luckipore [Jugdea]

Officers and soldiers,	Europeans	20
	Eurasians	11
		31

| | Total | 602 |

22. While Captain Grant, who had earlier served in Madras was wont to refer to them as *Peons*, they were strictly speaking *berkanduz* or gunmen. *Buxarries*, so-called because they were traditionally recruited in the province of Buxar, appear to have enjoyed a rather better reputation than their southern counterparts and when regularly engaged as sepoys some later became the 1st Bengal Native Infantry.

23. Hill, Vol. 1, pp. 130 & 137 (Drake, *Narrative of the succession of Sourag ud Dowlet to the provinces of Bengal, Bahar, and Orixa, and of the siege of Calcutta taken by escalade the 20th June, 1756*). A return compiled by Captain Grant showed that as of 11 June they numbered a total of 515 men comprised as follows, although it is unclear whether the 70 sick in hospital or in their quarters are included or whether it records only the effectives:

Military (Of these not above 45 Europeans)	180
Volunteers (Europeans)	50
Militia (Europeans)	60
Militia (Armenians and Portugueze)	150
Artillery (Europeans)	35
Volunteers (consisting of sea officers and Portugueze helmsmen*)	40

*i.e. Hoogli river pilots

24. Hill, Vol. 2, p. 27 (Holwell to Court of Directors, Fulta 30 November 1756).
25. He was in fact a former regular officer who had served with 2/Royal Scots at Culloden.
26. Hill, Vol. 1, pp. 200–1 (Fulta consultation 20 August 1756). It would be interesting to learn how he came by this reputation. All that is known with any certainty is that he had served in the rebel army during the Jacobite Rising of 1745–6, and afterwards under Boscawen at Pondicherry in 1748. He had then been a lieutenant and must have gained his promotion – and reputation – during the Carnatic wars, before coming to Bengal, perhaps with Caroline Scott.

Chapter 3

1. Lieutenant Le Baume had left Chandernagore on what was delicately referred to by Grant as a point of honour – seemingly he had allowed himself to be thrashed without demanding the satisfaction of a duel. He thereafter served the Company faithfully even after falling under suspicion for a time after Britain and France went to war. Accounts vary as to whose idea it was to occupy the jail but most likely Clayton asked for a volunteer and Le Beaume was the one who stepped forward.
2. Hill, Vol. 1, p. 256 (William Tooke's account). There is some confusion as to the identity of the *Prince George* with Holwell constantly referring to her as the *St. George* – perhaps on account of her belonging to Madras. Grant certainly refers to her as a sloop and Orme notes she had 18 guns. Despite sharing a name she should not be confused with the 499-ton Indiaman *Prince George*, which made four voyages to India between 1750 and 1762, but was a much smaller vessel based at Madras and normally employed in the 'Country Trade'.
3. Although the little fort was pierced with embrasures for seven guns, six of them were sited to cover the river and consequently Piccard could only point one of his 3-pounders directly towards the enemy.
4. Hill, Vol. 1, pp. 256–7. William Tooke was a factor who had joined the military as a volunteer and his narrative is generally well-informed and indeed quite invaluable. At this time he was serving under Lieutenant Blagg and almost certainly therefore an eyewitness, but not until after his arrival at the Chitpur bridge that evening.

5. Hill, Vol. 1, p. 78 (Grant).
6. Ibid., p. 40 (Mills) and pp. 78–9 (Grant).
7. Edwardes, p. 45. Lest this incident be taken as an example of Bengali ineptitude, it should be noted that Colonel Clive's men very nearly suffered exactly the same fate in the fight outside Budge Budge in January 1757, when they too scattered themselves to sleep without bothering to post sentries; as we shall see in the next chapter.
8. At this point it is worth inserting the story of Amir Chund and his *jemadar*. On 13 June two letters addressed to him had been intercepted on a boat and although their meaning was unclear their very existence was sufficient to justify raids on both his town house, and on his summer house out by the Maratha Ditch. The first netted Amir Chund himself, together with a surprising stockpile of weapons, while the opportunity was taken to arrest Krishna Das at the second. Both men were imprisoned in Fort William throughout the siege but in the meantime Amir Chund's *jemadar*, Jagernath Singh, entered his private apartments and proceeded to execute thirteen women and children before rounding off the performance by setting fire to the house and stabbing himself in the chest. Contrary to his apparent intention, this wound did not prove fatal and supposedly in accordance with his master's instructions the *Jemadar* subsequently recovered so far as to ride to Siraj-ud-Daula with information as to the other crossing points on the ditch. The first part of the story was widely broadcast and seemingly true, but it is hard to believe that the Bengalis were so ignorant of the state of the ditch as to depend on such an eccentric source of information.
9. The jail was strategically placed on a crossroads where the Avenue and its eastward extension, the Lal Bazaar, met the north-south axis of the Chitpur Road; hence the importance of securing it.
10. That is, the *buxarries*.
11. Fringys – *Feringhees* – Eurasians, not as it later became a term for Europeans. Muxadavad was how Murshidabad was spelled in almost all contemporary accounts.
12. St. Jacques had earlier offered his services to the East India Company, but the Council was warned off him by Pierre Renault, the French Director at Chandernagore, who damningly advised that 'Monsieur St. Jacques had been an officer and was turned out of Pondicherry with disgrace, and that he had likewise committed great enormities in Chandernagore and was a flighty hair brained man not in the least to be depended on or regarded.' He is said to have commanded the Nawab's artillery at the taking of Calcutta but thereafter disappears completely from the story: Hill, Vol. 1, p. 143 (Drake).
13. The British believed that the ranks of the Nawab's army were swollen by several thousand 'professional plunderers'.
14. Hill, Vol. 1, p. 258 (Tooke).
15. Hill, Vol. 2, p. 36 (Holwell).
16. Drake himself was positive that Holwell had *demanded* '(when he repaired to the Factory in the afternoon of the 18th June) that the battery which Captain Clayton and he commanded at should be immediately withdrawn.' Hill, Vol. 2, p. 154 (Drake 17–25 January 1757).
17. Hill, Vol. 1, pp. 260–1 (Tooke). According to Holwell, Wilkinson cried for quarter

but was cut to pieces, while Smith was offered quarter, but refused and killed five of the Bengalis before he was brought down (Hill, Vol. 2, p. 38). Orme, more plausibly tells it the other way around, saying that 'Smith and Wilkinson, separated from the rest, and were immediately intercepted: the enemy, however, offered them quarter, which Smith refused, and, it is said, slew five men before he fell; on which Wilkinson surrendered, and was immediately cut to pieces (Robert Orme, *A History of the Military Transactions of the British Nation in Indostan*, Madras, Pharoah and Co., 1861, Vol. 2, pp. 67–8).

18. Hill, Vol. 3, p. 386 (Rennie).

19. Of itself, evacuating the European women and children [(and the wounded) was only sensible and even overdue, but rather more controversial was the agreement that they be escorted by Messrs. Manningham and Frankland. The two were expected to return after seeing them safely aboard but instead they refused to do so on the spurious grounds that they were waiting for a promised escort of thirty soldiers to replace them. Whilst their conduct was regarded unfavourably both at the time and by generations of historians afterwards, it is worth remembering that in reality one was no more than the Export Warehouse Keeper and the other the Import Warehouse Keeper. As noted earlier, their exalted but temporary military ranks in the militia were merely a direct reflection of their status as Company servants and that neither actually exercised any command or military responsibility. Their desertion might be deplorable but in truth they were no loss to the defence.

20. This is the slightly more detailed version from Grant's second account.

21. Hill, Vol. 1, p. 166 (William Lindsay to Robert Orme).

22. Ibid., p. 262 (Tooke). It is doubtful that Tooke himself was present and neither Grant nor anyone else who was known to be present mentions this dramatic interruption, but it does make a splendid story.

23. By his own account Drake found himself there not by design but after responding to the same false alarm as to the enemy getting into the Company house (Hill, Vol. 2, pp. 142–3). Ironically it is just possible that the boat in which Drake and Grant escaped may have belonged to Holwell, for afterwards William Lindsay cattily remarked that when the magistrate took charge of the defence after they had gone 'It was much against his inclination being there, two gentlemen having carried away the budgerow he had waiting for him. I mention this as I understand he made a merit in staying when he found he could not get off.' Whilst it would certainly add some bite to the animosity which Holwell afterwards displayed towards Drake, it is more likely that the reference was actually to Minchin and Macket, for according to Grant's account the pair did indeed escape in a budgerow, while Drake, Grant and O'Hara had a much smaller boat (Hill, Vol. 1, p. 168 [Lindsay]). The story that the sanctimonious Holwell was only prevented from abandoning the Fort was evidently well-known, for see also Robert Clive's letter of 31 January 1757 (Hill, Vol. 2, p. 186), in which he writes 'Mr Holwell is a specious and sensible man, but from what I have heard and observed myself I cannot be persuaded he will ever make use of his abilities for the good of the Company. I am well informed there is no merit due to him for staying behind in the fort, nothing but the want of a boat prevented his escape and flight with the rest.'

24. Hill, Vol. 1, pp. 200–1 (Board at Fulta 20 August 1756).

25. Ibid., p. 263 (Tooke).
26. 'We got on board the *Dodly*, where Messrs. Manningham and Frankland with most of the women were. I then represented to the Governor the cruelty of abandoning so many gentlemen to the mercy of such an enemy, and requested he would order the ships and sloops to move up before the fort, by which means we should be able to send the boats under their cover, to bring off our distressed friends; but the captain of the ship representing the danger it would be attended with, and the impossibility of getting the ships back, in case they went up again before the fort, the Governor thought proper not to insist upon it.'
27. There was a quite unedifying row afterwards. No-one disputed that Grant had wanted to return and take off those still in the Fort, but Young claimed that he was acting under orders from Manningham, who had been given authority by Drake over the shipping. Drake denied that Manningham had been given any such authority over anyone and placed the blame squarely on Young, while at the same time side-stepping the question of why he himself had not ordered Young to take his ship inshore!
28. Hill, Vol. 1, p. 114 (Holwell).
29. Captain Hague and his officers escaped ashore and sought refuge with the Dutch, only to be handed over to the Nawab, but were eventually released unharmed.
30. Hill, Vol. 1, p. 59 (Watts to Council at Fort St. George, 7 July 1756). Many if not most of the military rank and file under Sergeant Hedleburgh were Dutch and other European mercenaries who found no difficulty in enlisting with the French. Later they played an active role in defending Chandernagore from their former employers, and having made their escape from that debacle as well, served on under Jean Law.

Chapter 4

1. 450,000 rupees apiece were demanded from both, although a fortunately-timed bullion shipment meant that the French were able to secure a substantial discount by offering an immediate cash payment.
2. Hill, Vol. 1, p.161 (Drake).
3. Hill, Vol. 2, p. 144. Even Drake lamented his having to sleep on an open deck with only the edge of a hatch cover for his pillow!
4. Orme, Vol. 2, p. 81.
5. Richard Becher, so far not encountered in our story, had been the chief of the factory at Dacca, arriving at Fulta on 26 August. Manningham was also a member of the committee for a time but contrived to be sent to Madras and was replaced by Holwell. Major Killpatrick was also co-opted on to the committee for a time but largely dropped out of the picture after Colonel Clive and Admiral Watson arrived.
6. An otherwise unexpected sense of humour is revealed by his choice to base himself on board the *Fort William*! In honour of its status as the new gubernatorial seat, the carpenter of the *Delaware* was employed in making a suitable flagstaff for it.
7. Hill, Vol. 1, p. 193 (Killpatrick to Council at Fort St. George 5 August 1756). Some contemporaries and most historians render the gallant Major's name as Kilpatrick, but as Hill points out he himself spelled it as here.

8. Ensign Edward Walcot also managed to turn up at Fulta, having survived the Black Hole, but died soon afterwards.

9. Hill, Vol. 1, pp. 200–1 (*Extract from the Fulta Consultations, 20th August 1756*). The only dissenter was a Mr Pearkes who tried to claim that Grant had effectively dismissed himself by *not* requiring returns from Keane and Muir, and sourly grumbled that Grant should have been required to serve as a volunteer until such time as he proved his courage. The rest took a more pragmatic view. Killpatrick's involvement is speculative but consistent both with his need at that time to re-organise the remaining Bengal forces and the very strong impression in the minute that the rest of the Council was being heavily leant upon. Minchin by contrast made no attempt to rehabilitate himself and was indeed dismissed and ordered home, although being afraid to do so he in fact died in Calcutta in April 1758.

10. Regimental tradition claims that Killpatrick's men from Madras became the grenadier company of the new battalion, but there is no contemporary evidence of this and the only grenadiers referenced in accounts of the campaign were Captain Pye's men who came later from Madras with Clive. Killpatrick did have them under his command from time to time and that association probably gave rise to the legend.

11. Muir was in fact the son of Major George Muir, who had commanded the Scotch Battalion of Independent Companies at Pondicherry in 1748. Like Grant, both father and son remained in Madras at the end of the war where the elder Muir died soon afterwards and the younger Muir went to Bengal as a writer on the Company's civil establishment. Not liking the job he obtained a transfer to the military in 1754 and eventually died as a Colonel in 1782 (John Philippart, *East India Military Calendar: containing the services of General and Field Officers*, London, 1826, Vol. 3, pp. 212–14).

12. *A General Return of All the Troops under the Command of Lieutenant-Colonel ROBERT CLIVE 22nd February 1757.*

13. Hill, Vol. 3, p. 82 (10 October 1756).

14. Hostilities had in fact begun in April 1756 with a successful attack on Britain's Mediterranean garrison of Minorca but otherwise both countries were somewhat tentative about going to war and it was not to spread to India until the following year.

15. The curiously-named Mutiny Act which had to be passed by Parliament each year provided the legal authority for the army to exist by affirming the size or Establishment of the army and estimates of the costs involved, it also set out the legal code or Articles of War under which it operated – hence the 'Mutiny' Act. This Act only applied to troops serving in or at least based in mainland Britain, paid for by the British Exchequer. Ireland had its own Mutiny Act, as did the North American colonies.

16. A. J. Guy, *Colonel Samuel Bagshawe and the Army of George II 1731-1762*, London, Army Records Society, 1990, p. 122.

17. Henry Fox to Colonel Adlercron 13 October 1755, quoted in Guy, p. 290. The letter arrived very timeously in April 1756.

18. Having made his reputation in the Carnatic, most famously in his defence of Arcot, Clive had returned in triumph to England in 1753, sat briefly in

Parliament and then came out to India for a second time in July 1755 as Deputy Governor of Fort St. David and heir presumptive to Governor Pigot at Madras. Just as importantly as it was to turn out, he also had his King's commission:

> George the Second, by the Grace of God. King of Great Britain, France and Ireland, Defender of the Faith, &c. To Our Trusty and Well Beloved Robert Clive Esq. Greeting: We, reposing especial Trust and Confidence in your Loyalty, Courage and Experience in Military Affairs, do by these Presents, constitute and appoint you to be Lieutenant Colonel of Foot, in the East Indies only; You are therefore to take upon you the Charge and Command of Lieutenant Colonel of Foot, in the East Indies only, as aforesaid, and carefully and diligently to Discharge the Duty thereof, by doing and performing all, and all manner of Things thereunto belonging; and We do hereby, Command all Officers and Soldiers to obey you as Lieutenant Colonel of Foot, in the East Indies only; And you are to observe and follow such Orders and Directions, from time to time, as you shall receive from Us, Our Captain General of our Forces, or any other your superior Officer, according to the Rules and Discipline of War, in Pursuance of the Trust we hereby repose in You. Given at our Court at St. James's the Thirty first day of March 1755 in the Twenty Eighth Year of our Reign.

19. Stringer Lawrence was senior to Clive and briefly considered for the job, but his health was not thought equal to the climate of Bengal.
20. The *Cumberland* (70), the *Tyger* (60), the *Salisbury* (50), the *Bridgewater* (20) and Watson's own flagship, the *Kent* (64). In addition there was a fireship, named the *Blaze* – presumably an old and expendable vessel acting as a tender. The latter proved unequal to the monsoon and was diverted to Bombay, but her captain, William King, sailed to Bengal as a volunteer on HMS *Kent* and distinguished himself as the commander of the various naval contingents landed from time to time.
21. The three companies chosen were commanded (in order of seniority) by Captain Archibald Grant, Captain Nicholas Weller and Captain Eyre Coote. What was more all of them were completed to their full wartime establishment of ninety rank and file apiece by drafting men from those companies staying behind in Madras.
22. Hill, Vol. 1, p. 228 and Vol. 3, p. 30.
23. Hill, Vol. 3, p. 30. All in all there were 97 officers and men of the 39th Foot, 150 Madras Europeans and 67 sepoys on the *Cumberland* and another 360 sepoys and lascars aboard the *Marlborough*. Of those however at least 100 of the Madras Europeans were snaffled for the garrison of Vizapatnam when the *Cumberland* put in there and the remainder afterwards landed again at Madras and so never made it to Bengal.
24. Hill, Vol. 2, p. 89 (Clive to Select Committee Fort St. George 8 January 1757).
25. Ibid., p. 73 (Account of [Bengali] forces in Calcutta and other Forts, appended to Select Committee Proceedings, 22 December 1756):

In Calcutta	...	...	...	332 horse
	...	...	...	1,100 burgundasses [*berkanduz*]
	...	...	...	500 pykes and peons
At Tannah's		...	...	300
Opposite Tannah's		...	...	6 guns
At Tannahs	...	...	...	9 guns
Mr Holwell's Garden		...	...	5 guns
Surman's do.	...	...	...	4 guns
At the Carpenter's yard	...		...	2 guns
By the Waterside the same as formerly				
On the Bastions the same				
Mr Watts' his house		...	...	2 guns
Seats gaut	...	...	...	2 guns
Margas's gaut	...	...	...	2 guns
At the Gunge	...	...	...	4 guns

Ominously it was added that 'Opposite Tannah's 3 sloops and 2 brigantines filled with earth. They are teaching people to play bombs.'

26. Ibid., pp. 73–4 (Clive to Killpatrick at Fulta, 23 December 1756).
27. Hill, Vol. 3, pp. 33–4 (*Journal of the expedition to Bengal*).
28. Orme, Vol. 2, pp. 122–4.
29. The 'Volunteers' in question were actually the rump Bengal Europeans, recruited around a nucleus of Keene and Muir's companies, but including volunteers from amongst the Company's civilians and a fair number of Eurasians. See Appendix 1.
30. In a number of other accounts, including Clive's, this happy near-miss was improved by claiming that a ball had actually gone through Manik Chand's turban!
31. E. Ives, *A Voyage from England to India in the year 1754*, London, Edward and Charles Dilly, 1773, pp. 99–100. Strahan is not explicitly identified as a Scotsman, but his name was an Aberdeenshire one. Ives was the surgeon of HMS *Kent* and a witness to the proceedings.
32. Hill, Vol. 3, pp. 40–1 (Coote). The various naval officers recounting the storming of the fort represent the affair as having been carried out all according to order, while Coote claims it was HM 39th who followed Strahan in!
33. Campbell's history is uncertain, but it would appear that he come to Fulta as a lieutenant under Killpatrick and was promoted on 13 August 1756, probably to replace William Keane, who had died of fever (Hill, Vol. 1, p. 202 and Vol. 2, pp. 190, 197). He is not therefore to be confused with the Captain *Robert* Campbell listed as a company commander in Clive's embarkation return of 8 October 1756 and who later served at Plassey. At any rate, Campbell was shot and killed while posting sentries and while this supposedly occurred by accident, there were suspicions it was 'designed' by his own men. One account states that, 'At ten we stormed and took it, when our friend Captain Dugald Campbell going on the bastion to forbid the sailors and seapoys firing from without, as they were killing our men, was shot dead on the spot, being wounded in five places, and died universally esteemed and regretted' (Hill., Vol. 3, p. 34).
34. Hill, Vol. 3, pp. 2–3 (*Kent* minute).
35. Ibid, p. 41 (Coote).
36. Hill, Vol. 2, p. 96 (Clive to Pigot, 8 January 1757).

37. Ibid., p. 77 (Watson to Clive, 2 January 1757).
38. Hill, Vol. 3, p. 309 (Clive's evidence to *Committee appointed to enquire into the Nature, State and Condition of the East India Company, and of British Affairs in the East Indies*, reported 26 May 1772).
39. Hill, Vol. 2, p. 96 (Clive to Pigot, 8 January 1757).
40. Hill, Vol. 3, p. 309 (Clive).

Chapter 5
1. Hill, Vol. 2, pp. 98, 99, 108–9.
2. Hill, Vol. 3, p. 14 (*Bridgewater* Log) Naval casualties were light with three men killed and wounded aboard both the *Bridgewater* and the *Kingfisher*, with another three seamen killed and twelve wounded ashore.
3. Ibid., p. 42 (Coote).
4. Ibid., p. 43 (Coote).
5. See Hill, Vol. 2, pp. 106–10, 111–12 for another unhappy exchange of correspondence.
6. Hill, Vol. 2, pp. 176–7 (Clive to Select Committee, Fort St. George, 28 January 1757) 'I have the pleasure to acquaint you that a ditch of 30 feet and 12 deep is finished. An esplanade of 200 yards and a glacis will likewise be completed in five or six days. To the southward the wall of the godown is raised equal to the curtain, and a strong battery will be erected at the southern barrier by the waterside which will flank at that face. Another at the northern barrier by the waterside will flank the northern face. To the east a ravelin, which had been begun by the gentlemen of Calcutta, will be made a large and fine battery, which will flank all that face. From the western side there is nothing to fear, being well secured by the river and a strong Line of guns. All this work I am positive will be completed in less than ten days. The ditch will be palisaded and may be kept wet or dry with great ease. In short, I may assure you, Fort William cannot be taken again by the Moors, but by cowardice.'
7. Hill, Vol. 3, p. 58. Tanks were water reservoirs, generally rectangular in shape with an earthwork perimeter wall which lent itself very well to being turned into an improvised fortification.
8. Captain Pye and his grenadier company had not of course returned downstream from Hugli at this point.
9. Hill, Vol. 2, pp. 123–4.
10. Ibid., p. 133 (Clive to Pigot, 25 January 1757). Determined to stand no nonsense, Clive fully integrated the regulars into his little army. While they remained in their own companies under their own officers, it is clear that Clive was not prepared to allow King's officers to claim any superiority over Company officers of the same rank, other than by straightforward seniority. Having made his point, however, he subsequently granted local brevets on 15 and 16 June respectively, to Archibald Grant and Eyre Coote, to serve as majors in Bengal.
11. Ibid., p. 97 (Clive to Pigot, 8 January 1757). 'In the Company's present distressed circumstances they [the Bengal committee] propose giving the sailors 50 bales of broad cloth which I think might well be spared, however if they do I shall insist upon something of the same nature for the military, otherwise the Service may suffer.'
12. Ibid., p. 123 (Clive to Select Committee, Fort William, 20 January 1757).

13. Hill, Vol. 3, p. 37 (*Journal of the expedition to Bengal*). Weller was at this time the senior officer of HM 39th Foot but a rather unfortunate one, with a knack for falling ill or getting himself wounded every time glory beckoned. This time, according to Coote, he was wounded in the thigh.

14. Captain King, who had previously been commanding the landing parties, was sent home after the Hugli expedition, carrying the admiral's dispatches and warmest recommendations. Warwick was another of the admiral's protégés, having formerly been the First Lieutenant of the *Kent*.

15. Hill, Vol. 2, p. 238 (Clive to Secret Committee, London, 22 February 1757). The '*bucksaries*' were presumably the recruits for the Bengal sepoys. While the camp was to be thus guarded there is, curiously, little mention of a garrison for Fort William, but see Appendix 1. Clive's military journal merely relates that on arriving safely at the fort 'a subaltern with forty-five military and 100 *seapoys* fresh from the garrison were detached immediately by boat to secure our camp' (Hill, Vol. 3, p. 59).

16. Coote on the other hand ascribes this minor disaster to Captain Pye's grenadier company (Hill, Vol. 3, p. 44): 'the alarm was soon given, and some popping shots fired at us, upon which our *seapoys* in the front began firing but with some confusion. As I had a company of grenadiers formed out of the King's troops, and my post being next to them, I was not without some apprehension of being broke by them; I therefore endeavoured to make them advance as fast as I could and sent for a piece of cannon to come in my front; while this was doing a shower of arrows came among us with some fire rockets, one of which unfortunately fell on one of the Company's grenadiers (who were in my rear) and blew up almost the whole platoon.'

17. Coote characteristically claims they came much closer: 'a body of their choice horse came riding down upon us sword in hand; as there was a very great fog we could not perceive them until they were within ten yards of us, upon which our battalion faced to the right and gave them a full fire, which destroyed almost the whole of them.'

18. William Pye was of course the commander of the Madras Europeans' grenadier company, which suggests that Coote was correct in stating it was the grenadiers who suffered from the rocket strike, rather than the sepoys identified by Orme. Timothy Bridge or Bridges is unidentified but may have been serving as Clive's aide de camp. Other named casualties were Clive's secretary William Belches, who was killed and four officers wounded; Subedar Kirza Singh, the commander of the Madras Sepoys, Captain Guappe, commander of Clive's Swiss company, Lieutenant Thomas Rumbold, another Madras officer and Ensign William Ellis, a writer from Calcutta, who lost a leg. Admiral Watson also noted that Lieutenant Lutwidge of the *Salisbury* was wounded – fatally as it turned out.

19. Orme, Vol. 2, pp. 131–4.

20. Hill, Vol. 2, pp. 215–17.
    Briefly, the Nawab agreed that:

    1. The original Imperial *firman* to the East India Company should be respected
    2. No taxes or duties should be imposed on goods passing with English *dustucks*

3. The Company's factories, and any of its monies goods and effects, seized by the Nawab should be restored and likewise those pillaged from its servants and tenants, or compensation paid in lieu. (This alone proved controversial in that the Nawab was willing to restore any goods seized by his orders and therefore properly accounted for, but was understandably evasive as to anything which might [or might not] have been seized by others and so unverifiable. In this he was not unlike an insurance claims adjuster looking narrowly at inflated claims for loss and damage. It will be noted that no 'justice' or compensation was demanded for those who died in the Black Hole.)

4. That permission be granted to fortify Calcutta

5. That the Company be permitted to operate a mint

21. Hill, Vol. 2, pp. 264–5 (Siraj-ud-Daula to de Bussy, February 1757).
22. Ibid., pp. 223–4 (Nawab to Clive, 14 February 1757). As the muster rolls confirm, an officer (Lieutenant Cassells) and fourteen men were sent to Cossimbazar, ostensibly for that purpose, but were recalled on 25 May.
23. Ibid., pp. 281–2. Once again the Company's readiness to ally with the Nawab in its own interest is evident.
24. Born in Paris in 1719, Jean Law was the nephew of the economist John Law of Lauriston. His brother, Jacques-François Law, with whom he is sometimes confused was a French commander in the Carnatic. He himself had at one point served in the Franco-Irish Regiment Dillon, and his status at this point was a touch ambiguous.
25. Hill, Vol. 2, p. 279 (Siraj-ud-Daula to Admiral Watson, 10 March 1757).
26. Hill, Vol. 3, pp. 267–8.
27. Ibid., p. 418.
28. Hill, Vol. 2, p. 311 (Watson to Cleveland, 31 March 1757).
29. Hill, Vol. 3, pp. 47–8.
30. Ibid., p. 39.
31. Ibid., pp. 49–50.
32. Ibid., p. 275.
33. So badly damaged was the *Kent* that she never sailed out of the river but was condemned at Calcutta.
34. Hill, Vol. 3, p. 50.
35. Ibid., pp. 420–1 (a rather confused list of the garrison compiled by a French officer).
36. These were the largely the Dutch and other European mercenaries who either deserted during the defence of Calcutta or escaped afterwards and found refuge in Chandernagore. Most took service under Law, although some may have been with St. Frais at Plassey.

Chapter 6
1. Hill, Vol. 2, pp. 354–5 (Clive to Collet, 23 April 1757).
2. Ibid., pp. 367, 369.
3. Ibid., p. 376 (Clive to Nawab, 4 May 1757).
4. Ibid., p. 464 (Clive to Orme, 1 August 1757).
5. In responding, Watson replied that he would do his best to secure sufficient

volunteers, but warned that: 'I must desire that those who accompany you on your march may not be made use of as cooleys for I have too much reason to fear it would occasion a mutiny among the seamen, who made great complaints at the fatigue they underwent when they marched through the Nabob's camp.' Clive hastily assured him that they were only wanted to help fight the artillery or make use of their small arms. Nevertheless, although enough were found to serve as a garrison for Chandernagore, only about fifty men under Lieutenant Richard Hayter RN could be persuaded to march with Clive as artillerymen (Ibid., p. 395).

6. The latter were soldiers found unfit for active service, whether due to illness, injuries or even old age, but still reckoned to be capable of standing guard and carrying out light duties in a garrison.

7. As was customary in India, the army was accompanied by its own bazaar, civilian merchants who supplied the needs of the sepoys and everyone else. Some may have carried bulk goods such as flour and rice in their own boats, but most of the bazaar was carried on pack bullocks.

8. Hill, Vol. 3, p. 51.

9. The escape was not quite as dramatic as was afterwards related. Watts and his companions certainly galloped off into the darkness in approved fashion, but later rendezvoused with the soldiers earlier sent off from Cossimbazar who safely convoyed them to the camp.

10. The 15 June return signed off by Captain Fraser tabulated the two battalions thus:

		Officers	Vo.unteers	NCOs	Drummers	European Centinels	Eurasians	Train	Total men
	HM 39th	9	–	5	6	194	–	–	215
1st Battalion	Bengal troops	21	3	21	11	120	48		200
	Train	9	–	8	2	–	–	84	94
	Madras troops	19	7	40	14	218	–	–	272
2nd Battalion	Bombay troops	8	1	17	4	81	43	–	145
	Train	8	–	8	1	–	–	87	96

11. '*June 15th.* – The Colonel thought proper to appoint Captain Archibald Grant a Major.' Coote's jealousy however was somewhat assuaged when he himself was also promoted to the rank of major the following day. Both appointments were of course local brevets rather than substantive promotions.

12. The howitzer was effectively a small mortar mounted on a field carriage and used for throwing explosive bomb-shells. It was still something of an innovation in the British service and normally known by its German designation as a *haubitzer*, hence the frequent references to it in narratives of the campaign as a 'hobit'!

13. Hill, Vol. 3, p. 53. According to Coote's description: 'The Fort of Cutwah is about half a mile in circumference, made of earth with eight round towers, situated on the bank of the Cossimbazar river, which covers the east face, with a large creek that covers the south face, which we were obliged to cross and found it very deep and rapid; this face with the other two are surrounded by a deep dry ditch having a narrow passage to walk over without a drawbridge.'

14. Ibid., p. 52. Extraordinary as the story sounds, it is confirmed by the 3 August return which records that Moses Ford, centinel in Captain Coote's company, died on 19 June 1757.

15. Ibid. Whilst Coote was understandably upset and no doubt expressed himself so in his usual soldier-like fashion with frequent exclamations of 'Damme!', the debacle may not entirely have been the fault of the un-named artillery officer. In his letter of 29 May to Admiral Watson, Clive related inter alia that, 'We have discovered a great scene of villainy amongst several of the military. It seems a boat has constantly come in the night from Chinchura to receive stolen goods, and at last one Trenchard was catched in the fact of stealing a small cohorn. One had been missing before and a small brass field-piece. A General Court Martial has sentenced two of them to be hanged, which is to be put into execution on Friday morning. One belongs to the King's, and other to the Company' (Hill, Vol. 2, p. 395). It is quite likely therefore that the missing limber and wheels may in fact have been stolen from the boats by Trenchard and his accomplices, rather than carelessly misplaced by the gunners!

16. Coote's spelling of Indian names is typically eccentric, but this would appear to be a Bengal officer, *Subadar* Moideen Saib.

17. Hill, Vol. 2, p. 419 (Coote to Clive 19 June 1757): 'Sir – this morning about seven o'clock took the Fort of Cuttwa by storm, The timidity of the defenders gave me an easy entrance. The particulars I will let you know when I have the pleasure of seeing you, which I hope will be soon, and am, &c. &c. EYRE COOTE.'

18. Clive, as it happens, had written to the Nawab on 14 May, saying that 'I hear a report of the Marattoes having a design to enter the country. Your excellency may be assured of my best endeavours to prevent their coming in' (Hill, Vol. 2, p. 380).

19. Hill, Vol. 3, pp. 53–4.

20. See Coote's account in Appendix 6 for the full list of the voting. The only officer in the Bengal service to vote against immediate action was Captain Melchior Le Beaume. He, as it happens, had been rather arbitrarily dismissed by Clive after the capture of Chandernagore, losing his company. Only recently restored to duty and allowed to recruit a new company he may have been wary of crossing Clive a second time.

21. Hill, Vol. 3, pp. 55.

22. Orme explains: 'All were landed on the opposite shore by four in the afternoon, at which time another messenger arrived with a letter from Jaffier, which had likewise been dispatched on the 19th, but had taken bye-roads, and was delayed by other precautions. The purport was, "That the Nabob had halted at Muncara, a village six miles to the south of Cossimbuzar, and intended to entrench and wait the event at that place, where Jaffier proposed that the English should attack him by surprize, marching round by the inland part of the island" [see Hill, Vol. 2, p. 240 for transcript]. Colonel Clive immediately sent back the

messenger with this answer, "That he should march to Plassy without delay, and would the next morning advance six miles farther to the village of Daudpoor; but if Meer Jaffier did not join him there, he would make peace with the Nabob".' Hill, Vol. 2, p. 423 provides a transcript of the letter, which confirms the accuracy of Orme's version of the text, but hopelessly confuses matters by recording that it is endorsed as having been sent off at 7am the next morning! By that time the battle was well underway.

23. Ibid., p. 426 (Mr Vernet to Dutch Director and Council at Hughli, 24 June 1757).
24. Orme, Vol. 2, pp. 172–3.
25. Corneille, pp. 120–1. See Note 11 above.
26. All of this was in accordance with Humphrey Bland's *Treatise of Military Discipline*, the drill book adopted by the Company's forces. The King's Regulations used by HM 39th, having originally been based upon Bland's teaching, were very similar.
27. Whilst it might at first seem odd that none of the officers were commanding their parent units, this was once again in accordance with Bland's *Military Discipline*. The rank and file of a battalion were drawn up into a battle-line and told off equally into wings, grand divisions and platoons without regard to company affiliations. The Bengal Europeans and the detachment of HM 39th were pretty much the same size and could be left as they were, but as the Bombay Europeans were noticeably fewer, a number of the Madras Europeans will have needed to be temporarily transferred to Guapp's division in order to even it up.
28. Hill, Vol. 2, pp. 434. Other accounts state that two grenadiers were killed. A sergeant and three soldiers of Eyre Coote's company were afterwards named in the 3 August return as having been wounded, but none were killed, or reported dead of their wounds so presumably the unfortunate grenadier survived.
29. Other accounts make it clear that the Bengali infantry were all or most of them properly-organised units of *berkanduz* or matchlock men – see Appendix 2.
30. M. de St. Frais, the former secretary to the French Council at Chandernagore.
31. Orme, Vol. 2, pp. 173–4.
32. Ibid., p. 174. Coote on the other hand states that Clive called the captains together for a council but then changed his mind and dismissed them again without actually holding it. Presumably he simply informed them as to his intentions but declined to enter into any discussion.
33. The British gunners are said at this point to have promptly flung tarpaulins over their ammunition, while the Bengalis neglected to do so, thus rendering their artillery useless, but although Orme tells the tale there is no evidence that this was really the case.
34. The story originated with Mir Jafar himself, who subsequently wrote to Clive that 'He sent for me and flung his turband off before me' (Hill, Vol. 2, p. 423). Later versions are considerably embellished and none of them favourable to the Nawab.
35. Captain Arthur Broome, *History of the Rise and Progress of the Bengal Army*, Calcutta, Thacker & Co., 1850, p. 148, without giving a source identifies it as the Bengal Sepoys' grenadier company, which would be consistent with the Bengal sepoys suffering heavier casualties than the Madras ones.
36. Corneille, p. 123 ' ... the company of grenadiers belonging to the first battalion, with a couple of guns and some sepoys, were ordered to take possession of the

pond which the enemy had held that morning. This was immediately executed without any loss, the enemy having quitted it some time before.'

37. Orme, Vol. 2, pp. 176. Notwithstanding his friend Orme's defence, Clive and his partisans vigorously denied the imputation that he was asleep. Instead the eccentric explanation was advanced that having been soaked in the thunderstorm he had retired to shift (ie; change) his clothes. This has generally been accepted by historians but there is no mention of Clive running after Killpatrick half-dressed and it is far more likely that if he were not asleep, his changing of his clothes was a genteel euphemism for his sitting with his breeches round his ankles when it all kicked off. It will be noted inter alia that Clive *ran* to catch up with Killpatrick (which cannot have improved his temper) for neither he nor any of his officers had horses. Surgeon Ives (p. 152) appears to be the only source for the story that Clive initially arrested Killpatrick, but Ives knew Clive well and discussed the battle with him when preparing his narrative.

38. Corneille, p. 123. Presumably Coote and the Bengal Europeans were chosen as the nearest troops available. Killpatrick could hardly have sent off the remainder of his own division while remaining behind himself, and Corneille's account, although tolerably vague, appears to confirm that HM 39th Foot did not go forward at this point in time.

39. Orme, Vol. 2, p. 176 is the only source for this incident, but given the very particular circumstantial detail in naming the three officers concerned, there is no reason to doubt its authenticity. As noted earlier each of the four divisions will have been told off into four platoons for fire-control purposes. Grant was the senior captain in Coote's division and the logical choice to command this detachment. What is slightly puzzling is that the third platoon must have come from Captain Guapp's division of the 2nd Battalion, for Captain (not Lieutenant) Thomas Rumbold commanded a Madras company at that time. He gained a reputation as a bold and enterprising officer in the Carnatic and may simply have tagged along. The artillery commander, John Johnstone, had formerly been a writer at Dacca, but was named in returns as a lieutenant, commanding the Bengal artillery as early as February 1757.

40. Corneille, p. 124. This was probably the Madras Europeans' grenadier company.

41. Orme, Vol. 2, pp. 176–7.

42. Some accounts name the new commander as Mohul Lal, the Nawab's treasurer, but while he appears to have been a stout old gentleman and got himself wounded, his military son-in-law Bahadur Ali Khan is a much more plausible candidate.

43. There is some uncertainty as to exactly when the Nawab fled. Some hostile sources suggest that he may have done so shortly after Mir Madan fell and long before the fighting was over, but contemporary accounts are consistent in saying that he did not run until his army crumbled under Clive's final attack, and one states he took time to speak with St. Frais and order the French to retreat.

44. Corneille, p. 124.

45. Hill, Vol. 2, p. 425 (*A return of the Killed, Wounded and missing of the Two Battalions under the command of Lieutenant Colonel Clive 23 June 1757* and *General Return of Sepoys Killed and Wounded, June 23rd, 1757*).
   The subsequent 3 August return names all of the European and Eurasian casualties:

Killed
John Raison, Corporal in the (Madras) Grenadier company
William Bisenar, Centinel in Captain Muir's company (Bengal Europeans)
George Anderson, Corporal; John Brunt, Gunner; and Thomas Berry, Matross in the Madrass Artillery

Wounded
Lieutenant De Lubers (Captain Grant's company, Bengal Europeans)
Lieutenant Cassells and Lieutenant Holts (Madras Artillery)
Daniel Lyons, Serjeant; James Thorn, Peter Newby, and John Greenwood, Centinels in Captain Coote's company. (HM 39th Foot)
David Pridmore, Serjeant in Captain Guapp's company (Madras Europeans)
John Pringle and John Dyson, Serjeants in the Supernumeraries
Thomas Crowder, Centinel in Captain Grant's company (Bengal Europeans)
Thomas Lauder, Serjeant in Captain Le Beaume's company (Bengal Europeans)
Joseph Massey Wright, Sergeant in Captain Armstrong's company (Bombay Europeans)
Corporal John Potter; George Pitman, Bombardier; John O'Bryan, Bombardier; and William Lloyd, Gunner in the Madras Artillery.
Christopher Noste, Matross in the Bengal Artillery.

In addition, Coiton Disobree and John Lewis Gerald, Centinels in Captain Palmer's company (Bombay Europeans) were returned as having deserted during the battle.

46. Aside from Mir Madan, named Bengali casualties included, Mohan Lal's son-in-law, Bahadur Ali Khan, identified as a commander of *berkanduz* (and probable successor to Mir Madan) and the artillery commander, Nauwe Singh Hazari, who were both killed, while Mohan Lal, Manick Chund and Coja Haddie were all named in a Dutch report as being wounded.

Epilogue
1. Orme, Vol. 2, p. 178.
2. The treasury proved a sad disappointment, holding nothing like the fabulous sums rumoured to be piled up in its vaults. Instead of the eagerly anticipated 5,000 *lakhs* of rupees, there were only 140. There was a shrewd suspicion that a substantial part of the shortfall had been hurriedly moved by Rai Durlabh in the hours before Clive's arrival in Murshidabad, and secured in the zenana or women's quarters within the palace, but nothing could be proven and the British had to settle for half down and the remainder by annual instalments. It was still more than enough to make everyone rich and Corneille (pp. 133–7) records how a Council of War was necessary to determine the distribution of the riches to the army:

COPY OF A COUNCIL OF WAR held at Muxidavad the 3rd July 1757 –

Present

Robert Clive Esqr &c. PRESIDENT

MAJORS
James Kilpatrick
Archibald Grant
Eyre Coote

FROM THE KING'S DETACHMT
Captain John Corneille
Lieut Joseph Adnett
Lieut Martin Yorke

FROM THE BENGAL DETACHMT
Captain Alix Grant
Lieute Archd Keir
Ensn – Champion

FROM THE MADRAS DETACHMT
Captain Robert Campbell
Lieut Bryan Scotney
Ensn – Stringer

FROM THE BOMBAY DETACHMT
Captain Andrew Armstrong
Lieut Villars Walsh
Ensign – Robinson

OF THE ARTILLERY
Capt – Pashaud
Lieut Thoms Lewis
Lieut – Kinch

There being no regulation among the land forces on this expedition, for the division of plunder, or booty taken from the enemy, or for the gift made by the Nabob [Mir Jafar] this Council of War consisting of the Field Officers of the Army, and of the three officers chosen by each respective detachment is assembled to settle the same. After thorough consideration of the matter, It is agreed.

That everything in shall be determined in this Council of War by the Majority of votes.

That One Eighth part of the amount of the whole booty and gift be paid to the Commander in Chief and
Major James Kilpatrick: that is to say two thirds of the Eighth to the Commander in Chief, and One third to Major James Kilpatrick.
That four Eighths be paid to the Captains, Staff Officers, and Subalterns in such manner that the share of every Captain and Staff Officer shall be double to that of a Subaltern. The Staff Officers here

meant are the Aid de Camp, Secretary, Judge Advocate, Pay master, the Commissary on the Fort St. George establishment, the Commissary on the Bengal establishment, and the Commissary of Artillery. It is also meant that the Chaplain, Surgeons, Quartermasters, shall share as Subalterns.

That One Eighth and a half, or three Sixteenths, be paid to Volunteers, Non Commissioned Officers, Soldiers, Artificers &c. in the following proportion:
To each Volunteer, Surgeon's Mate, Conductor of the Train, Serjeant Majors, Quartermaster Serjts, Three times the share of an European private Sentinel.
To each Serjeant twice as much as a private Sentinel.
To each Corporal, Bombardier, European Drum and Artificer half a share more than a private Sentinel.
To each Gunner, Matross and Mustee [part-Eurasian] Sentinel, the same as a European private Sentinel.
To each Topaz and Black drum two thirds of the share of an European private Sentinel, the surplus third to be thrown into the three sixteenths.

That One Eighth be paid to the Seapoys, the Lascars in the following proportions:
To Keysar Sing the Commandant of the Madras Seapoys, and the Commandant of the Bengal Seapoys, One Sixteenth part of the Eighth to be shared equally between them, the latter to share from the date of his appointment.
To the Subhadars excluding Keysar Sing and the Commandant of the Bengal Seapoys, three Sixteenths.
To the Jammadars of the Seapoys and the Serangs of the Lascars, four Sixteenths.
To the Havildars, Naiques, and Colour men of the Seapoys and Tindals of the Lascars, all sharing equally two sixteenths.
To the Tom Toms, Trumpeters, and private Seapoys and the Lascars, all sharing equally six sixteenths.

One sixteenths of the whole plunder still remaining undivided, It is agreed that out of it the share of Major Archibald Grant be made equal to half the amount of Major James Kilpatrick's share, and that the rest of the sixteenth be thrown into the share of the Captains, Staff Officers, and Subalterns in consideration of the many Staff Officers who divide as Captains.

It is agreed that the detachment which did arrive on the Cumberland do share in the plunder taken from the French at Chandernagore, in consideration of that Ship then being in the river; but that the plunder taken from the Moors at Hughly, Calcutta, Bougie Bougie, &c. be only shared amongst the troops arrived at the time of those captures.

It is agreed that the Officers and Sailors belonging to the Squadron which came with the Army on the expedition to Muxidavad are not to receive prize money with the Military.

It is further agreed that no person shall share in two capacities, that whover shall be killed or die during a Siege or action, his share of the prize money acquired by such siege or action, shall be paid to his executors or agents. That Officers succeeding others killed during a siege or action shall be entitled only to the share due to his former post. That the prize money belonging to non-commissioned Officers and soldiers be paid to their respective Captains, and that the Agents for the Captors be allowed to draw 5 pr Cent on the sale of all goods, and one pr Ct on all money taken. That Jewels and plate are to have commission drawn but as for money.

It is unanimously desired that Colonel Clive shall negotiate for prompt payment with the Nabob, Juger Said – one of the principal merchants of the East, reckoned worth some millions of money – or others, in the best manner he is able.

3. Broome, p. 168.
4. Orme, Vol. 2, p. 186.
5. Major Archibald Grant was originally named to command, but no sooner was the advance guard sent off than he was replaced by Coote. There is no explanation for the change but it was presumably connected with a dispute as to the division of the monies reluctantly donated to the army by Mir Jafar. Grant contended that he should share as a major, but his fellow officers held that he should do so according to his substantive regimental rank of captain. Clearly he was reluctant to leave Murshidabad until the matter was settled; in which he was eventually disappointed and made himself unpopular in the process (Corneille, pp. 130–8 has a detailed account of the row).
6. Seemingly picked for his knowledge of the Ganges.
7. According to the 3 August return, Captain Alexander Grant; Captain Thomas Rumbold; Captain Robert Campbell; and Captain John Cudmore.

Appendix 1
1. Hill, Vol. 2, p. 413. This is clearly set out in a return of Clive's forces on 15 June 1757, signed off by Captain John Fraser as major of brigade.
2. Hill, Vol. 3, p. 408.
3. The 'Company's servants' were presumably employed as artificers etc. Captain Polier's Company was also noted as absent, having been 'sent to the assistance of Madras'. The Eurasians making up nearly half the total were actually identified in the return as 'blacks' which presumably meant 'Black Portuguese'; a euphemism for Eurasians, since there were no sepoys on the Bengal establishment at this time.
4. Hill, Vol. 1, pp. 97, 99 and 297, and Vol. 3, pp. 19–24 (The log of the *Delaware*).
5. Promoted 13 August 1756 (Hill, Vol. 1, p. 202).

6. The log entry is unclear as to Herdman's status: 'Departed this life one of the Honourable Company's sergeants, as also on shore Lieutenant Herdman and a corporal of the Train. Our own people very ill in general.' This suggests that he was an artillery officer although it is not certain.

7. February 22 1757, *Return of the Troops under the Command of Lieutenant-Colonel ROBERT CLIVE.*

8. A wholly unconvincing thirteen ensigns are recorded in the 22 February return but as only three ensigns appear six days later this is clearly an error or misprint.

9. Hill, Vol. 2, p. 263.

10. Wounded while serving as an ensign under Le Beaume in the defence of the Calcutta jail, and evacuated with him to Fulta.

11. Hill, Vol. 3, p. 344 (Le Beaume to Council, 18 April 1757) '. . . I have the honour to present before you a copy of the General Court Martial held over me by order of Colonel Clive, before which I was obliged to appear although I had already been broke and the European soldiers and topasses of my company incorporated with those of Captains Muier and Frazier without any crime I had before committed, although I have found that the General Court Martial have thought proper to acquit me.'

12. Cited as 'Dallabars' but obviously the De Lubers recorded in April.

13. Hill, Vol. 2, p. 190. This had been Dugald Campbell's company but he was killed at the taking of Budge Budge and was replaced by Captain John Fraser. The latter is usually referred to as 'Frazer', but he himself clearly signed himself as Fraser.

14. A Bengal volunteer, Rider was one of those who escaped from Calcutta on 19 June 1756.

15. Hill, Vol. 3, p. 20 (Log of the *Delaware*).

16. Formerly of Fraser's Company.

17. Probably Alexander (?) Champion, variously cited as captain of the *Chance* sloop, or as a ship's mate, who escaped from Calcutta to Fulta.

18. Hill, Vol. 2, p. 412.

19. Ibid., p. 413. For the avoidance of doubt it should be noted that these figures applied only to the infantry. The artillery were counted separately but no distinction was made as to which Establishment they belonged to.

20. W. J. Wilson, *History of the Madras Army*, Madras, E. Keys, 1882, Vol. 1, pp. 375–6. Exactly when Le Beaume's new company was raised is unknown, but he himself took part in the council of war two days before the Battle of Plassey and a Sergeant Thomas Lauder of his company was returned as wounded there.

21. He was in fact serving as second-in-command to Major Coote, in the expedition which unsuccessfully pursued the French, under Law, towards Patna.

22. Returned as wounded at Plassey on 23 June and still at this time on the sick list.

23. It seems a little odd that Grant's company which had mainly comprised Eurasians in April should now be an all-European unit. It seems more likely that this is an error and that no distinction was made in the return between Europeans and Eurasians.

24. Both ensigns were returned as sick.

25. A son of Sir James Johnstone of Westerhall, Dumfries. His brother Patrick died in the Black Hole, and he himself had been a writer at Dacca.

26. Matrosses were semi-skilled artillerymen serving as military labourers, moving

the guns and carrying ammunition until such time as they could pass as gunners.

27. Wilson, Vol. 1, p. 373.
28. Hill, Vol. 2, p. 412.
29. Wilson, Vol. 1, p. 377.
30. Hill, Vol. 1, p. 228.
31. Commanded by Captain William Pye, killed in action at Calcutta, 5 February 1756.
32. Captain George Frederick Guapp.
33. Robert Campbell; not to be confused with Dugald Campbell, killed at Budge Budge.
34. These were presumably supernumeraries and included the newly-promoted Captain Melchior Le Beaume of the Bengal Establishment.
35. Hill, Vol. 1, p. 233.
36. Hill, Vol. 3, p. 30.
37. Ibid., p. 32.
38. Orme, Vol. 2, p. 174.
39. Died 10 June 1757 according to the 3 August return.
40. The tables of the returns are slightly misleading in that adjutants and quartermasters are enumerated and counted in the eventual totals of officers. In this case Campbell is counted twice, first as a lieutenant and again as a quartermaster.
41. It will be noted that with all the European troops consolidated into a single battalion at this time, Major Killpatrick had reverted for the purpose of pay and allowances to the Madras Establishment (a rather sore point, as it happened).
42. Captain Maskelyne himself was actually serving on Clive's staff, but in any case due to illness was forced to return to Madras on 16 March 1757 (Hill, Vol. 3, p. 60).
43. A Swiss officer commissioned 2 August 1752 (*List of Officers doing duty upon the Coast of Coromandel in the Service of the Honble the United East India Company, 1st January 1756*). Wounded in action at Calcutta on 5 February 1757.
44. Wounded as a lieutenant in the action at Calcutta on 5 February 1757.
45. Wrongly identified by Broome as an officer of HM 38th, Waggoner or Wagner was one of the Swiss mercenaries.
46. A Danish officer commissioned 7 February 1757, according to Broome (p. 133), who places him with the Bengal battalion. In actual fact he does not appear to have joined it until the post-Plassey re-organisation amalgamated all three European contingents into a single regiment.
47. Still listed as a company commander in the Bengal Europeans.
48. Hill, Vol. 2, p. 412.
49. Ibid., p. 413.
50. Taking part in the pursuit of M. Law, under Major Coote and Captain Grant.
51. This was probably Lieutenant Robert L. Knox, who according to Broome (p. 133) was placed in charge of the Bengal Sepoys. If so, the seven serjeants were with him to assist in disciplining the sepoys.
52. Returned to Madras to assume command of the artillery there, leaving Jennings in charge (Broome, p. 132).
53. Swiss officer.
54. Said to be a one-armed French officer who deserted from the garrison of

Chandernagore (Broome, pp. 110–11). But notwithstanding a legend that he hanged himself after being reproached by his father as a traitor, he subsequently transferred to the Royal Invalid Artillery and was still serving with it in 1777.

55. Wilson, Vol. 1, p. 373.

56. Hill, Vol. 2, p. 412.

57. Hill, Vol. 3, p. 62. These figures, although presumably based on returns provided by the conducting officers, are evidently incomplete, as can be seen by the muster figures below. It will also be noted that Captain-lieutenant Egerton and Lieutenant Molitor were in fact artillery officers. Coote's journal confirms their arrival in three discrete contingents but cites quite different numbers and slightly different dates:

> *March 4th.* – The first division of the Bombay troops consisting of 150 men, joined us, under the command of Captain Andrew Buchannan.
> *March 11th.* – Halted; 2nd division of the Bombay troops consisting of 150 men, joined us, under the command of Captain Andrew Armstrong.
> *March 14th.* – ... the 3rd division of the Bombay troops consisting of 100 men, joined us;

The discrepancy between the two sets of figures for the 14 March arrivals can only be explained by Clive's official journal recording a party of artillerymen under Egerton rather than the whole of the third division.

58. Hill, Vol. 2, p. 412.

59. Ibid., p. 413.

60. Broome, p. 132.

61. Until 1748, marines were army units raised for the Sea Service, but such were the administrative difficulties of keeping track of men scattered over dozens of ships that ownership of them was then passed to the Royal Navy – who promptly disbanded the lot on the happy outbreak of peace. Having realised that this was a mistake, the navy began forming its own companies of marines in 1755, but this was too late by a year for Admiral Watson, who had sailed for India in March 1754. His insistence that Colonel Adlercron supply him with three companies of the 39th Foot to serve as marines was not therefore a subterfuge to increase Clive's forces, but represented a legitimate requirement.

62. Weller was evidently still not fit for duty at this point, which probably explains why a memorandum to the muster notes Lieutenant John Corneille of the King's troops being appointed to do duty as captain. Corneille states that he himself was appointed by Colonel Clive to act as captain on 27 March 1757 (Corneille, p. 114).

63. Hill, Vol. 2, p. 412.

64. Ibid., p. 413.

65. Clive's promotions of both Grant and Coote were local brevets and did not change their substantive or regimental rank. Corneille states that Grant was appointed major to be commanding officer of HM 39th Foot – a position he already held by seniority – and instead his promotion was necessary in order to place him in command of the newly 2nd Battalion.

66. This was still his regimental rank. He fought at Plassey as a captain and retained that brevet rank afterwards.

Appendix 2

1. Orme, Vol. 2, pp. 173–4.
2. Ibid.
3. Ibid., pp. 176–7.
4. It is worth noting that during the American Civil War just over a century later one Confederate artillery officer opined that firing roundshot at close quarters was actually more effective than grapeshot or canister. Fewer casualties might be inflicted but this was by far outweighed by the moral effect of the great crashing sound of the roundshot being fired.
5. Orme, Vol. 2, pp. 173–4.

Appendix 3

1. V. C. P. Hodson, 'Captain Alexander Grant, Adjutant General during the siege of Calcutta 1756', *Bengal Past and Present* XLI (1931), pp. 141–2. Also Janot Arnot and Gordon Seton, *Prisoners of the '45*, Edinburgh, Scottish History Society, 1929, Vol. 2, pp. 248–9. There is some confusion here with another Alexander Grant, referred to in the published account of the trial as brother to Patrick Grant of Glenmoriston. However, the circumstance of Grant's obtaining a commission immediately afterwards seems decisive. The circumstances of his surrender are unknown, but he may have done so following the death of an elder brother at Falkirk in January 1746.
2. Hill, Vol. 1, pp. 73–89 and Vol. 3, pp. 379–82. The original draft is to be found in BM Addl. MS 29:209. Hill opines that it was written for Robert Orme.
3. The *Success* was being employed as a hospital ship at the time.
4. Hill, Vol. 1, pp. 89–95 and Orme MSS OV 19, pp. 173–80.
5. No trace can be found of the 20 August letter but this narrative probably does not differ materially in content. At any rate his explanation was judged sufficient to exonerate and reinstate him, only Mr Pearkes dissenting (Hill, Vol. 1, pp. 200–1).
6. In the list of those voting to fight at Plassey, Grant came second in seniority after Coote, and according to family tradition he was instrumental in persuading Clive to change his mind and fight after all, but this probably rests on no more than his voting to fight.

Appendix 4

1. Hill, Vol. 3, p. 153 (Holwell to Davis, 28 February 1757). However, see also Watts' statement as to seventy-nine soldiers and others having escaped to Chandernagore (Hill, Vol. 1, p. 59).

Appendix 5

1. Hill, Vol. 3, pp. 30–9 (Captain Neville Maskelyne).
2. This appears from the remainder of the entry to be an error and that the European infantry are intended.
3. Maskelyne's war diary is substantially duplicated for the period 19 January to 18 February 1757 by a *Journal of the Proceedings of the Troops commanded by Lieutenant-Colonel Robert Clive on the expedition to Bengal* by a correspondent identified only as J.C. (John Cudmore?). Most entries are substantially the same although the wording is occasionally different. At times also some different information is given as in this entry:

'*Jan. 19th.*– Whilst these things were transacting at Hughley the remainder of the troops marched out and encamped under the bank of Chichapore Tank which was fortified immediately for the reception of our bazar, cooleys and baggage, in case the Nabob should make an attack upon us. The Salisbury anchored off the avenue that leads to the river side in order to keep open our communication with it and to facilitate it, we erected a battery about 400 yards to the westward of the camp. Another battery was also raised about the same distance north-east of the Tank to scour the plain leading to Dumdumma Bridge and an epaulment thrown up on the right and left flanks of our encampment, in which situation we waited for the Nabob till [February 2nd.]' (Hill, Vol. 3, p. 58).

4. C.'s version is slightly different and more detailed: ' At daybreak we arrived close to the Nabob's camp before we were challenged, when we received a brisk fire from several quarters, which was returned by our advanced *seapoys*. The enemy retreated, and we pursued our march through their camp undisturbed, till on reaching the centre of it, a body of 300 horse appeared in the fog within ten yards of the battalion and being pressed on by those in the rear (who were ignorant of their being so near) were obliged to pass along our right flank as we were marching by files, but on facing the battalion to the right and giving them two fires by platoons, such havock was made amongst them, that by all accounts not above thirteen escaped, some of the platoons being obliged to open to let them drop clear of them. After this the whole army began to encompass us in great bodies, which obliged us to keep them at a distance by a constant fire of musquetry and artillery. We were full two hours in marching through their camp, several charges were made upon our rear by the horse, but not with equal courage to that of the first. About 11 we arrived at the Fort from whence a subaltern with forty-five military and 100 seapoys fresh from the garrison were detached immediately by boat to secure our camp, which the enemy had not made the least attempt upon, though only 300 buckdarries, 100 seapoys, and a few seamen besides the sick were left to guard it. In the evening the troops being a little refreshed, marched back also to camp where they arrived about 7 at night. An unlucky fog prevented our attack upon the Nabob's head quarters, which if successful would have made the action more decisive; however, as it was, the enemy suffered very considerably; the sailors and *seapoys* in the rear destroyed everything which the van had passed. The Nabob's army consisted of 20,000 horse and 30,000 foot with 50 pieces of cannon, and by the best accounts 1,300 were killed and wounded including 22 officers, some of which were of great distinction. Upwards of 500 horse were counted upon the spot with four elephants, some camels and a number of bullocks. The loss on our side amounted to 39 Europeans killed and disabled, 20 seamen and 26 seapoys, and 113 of all kinds wounded, most of whom are in a fair way. Captains Pye and Bridge with Mr Belches the Colonel's secretary fell in the beginning of the action. The enemy's apprehensions of another attack (which was indeed intended) were so great that they kept up a constant fire all night.'

5. The Journal ends at this point and the copy by J.C. notes: 'Thus far Maskelyne who returned lately to the coast in the *Walpole*, having been much indisposed by a flux. He left Calcutta, I mean the river, the 16th of March.' J.C.'s version then jumps to 8 March, covering the campaign against Chandernagore but adds nothing of substance.

6. i.e., for Madras.
7. Presumably instead of going on board the ships?
8. 100 *lakhs*.
9. A tax or rather protection money.

Appendix 6

1. Hill, Vol. 3, pp. 39–58.
2. i.e., ran aground and fired guns as a signal of their distress – and embarrassment.
3. This was to facilitate platooning, which was the British Army's favoured method of fire control. All the available men would be told off into equal-sized platoons, usually of about thirty men, which were then in turn allocated to one of three firings. On the word of command being given, only those of the first firing would deliver a volley, followed by those of the second firing and then the third. By the time the latter had fired it was expected that the platoons of the first firing would have reloaded and be ready to continue the cycle if need be. Although the platoon exercise was practised incessantly the system was unsatisfactory in execution and effect and in England the much simpler alternate firing was already being introduced by an officer named James Wolfe. This paired off platoons which then fired alternately without trying to keep pace with the other pairs, but having come out to India in 1754 the 39th will have been wholly unacquainted with it.
4. Street firing was a relatively simple procedure in which the battalion or company was formed up in a column on a front close to the width of the street. The leading ranks would deliver a volley then file to either side of the street to reload while the next platoon pressed forward, each one following the other.
5. This, alas, was the same William Tooke who provided such a useful account of the battle for Calcutta in 1756.
6. Captain Archibald Grant, HM 39th Foot.
7. It would appear that Clive primarily wanted to appoint Coote as a major, but was obliged to first promote Archy Grant as he was regimentally senior to Coote.
8. The list is useful in recording the relative seniority of the officers. Traditionally when votes were cast the most junior officer present offered his opinion first and so on up the ladder of seniority, in order that the president did not unduly influence the vote. In this case however, as Coote relates, Clive opened the proceedings by declaring his opinion and then inviting everyone else to agree with him. It will be noted that for the most part regulars took their proper turn instead of asserting precedence as King's officers. Coote's copy of the list does not identify the service to which they belonged, that information being very helpfully interpolated by Hill.
9. A Swiss officer, wrongly identified by Hill as an officer in the 39th Foot.
10. When sea officers served on land, captains ranked as colonels or lieutenant colonels in the army and lieutenants as captains.
11. Swiss artillery officer – one of those injured when the veranda collapsed at the siege of Chandernagar.
12. Swiss officer.

Appendix 7
1. Orme, Vol. 2, pp. 168–79.
2. Orme appears to be a little mistaken as to the timing of this episode. Grant was the senior officer of the Bengal Europeans and will have gone forward as part of Coote's division as described in the text, rather than with the main body of the army some time afterwards. The most likely explanation is that his detachment was dropped off by Coote and was still occupying a covering position when the main body came up.
3. Hill, Vol. 2, pp. 433–6.
4. Apparently a copy of one attributed to Clive himself.
5. Corneille, pp. 120–5 – the spelling appears to have been modernised by Corneille's editor, Professor Michael Edwardes.
6. Picquets were formed of detachments from every unit and formally relieved at noon each day – if practical – aside from providing security details during the hours of darkness they customarily formed a headquarters reserve.
7. Hill, Vol. 2, p. 426.

Appendix 8
1. Orme, Vol. 2, pp. 186–7, 189–95.

Bibliography

Barber, Noel, *The Black Hole of Calcutta*, London, Collins, 1966.

Broome, Capt. Arthur, *History of the Rise and Progress of the Bengal Army*, Calcutta, Thacker & Co. 1850.

Callahan, Raymond, *The East India Company and Army Reform 1783-1798*, Harvard, 1972.

Corneille, John, *Journal of my Service in India*, London, Folio Society, 1966.

Edwardes, Michael, *The Battle of Plassey and the Conquest of Bengal*, London, Batsford, 1963.

Forrest, Sir George, *The Life of Lord Clive*, 2 vols, London, Cassell, 1918.

Guy, Alan J. (ed.), *Colonel Samuel Bagshawe and the Army of George II 1731-1762*, London, Army Records Society, 1990.

Hill, S. C. (ed.), *Bengal in 1756-1757*, 3 vols, London, John Murray, 1905.

Hodson, V. C. P., *Officers of the Bengal Army 1758-1834*, Vols 1–2, London, Constable & Co., 1927,

Ives, Edward, *A Voyage from England to India in the Year 1754*, London, Edward and Charles Dilly, 1773.

Keay, John *The Honourable Company*, London, HarperCollins, 1991.

Lawford, James P., *Britain's Army in India; From its Origins to the Conquest of Bengal*, London, Allen & Unwin, 1978.

Love, Henry Davidson, *Vestiges of Old Madras*, 4 vols, London, John Murray, 1913.

Orme, Robert, *A History of the Military Transactions of the British Nation in Indostan*, 3 vols, Madras, Pharoah & Co., 1861.

Reid, Stuart, *Armies of the East India Company 1750-1850*, Oxford, Osprey, 2009.

Wilson, W. J., *History of the Madras Army*, Vol. 1, Madras, E. Keys, 1882.

Index

Adlercron, Colonel John (39th Foot), 55-6

Aliverdi Khan, Nawab of Bengal, 20

Amir Chund (Omichand), 22, 87

Anwar-ud-Din, Nawab of the Carnatic, 7, 8, 10, 12, 15

Bagh Bazaar Fort, 29, 35-7, 38, 44

Bagshawe, Lieut. Colonel Sam (39th Foot), 56

Bahadur Ali Khan (Bengali general), 99

Bannatyne, Captain Robert EIC, 6

Barnet, Commodore Curtis, RN, 7-8

Becher, Richard, 53

Bengali Army, 22-6, 35, 37, 39, 58, 61-2, 67, 72-3, 79, 80, 95-6, 97-100, 102

Best, Captain Thomas (*Lively*), 35

Black Hole, 50

Blagge, Lieutenant Thomas EIC, 37-8, 43, 44, 45, 49

Boscawen, Rear Admiral Edward RN, 12-3

Bridges, Captain Timothy EIC, 74

British Army,
   39th Foot, 55-7, 61, 63, 66, 67, 72, 74, 80, 81, 82-3, 87, 88, 89, 94-5
   Independent Companies, 12-3, 14
   Royal Artillery, 13, 55, 56

Buchannan, Captain John EIC, 31, 34, 41, 42-3, 49

Budge Budge, 51, 58, 59, 61-2

Bussy-Castelnau, Marquis de, 15, 21, 78

Calcutta, 17-9, 21,
   defences 25-30, 32
   garrison, 30-5
   siege, 34-50,
   recapture, 63-5, 68, 86

Campbell, Captain Dugald EIC, 62

Carstairs, Ensign Peter EIC, 40, 53

Chance (sloop), 37

Chanda Sahib, Nawab of Carnatic, 15

Chandernagore, 21, 37, 50, 78-9 80-4, 86, 87

Charnock, Job, 17-9

Chinsura, 68

Clerke, Lieutenant John RN, 67, 87

Clayton, Captain David EIC, 31, 34, 37-8, 40, 41-2, 43

Clive, Robert EIC, 8, 11, 14-6, 56, 57, 58-65, 68-9, 70-1, 72, 78, 81, 83, 84, 85-8, 89, 90-2, 94-102, 104

Compagnie des Indes troops, 10-1, 80, 84

Coote, Major Eyre (39th Foot), 61-2, 63-5, 67-8, 72, 81-3, 87, 89, 91-2, 95, 98, 99, 100, 103

Corneille, Captain John (39th Foot), 94-5, 98, 100

Cossimbazar, 22-4, 85-6, 88

Cuddalore, 11-2

Cudmore, Captain John EIC, 54

Culnah, 87, 88

Cutwa (fort), 89-90, 91

Cypayes (sepoys), 10-1

Daudpore, 100, 101

De Ryder (merchantman),66

Delaware Indiaman, 34, 53

Dodaley (merchantman), 35, 47, 48, 54

Drake, Roger (governor of Calcutta), 21, 30-1, 32-3, 40-1, 42, 45, 47-9, 52-3, 54, 58, 65, 78-9

Dumas, Pierre Benoit, 10-1

Dupleix, Joseph-Francois, 7, 8, 9-10, 11, 12, 15, 16

East India Company Forces,
Bengal Artillery, 30, 32, 33, 34-5, 60, 98-9
Bengal Europeans, 4-5, 23, 30, 37, 54, 59, 78, 80, 86, 88, 95
Bengal Sepoys, 30, 34, 37, 39, 69, 78, 80, 90, 95, 98, 100, 103
Calcutta militia, 27, 30-2, 34-5,
Madras Artillery, 4, 8, 13, 15, 79
Madras Europeans, 4, 12, 13, 34, 53, 54, 57, 58, 59, 61, 62, 66, 67, 69, 80, 88-9, 95, 103
Madras Sepoys, 15, 57, 58, 59, 66, 67-8, 70, 72, 73, 78, 81, 87, 95, 100
Bombay Europeans, 4, 14, 86, 87, 88-9, 95 103,
Swiss mercenaries, 6
Elliot, Lieutenant John EIC, 24

Fort d'Orleans (Chandernagore), 80

Fort St. David   (Madras), 4, 8, 11, 12, 13

Fort St. George (Madras), 4, 8

Fort William   (Calcutta), 18, 21, 25, 28, 34, 44, 51, 63-5, 68

Fortune (ketch), 37

Frankland, William, 32, 33, 45, 47

Fraser, Captain John EIC, 70

Fulta, 52-3, 57

Grant, Captain Alexander EIC, 6, 14, 23-4, 25-6, 27, 30, 31, 32-3, 34, 37-40, 41-2, 46, 47, 48-9, 53-4, 86, 98, 103

Grant, Major Archibald (39th Foot), 84, 89, 95

Griffin, Commodore Thomas RN, 12

Guapp, Captain George Frederick EIC, 6, 95

Hay, Lieutenant RN, 84

Hayter, Lieutenant Richard RN, 67

Hedleburg, Sergeant, 49

HM Ships,
HMS *Bridgewater*, 62, 66-8
HMS *Cumberland*, 57
HMS *Kent*, 61, 63, 83, 84
HMS *Kingfisher*, 62, 67
HMS *Salisbury*, 62, 83, 84
HMS *Thunder*, 67
HMS *Tyger*, 62-3, 83, 84

Holwell, John Zephaniah, 31, 34, 40-1, 42, 46, 47, 49, 50, 52-3

Hugli, 17, 66-8

Hunter (schooner), 49

Johnstone, Lieutenant John EIC, 98, 99

Keene, Lieutenant William EIC, 64

Killpatrick, Major James EIC, 34, 53, 54, 58-9, 61, 64, 66, 67, 68, 81, 86, 87, 88, 95, 98-9

Kinch, Lieutenant John EIC, 103

King, Captain William RN, 63, 67

La Bourdonnais, Francois Mahe, 8-10

Latham, Captain Thomas RN, 63, 64

Law, Jean, 80, 85, 90-1, 102, 103

Lawrence, Major Stringer EIC, 13-4

Le Beaume, Captain Melchior EIC, 34, 38-9, 40, 53, 70

Linn, Captain William EIC, 81

Lively (ketch), 35

Lutwich, Lieutenant RN, 67

Mackett, William, 34, 48

Mafuz Khan (Carnatic general), 10, 11-2, 54

Madras , 8-10, 11, 34

Manik Chand, (Bengali general), 58, 60-1, 63, 67, 89

Manningham, Charles, 31-2, 33, 45, 47, 48-9, 53

Mapletoft, Rev. William, 34-5

Marlborough (Indian), 57

Minchin, Captain George EIC, 31, 32, 33, 34, 48, 53

Mir Jafar (Bengali general), 72, 86, 87,

88, 89, 92, 94, 97-9, 100, 101-3

Mir Madan (Bengali general), 92, 96, 97-8

Mirza Shah Abbasbeg (*Jemadar*), 90

Moideen Saib, 90, 103

Mompesson, Major John, 13

Morgan, Lieutenant RN, 67

Morse, Nicholas (governor of Madras), 7, 8, 9-10

Muhammad Ali, Nawab of Carnatic, 11-2, 15, 16

Muir, Captain George Grainger EIC, 54

Muir, Major William, 12

Murshidabad, 79, 85

Nawabgunj, 58

Nazir Jang, 15

Neptune (merchantman), 35, 51

Niaserray, 87

O'Hara, Charles (engineer) EIC, 48

Omar Beg (Bengali officer), 22, 101

Omichand, *see* Amir Chund

Paradis, Major Louis, 10-1

Patna, 85, 103

Pearkes, Paul, 103

Pepper, Major Park, 13

Perreau, Lieutenant Samuel RN, 84

Perrin's Redoubt, *see* Bagh Bazaar Fort

Peyton, Captain Edward, RN, 8, 12

Piccard, Ensign John Francis EIC, 37-8, 44, 46

Plassey, 86, 92-100

Pocock, Admiral Sir George RN, 84

Pondicherry, 7-8, 12, 13

Prince George (merchantman), 35, 49

Pye, Captain William EIC, 61, 66, 67, 74

Rai Durlabh (Bengali general), 38, 86, 92, 94, 101, 102

Renault, Pierre   , 78, 79, 81, 83-4

Rennie, Captain David, 28, 35

Rumbold, Lieutenant Thomas EIC, 98

Seamen, 61-2, 67-8, 70, 72-4, 87

San Thome, Battle of, 10-1

Scrafton, Luke   , 70, 101

Shaista Khan, Nawab of Bengal, 17-8

Shaukat Jang, governor of Purneah, 20-1, 57-8

Siraj-ud-Daula, Nawab of Bengal, 20-5, 38, 45, 50, 51, 57-58, 65, 68, 70, 72-5, 78, 85, 86, 88, 92, 96-97, 100, 101-2

Smith, Captain Henry RN, 66

Smith, Captain-Lieutenant Peter EIC, 31, 39, 42

Speke, Captain Charles RN, 64, 84

St. Frais, M. de, 96, 97, 99

St. Jacques, Marquis de, 39

Strachan, 62

Success (galley), 51

Tanna (fort), 35, 51, 62

Tooke, William, 43-4, 46, 48, 81

Walcott, Ensign Edward EIC, 39-40

Walsh, John, 70

Warwick, Captain Thomas RN, 70

Watson, Vice Admiral Charles RN, 55, 56-7, 58, 61, 64-5, 66, 69, 78-9, 81, 82-3, 87

Watts, William, 22-4, 50, 53, 79, 80, 85, 87, 88

Weller, Captain Nicholas (39th Foot), 61, 69, 70

Winter, Captain Thomas (*Delaware*), 53

Witherington, Captain Lawrence EIC, 32, 33, 45-6

Yar Lutuf Khan (Bengali general), 94, 101

Yorke, Ensign Martin (39th Foot), 74

Young, Captain Andrew (*Dodaley*), 48-9